P9-CLH-745

Marketing in a Developing Nation

Marketing in a Developing Nation

HF
54,5.12
P4
M35

ST. JOSEPH'S UNIVERSITY   STX
HF5415.12.P4M35
Marketing in a developing nation;

3 9353 00147 6579

141548

The Competitive Behavior of
Peruvian Industry

William P. Glade
William A. Strang
Jon G. Udell

University of Wisconsin

James E. Littlefield

University of North Carolina

Heath Lexington Books
D. C. Heath and Company
Lexington, Massachusetts

Copyright © 1970 by D. C. Heath and
Company

All rights reserved. No part of this publication may be reproduced or transmitted in
any form or by any means, electronic or
mechanical, including photocopy, recording,
or any information storage or retrieval
system, without permission in writing from
the publisher.

Printed in the United States of America

Library of Congress Number: 79-121405

To Our Wives
Marlene, Audrey, Susan,
and Joyce

Contents

Tables and Figures

Figures

Preface

In a recent essay, inspired by extensive comparative and longitudinal studies of communities in Peru, William F. Whyte and Lawrence K. Williams observed that agricultural modernization in that country has often been impeded by the inability of farmers to obtain the new supply inputs they need from local dealers. Not only is it difficult to obtain these inputs when they are needed, but when they are obtained the farmers seldom receive adequate instructions for their use.[1] Doubtless it was the latter point that led Arthur T. Mosher some years ago to suggest that governments in the less developed regions should consider launching publicly supported advertising programs for selected and tested agricultural production requisites in the interest of improving the coverage and quality of marketing communications and the "agricultural extension" efforts of private enterprise.[2] As if to emphasize the possible role of better marketing, one of the most analytically rigorous development economists has gone so far as to say that public subventions for distributional outlets might even be appropriate in the marketing of consumer goods (i.e., incentive goods) among the rural populace as well as for the advertising of agricultural production requisites.[3]

Whatever may be said for and against such proposals, they do at least illustrate that occasionally, though not frequently, the effects of marketing problems on economic growth are recognized in the now rather formidable literature of development. With the hope of clarifying certain organizational and behavioral aspects of the marketing process in less developed countries, the writers of this study — all associated, at the time of the field research, with the Center for International Business Research of the University of Wisconsin at Madison — undertook to examine the principal features of the marketing of industrial sector output in Peru. While no claim is made that the results of this research provide an exhaustive and detailed account of the subject, it is believed that they can serve an heuristic purpose in revealing salient dysfunctions in the marketing system studied, and that they provide an understanding of how marketing is actually conducted in Peru. Excessive generalization from the case of a single country would be unwise. Yet, to the extent that many aspects of Peruvian marketing were derived from environmental characteristics which are rather common among low-income countries, the findings distinctly suggest lines of inquiry which should be fruitful for comparative study in other national settings.

As is true with other countries, including the United States, much information on business operations is not available in published form. To obtain most of the data desired on marketing operations, it was necessary to go to the source of the data — the individual business firm. Our main debt, then, is to the more than one-hundred firms in Peru whose executives gave so unstintingly of their time during the nearly five months of field research conducted in 1966. Because of the anonymity promised to each of these firms, we are, unfortunately, precluded from listing each of them. We trust that our use of aggregation and our deliberate delay in making the results of our study available in published form — a delay which in no way, we feel, detracts from the usefulness of our findings — will adequately insure the confidentiality of their replies to our questions.

Dr. Juan Ignacio Elguera, Sr. Pablo Carriquiry, the late Sr. Juan Pardo H., Sr. Enrique Novak, Rev. Raimundo Villagrasa, S. J., and Rev. Alberto Rodríguez, S. J. — all of the 1966 Administration of the Universidad del Pacífico — were extremely helpful in providing office space, duplication services and general advice for the study. Dr. Alberto Bedon G. of Instituto Peruano de Administracion de Empresas (IPAE), the Peruvian complement of the American Management Association, was helpful in publicizing the study and setting up interviews in Arequipa and Trujillo. Sr. Roland Meyer, a management consultant, helped in sample selection and provided advice and information in other areas.

A special note of thanks should go to Dr. Pablo L. Harms, former Director of the Asociación de Dirigentes de Ventas del Peru (ADV), the Peruvian equivalent of the Sales and Marketing Club. Dr. Harms, an enthusiastic supporter of modern marketing in Peru, spent many agonizing hours helping to translate our questionnaire into Spanish and suggesting firms and individuals to interview. He also provided the typing facilities for the letter of introduction and questionnaires, and allowed us to use one of the monthly ADV meetings to announce our study.

Others who patiently listened to our story, offered suggestions, and gave helpful information were:

Sr. Eduardo Alegria M. of Enrique Ferreyros y Cia. S.A.
Mr. John Barrett of the U. S. Embassy, Lima.
Sr. Juan Bassio of the Sociedad Nacional de Industrias.
Sr. Juan Basso of the Instituto Nacional de Promocion Industrial.
Mr. T. J. Bayliss of Price Waterhouse Peat & Company, Lima.
Sr. José Berckemeyer of G. Berckemeyer y Co. S. A.
Mr. Arthur James Boyd of Artesanias del Peru.
Sr. Daniel Camino Brent of the Comité de Fabricantes de Cerveza.
Mr. John Chamberlin of the Peace Corps, Ica.
Sr. Napoleon J. de la Colina of Consultores de Seguros S. A.
Sr. Guillermo Cruz Gallo of Corporacion Nacional de Comerciantes.
Sr. Konrad Fischer Rossi of the Escuela de Administracion de Negocios Para Graduados (ESAN).
Sr. Luis Galliani Sologuren of Publicidad Mercurio S. A.
Sr. John Gardner of Sears Roebuck del Peru S. A.
Sr. Christian Hamman of McCann-Erickson Publicidad S. A.
Ing. Francisco Ponce de Léon G. of CRIG, Cuzco.
Sr. Augusto Llosa Llosa of the Ministerio de Hacienda.
Sr. Eduardo Lopez-Guerra E. of Publicidad Causa S. A.
Ing. Pablo de Lorenzi S. of the Centro Nacional de Productividad (CENIP).
Sr. Carlos Maurer of A. y F. Wiese S. A.
Ing. Jorge Pflucker Holguin of the Ministerio de Fomento y O. P.

Mr. George Phillips of the USAID, Lima.
Dr. Antonio Pinilla of the Universidad de Lima.
Sr. Gotthilf Ph. Schmid of Arthur Young and Company, Lima.
Dr. Roy Shaw of the Escuela de Administracion de Negocios Para Graduados (ESAN).
Sr. Willy Soenens of Publicidad Ross S. A.
Sr. José Taboada G. of J. Walter Thompson Peruana.
Mr. William Tait of TODOS, Lima.
Sr. Alberto Torres V. of Distrubuidora Necchi de la Victoria.
Sr. Carlos Uriarte T. of Carlos Uriarte & Associates.
Srta. Mercedes Vergara Mejía of La Universidad del Centro, Huancayo.

Thanks are also due to the chambers of commerce and their directors in Chiclayo, Cuzco, Huancayo, Ica, Lima and Trujillo, to the Instituto Nacional de Planificación and to the Dirección Nacional de Estadística y Censos.

Financial support for the project was supplied by the Center for International Business Research of the University of Wisconsin, from a grant from the Ford Foundation, and by the Bureau of Business Research and Service of the University of Wisconsin. It need hardly be added, however, that the views and conclusions expressed herein remain solely the responsibility of the authors and do not imply any necessary concurrence by any of the institutions and individuals whose assistance has been acknowledged above.

**Marketing
in a
Developing
Nation**

Section I: Perspective for Marketing in Peru

In order to properly evaluate the results of empirical studies, one must have enough background knowledge to view the subject with perspective. The first five chapters of this book are designed to provide the background essential to understanding marketing in Peru.

The relationship between marketing and economic development is discussed, with a brief survey of the more important literature. In this context, the basic objectives of our research are presented to provide a focus for the reader.

A major portion of this section is devoted to the environment for marketing in Peru, with the assumption that marketing strategies and practices are necessarily reflective of the socio-economic surroundings. A brief history of the development of business in Peru gives the reader some understanding of the past environments that have influenced the attitudes of businessmen in Peru. Then, the presentation of the most important characteristics of the present day environment for business in Peru, including a discussion of the characteristics of the market, provides the reader with the perspective to evaluate current marketing practices.

Finally, a brief presentation of research methodology, including a discussion of the sample characteristics, completes the foundation necessary for evaluation of the study results.

1 Introduction

Growing Concern With Development

Since the end of World War II the economically advanced nations, and particularly the United States, have poured considerable resources into the less-developed nations. An immediate goal of this aid has been to improve living standards through increased economic growth. The fact that many of the aided economies have not responded as rapidly as was hoped has led to the realization that the economics of development requires consideration of elements outside the traditional scope of economic theory.

Generally speaking, the concept of economic development focuses on two major themes: 1) the growth of national income, usually measured in per capita terms to eliminate the impact of population growth; and 2) changes in the sectoral distribution of income. A high per capita income is, thus, a rough indication of advanced economic development, and a more developed country will normally be more dependent upon manufacturing than upon agriculture, mining, and fishing, which are crucial to the underdeveloped nation. In addition to these measurable differences, however, changes which are less readily quantifiable are also involved in the development process. Changes in attitudes and behavior, changes in the channels and degree of social mobility and similar elements are inherent in the development process. Moreover, the whole quality or character of economic organization, at both macro- and micro-economic levels, distinguishes the advanced country from the country still operating at low per capita income levels.

During the past two decades, the subject of development has involved many men in an enormous amount of study. But much of the economic research to date has concentrated on such problems as capital formation, fiscal policy, intersectoral shifts of resources, commodity pricing problems, monetary policies, and improvement of production techniques. To some extent, the emphasis which has been placed upon the increasing of investment and production is justified by the reasonable argument that only when output grows at a rate exceeding population growth can living standards be raised.[1]

Unfortunately, many of the less-developed economies continue to experience serious growing pains or even find it difficult to initiate a viable growth process at all, despite the growing body of relevant literature and the increasingly widespread decision to resort to various types of economic planning aimed at fostering change and expansion. The reasons for this are multiple and complicated, and the blame can be laid to many causes.

Marketing and Development

An increasing number of observers and students of development have suggested that a major difficulty is that too little attention has been given to the problems of distribution. Peter Drucker, for instance, noted several years ago that in underdeveloped countries, marketing is often neglected in favor of the more "glamorous fields of manufacturing and construction."[2] Similarly, a specialist in international economics, Charles Kindleberger, has written: "Whether markets pull development or lag behind it, it is evident that much planning in the area of economic development today neglects distribution. . . ."[3] That a wider availability of incentive goods might be crucial in development was argued by Arthur Smithies in 1961.[4] During the 1960's, in fact, insufficient concern about improved market structures as an element of development came to be recognized as a significant shortcoming of past foreign aid programs. Walt Whitman Rostow, by then a prominent member of the foreign economic policy group of the federal government, was repeatedly calling for action to remedy the situation.[5]

The dimensions of the gap to which these men and others have referred were suggested by Reed Moyer, who noted that the journal, *Economic Development and Cultural Change*, devoted exclusively to the economic development field, published nothing about marketing between 1952 and 1965.[6] Further, Hazelwood's annotated bibliography, *The Economics of Under-Developed Areas*, included only 21 of 1,027 entries under the heading of "Commerce and Marketing," and not even all of these really dealt with marketing systems and practices to any substantial degree.[7] Insofar as marketing has been considered, many studies of the subject have tended to concentrate on transportation and physical distribution, leaving a serious void in the knowledge of other aspects of marketing,[a] though this is somewhat less true of research in the field of agricultural economics.

This relative neglect of marketing can probably be attributed to a variety of factors. For one thing, it would appear that western economists tend to assume a more or less adequate marketing system as a "given" in their analysis, an assumption which has been, on the whole, a reasonable one to make within the institutional context of the more highly developed economies of the western world. This in turn has seemed to be closely related to a further assumption that the marketing system is essentially passive or adaptive in its relation to the economic system and the production aspects thereof — an assumption which is perhaps more dubious from an historical point of view when one remembers that the remarkable expansion of output which occurred during the industrial revolution was preceded by a lengthy era in which the marketing organization of Western Europe had undergone a considerable transformation.[b] The study of marketing in an analytic manner is, moreover, a comparatively new academic discipline, and given the rapid changes which have been occurring in the marketing systems of the advanced countries, the attention of specialists in the marketing field has been almost fully absorbed by the study of problems close at hand. As far as the underdeveloped countries are concerned, the marketing function seems often to have been viewed, mistakenly, as a quasi-parasitic activity which is not a source of value in the total economic process. Possibly

[a]For the purposes of this study, marketing will be defined as "a total system of interacting business activities designed to plan, price, promote, distribute, and service want-satisfying products and services to present and potential customers." The term will be used synonomously with "distribution."

[b]In this connection, the mainstream of economic analysis, through at least the

this attitude has developed in part because resented expatriate minorities have often tended to congregate in the marketing sectors of these economies.[c]

In any case, for a variety of reasons comparatively little action involving the improvement of marketing systems in underdeveloped areas has occurred during the postwar period, despite the fact that institutional marketing behavior sets a parameter within which economic policy must operate. Not only do costly inventories reflect the inability of marketing systems to distribute efficiently the output of the production system, but also investment, production, and employment are all affected adversely by the inadequate access of producers to consumers (both households and firms).

Objectives of the Present Research

The present research was undertaken in the hope that it would supplement the limited fund of knowledge about the forces which influence marketing and distribution in developing nations, with special reference to the manufacturing sector.

For a number of reasons, Peru seemed to be an especially suitable location in which to conduct this research. In the first place, as a low-income country in an intermediate stage of development, Peru affords researchers an opportunity to encounter the interesting problems of a "dual economy" (i.e., an under-developed sector alongside a relatively developed, "modern" one). For approx-imately a decade and a half, the Peruvian government has committed itself to promoting rapid industrial growth. But even though much progress has been made, the main experience with industrialization is still sufficiently recent that one can observe with considerable clarity the types of marketing problems which hinder the inception of manufacturing activity in the less-developed parts of the world. Further, different behavioral responses to these problems can also be examined, inasmuch as the country has firms in all ranges of ownership, from those completely nationally owned to those completely foreign-owned. That relations between Peru and the United States were, at the time of the study, generally cordial, appeared to be an additional advantage in that it made it more

---

classical and neoclassical writers, seems to have concerned itself chiefly with the negative aspects of mercantilist trade policy and bullionism and to have missed, accord-ingly, the great significance of the mercanti-list era in restructuring the institutional setting in a manner conducive to economic expansion. Gustav Schmoller, Eli Heckscher, Maurice Dobb, and others have, of course, done much to correct this rather one-sided interpretation of the period. Particularly significant, it appears, were the organizational changes effected in the realm of export marketing and interregional trade.

[c]Our colleague, Everett Kassalow, has suggested also that state planning of marketing, because of its direct connection with consumption and the distribution thereof, may well have involved greater social and political difficulties than the planning of production.

likely that the researchers would receive greater cooperation from the many persons it was necessary to interview.

In preparing the research design of this project, the research team concluded that in view of the lamentable scarcity of information on actual marketing behavior in underdeveloped countries, a major objective should be simply to obtain a reasonably adequate description of the marketing policies and strategies practiced by industrial firms in Peru. Not only was this prerequisite to understanding the workings of the Peruvian industrial sector; it was also felt to have great potential value in providing a base of data for additional research which could concentrate on in-depth studies of more narrow aspects of marketing in that country.

Inasmuch as firms must ordinarily adapt their behavior to their particular environment, a second research objective was to detect and explain some of the important relationships between social, political, and economic variables on the one hand, and marketing strategies and practices on the other.

Finally, the authors were concerned with examining the influence on marketing strategy of such variables as type of product and industry, value of the typical purchase, degree of competition, sales volume, and type of ownership. Although a rigorous testing of hypotheses was not feasible, there were seven working hypotheses against which the data were considered:

Hypothesis 1: Marketing strategies fall into certain patterns for similar industries within a given economic, political, and social environment.

Hypothesis 2: Foreign-owned firms tend to employ a more advanced marketing technology and to be more aggressive in their marketing than those owned by Peruvians.[d]

Hypothesis 3: Nonowner-managed firms tend to employ a more advanced marketing technology and to be more aggressive in their marketing than owner-managed firms.

Hypothesis 4: Firms with high sales volume tend to employ a more advanced marketing technology and to be more aggressive in their marketing than firms with low sales volume.

[d]A *more advanced marketing technology* is defined simply as a greater knowledge of the techniques used in marketing. For, instance, a firm utilizing marketing research and engaging in cooperative advertising is employing a more advanced marketing technology than one which only produces and sells. Marketing *aggressiveness* is defined as the firm's emphasis on marketing relative to other business functions. An advanced technology enables a firm to express marketing aggressiveness in more ways. For example, a corporation emphasizing dealer service and promoting heavily would be exhibiting aggressive marketing characteristics. The firm's actions imply a knowledge of the importance of dealer service and promotion. The knowledge is part of the firm's technology.

The authors intend no implication that either marketing technology or aggressiveness can be directly related to a normative judgment of the marketing manager's performance. Employment of many marketing techniques may be inappropriate for a given firm in a given environment. Aggressive marketing, for example, may be inappropriate where demand exceeds supply.

Hypothesis 5: Producers of consumer goods tend to employ a more advanced marketing technology and to be more aggressive in their marketing than producers of industrial goods.

Hypothesis 6: Firms facing heavy competition tend to employ a more advanced marketing technology and to be more aggressive in their marketing than firms facing slight competition.

Hypothesis 7: Firms selling a product with a low value of typical purchase will tend to employ a more advanced marketing technology and to be more aggressive in their marketing than firms selling a product with a high value of typical purchase.

While viewing the data through the prisms of these hypotheses, the authors were particularly interested in arriving at some assessment of both the evolutionary level of marketing management in Peru and the implications of that evolutionary level for the economic development processes of the country.

By "level of evolution," a notion which lies behind the second hypothesis stated above, we had in mind an adaptation of the "stages" classification suggested by William Stanton.[8] In view of the well-known objections which can be raised regarding any rigid "stages" classification of evolutionary social or institutional phenomena, however, we did not wish to imply the existence of a single sequential course of development over which all firms must pass in the organization and conduct of marketing management. What we wanted, rather, was a convenient range or scale of organizational possibilities, the various points on which serve to identify different degrees of sophistication in the conduct of marketing management. For the purposes of this study, then, the stages of development in marketing management organization were defined as follows:

Stage 1 — The general manager or president is responsible for most of the marketing functions in addition to his other duties.

Stage 2 — The sales manager is responsible for the field sales force; most other marketing activities are spread throughout the firm.

Stage 3 — Most marketing activity is grouped under one marketing executive, who is usually called the sales manager.

Stage 4 — Marketing management is fully integrated, often under a vice-president of marketing or a marketing manager; activities such as inventory control, transportation, warehousing, and aspects of product planning are the responsibility of the chief marketing executive.

Stage 5 — Marketing becomes the basic motivating force for the entire firm. All short-term company policies are highly conditioned by marketing. This stage cannot be represented on an organization chart. It is reached when attitudes of all company executives reflect the marketing concept.

In examining marketing activities and their implications for Peru's economic development, the authors were led to consider the potential relevance of the "marketing concept" to strategies of economic growth and change. While *marketing* consists of the planning, promotion, distribution, and servicing of goods and services desired by consumers (both firms and households), the *marketing concept* refers to an organizational pattern and managerial approach in which a strong consumer orientation is basic to the planning and execution of nearly all business activities.

While the marketing concept has come into usage chiefly in the United States in recent years, it became apparent in the course of this project that the marketing management system described by the marketing concept might well complement, at the micro-economic level, the macro-economic level development policies being pursued in low-income countries such as Peru. Indeed, if the behavior of the firm is viewed from the perspective of national development requirements, other patterns of marketing management would seem to be dysfunctional, albeit in perhaps varying degrees. The relevance of the marketing activities and the marketing concept to national economic development is explored at some length in the final chapter of this study.

2

The Evolution of the Peruvian Business Enterprise System

Although the belief that Peru is a bastion of traditional society is widespread (and partly justified), like most such opinions this viewpoint contains a great deal of oversimplification — and even inaccuracies. If one equates traditionalism, for example, with a precommercial pattern of social organization, the belief is quite in error, and has been for several centuries. While it is undeniable that a substantial segment of the Peruvian population has long lived in conditions tantamount to serfdom (retaining many culture traits from the Incaic period), since the arrival of the Spaniards there has been a considerable amount of market-oriented activity of a relatively more modern sort.

It is well known, for example, that during much of the colonial period the expanding mining industry constituted a mainstay of the export sector. Also during that period commercial agriculture began, with Spanish settlers establishing plantations in the various river valleys scattered along the arid Peruvian coast.[1] Throughout the Peruvian viceroyalty a wide variety of artisan industries developed, particularly in the Andean regions, and a considerable amount of interregional trade was a feature of the times.[2] In fact, until the empire was subdivided into additional viceroyalties during the latter half of the eighteenth century and new trade policies were introduced, the centralized and regulated commercial system of imperial Spain made Lima the wholesale emporium of most of South America. The wealthy aristocracy of Lima, based partly upon absentee ownership of land, also contained individuals whose riches derived from mining and the far-flung marketing activities.[3] Developments during three centuries of Spanish rule served to install at least the rudiments of a business sector in the territory which was declared a republic in June, 1821.

Business Developments in the Century Following Independence

Conditions in the unsettled early years of the new republic were hardly auspicious for business growth, although some minerals and sugar continued to be exported.[4] By the late 1830's, production of cotton on coastal plantations had increased to the point that exports of raw cotton began on a small scale.[5] Of considerable importance in this period was the establishment of European trading firms.[6] Operating mainly in the external sector, these firms provided vital institutional links with overseas markets and supply sources, and initiated a role which, in later decades, was to be of great consequence for the evolution of the Peruvian business system.

In 1841, a distinct new era of expansion emerged based on the export of guano fertilizer and nitrate, and there followed a long, if occasionally interrupted, period of commercial growth which came to an end in 1879 in a disastrous war with Chile. Notwithstanding this costly episode and in spite of the financial crises which had plagued the economy from time to time,[a] the basic outlines of the country's twentieth century economic and business structure began to appear.[7] In time, the economy recovered from the aftermath of war and resumed the expansionary course of the earlier period, one of the chief changes being the gradual rise of United States investment in the country.

While it is neither necessary nor desirable to dwell at length upon the events of this formative period, several of its more notable developments must be mentioned to explain more adequately the later course of business evolution. The growth of the period clearly had its origins in the expansion and the increasing complexity of the export sector. Guano, nitrates, sugar, cotton, copper, silver, lead, zinc, and petroleum all contributed in varying degrees to the country's earnings of foreign exchange.[8] Foreign-owned businesses had a hand in much of this new investment activity, and indeed assumed a dominant role in the capital-intensive mining industry of the present century. For that matter, foreign workers were even brought in from the Orient to provide a portion of the labor power needed in such fields as guano extraction, sugar and cotton production, and railway construction.[9] Yet it should not be overlooked that Peruvian nationals and resident immigrants also participated in the growth of the export sector, in both minerals and commercial agricultural operations.[10] From these activities, in fact, sprang a number of the more substantial accumulations of domestic capital and, no less importantly, accumulations of business experience.[b]

In the course of developing this diversified export sector, there was, of course, a buildup of infrastructure. Port and harbor facilities were improved, and

[a]Civil wars and political squabbles, *coups d' etat,* assorted international disputes, and the emancipation of the slaves in 1854 — all were disruptive of the economic development of the country during the early years of independence, but perhaps few factors were so inimical to a more satisfactory evolution than the disordered state of the fiscal system, and public administration generally. The handling (or, perhaps more accurately, the mishandling) of the government debt, both external and internal, was a source of scandal and caused grave difficulties for the nation in reaching a satisfactory external position, despite export growth. No less damaging were the government's unsound policy in the guano trade and the apparently widespread speculation which further weakened the flimsy revenue position of the state.

[b]The ranks of the admittedly small wealthy and middle classes were also swelled by those who became affluent by routes less related to business achievement, that is, by positions in the growing bureaucracy and access to an ill-protected public purse.

with a certain promotional and financial flamboyance, the main structure of the country's rather disconnected railway system was laid down: scattered narrow-gauge lines up the agricultural valleys of the coast and lines from the coast to the interior highlands in the central and southern parts of the republic. Here and there private short-haul lines were also built to serve the oil fields and particular mining operations. Telecommunications services were developed, though with limited geographical coverage, and various other types of public utility concerns were initiated in the few but growing urban centers of consequence — Lima, Callao, and Arequipa chiefly, and to a lesser extent in Trujillo, Chiclayo, Piura, Ica, and Huancayo. However embryonic it was for decades, the nucleus of a national market was at least beginning to take shape in the form of a major metropolitan market — Lima and Callao — linked quite imperfectly with a constellation of satellite provincial markets. These latter, in turn, served as the points of intersection which, even more imperfectly, linked the more modern and commercialized portions of the economy with the highly segmented, localized markets of the country's indigenous economic sector.

With the growth of the export sector, there was also a corresponding development of various business institutions. Mercantile firms active in that sector emerged as major focal points of domestic capital accumulation and developed rudimentary distributional networks serving the coastal markets and, to a lesser extent, scattered portions of the highlands. Frequently established by immigrant entrepreneurs, the mercantile concerns were local branches of foreign-based international trading firms. Providing institutional channels through which market information, knowledge of production techniques, and new business skills could flow into Peru from abroad, many of these trading houses (now properly designated as "old-line" mercantile firms) were often linked with the new banking and insurance institutions which they helped establish to provide the local financial services required for the conduct of foreign trade. In recent years these old-line firms have often used their advantages to diversify their holdings further by establishing new industrial undertakings. Of some consequence also were the retail establishments initiated in this long formative period, particularly those established in later decades by immigrant entrepreneurs in the Lima market.

Finally, mention should also be made of the incipient industrialization which took place in Peru in this early period. In 1847, the industrial age arrived when the first modern looms for cotton weaving were imported.[11] A second cotton mill was established in Ica in 1892, with others following. By 1902, when the Ministerio de Fomento published a survey of domestic industries, seven comparatively modern cotton mills were operating in the country.[12] The closing two decades of the 1800's was a period of special importance for Peruvian manufacturing, for by the time of the 1902 official survey, there were dozens of small-scale factories and mills operating in the country, using machinery to produce such varied lines as cottonseed oil, stearine for soap and candle-making, hats, shoes and leather goods, woolens, tobacco products, matches, lumber and furniture, paper, lard, wheat flour, bottled beverages (wines, beer, soft drinks), and pasta. Four petroleum refineries were operating in Peru as well. During the first 20 years of the present century manufacturing installations were also set up to turn out new products such as biscuits, candies, chocolate, pasteurized milk, glassware, shirts, aluminum ware, rubber goods, electric light bulbs, and a variety of the items customarily produced in knitting mills. During this period there were even the beginnings of a modest producer goods industry. Small foundries and machine shops were set up, and assorted smelters for processing the output of the mines were also established during the nineteenth and early twentieth centuries.

The Present Structure of the Peruvian Economy

Even though the importance of the foregoing developments should not be overemphasized (since the economy remained heavily dependent upon agriculture and, to a significant degree, upon export-oriented mining), the point is that Peru had acquired a modicum of industrial and manufacturing experience by the end of the 1920's.

During the 1930's and the 1940's, the interplay of both internal and external conditions resulted in further expansion of this industrial base. Domestically, the gradual growth of population and income, along with urbanization, had provided for a slowly widening home market, especially in the coastal region, which was the region best served by the distributional system. At the same time the evolution of an industrial labor force, the accumulation of domestic capital, and the perfection of business skills were increasing the country's potential to meet this demand from local production facilities — especially for lines in which international transport costs provided some protection from external competition. In addition, here and there the movement of import duties to somewhat higher levels, ostensibly for purposes of revenue, began to provide a measure of tariff protection, although Peru was much less aggressive in employing tariffs to promote domestic industrialization than many of the other Latin American republics were. A commitment to industrialization was symbolized by the creation of a government-sponsored Industrial Bank in 1936, although the modest amount of resources channelled through this institution suggests that for years it was not much more than a symbol.

It was, however, probably external events which, during the thirties and forties, supplied the main impetus to accelerated industrial development — just as they did in other countries in the hemisphere.[13] Foreign exchange shortages during the world depression, together with the general disorder afflicting the economies which traditionally served as the sources of Peruvian imports, favored some displacement of imports by home production. Further shifts in this direction occurred when World War II cut off for several years many of the erstwhile foreign suppliers of Peruvian imports and, temporarily at least, opened up foreign export markets for some Peruvian manufactures — older ones such as textiles and newer ones such as fish products. For a while during the middle forties Peru's government seemed disposed to employ a wide variety of interventionary measures to force the pace of internally oriented development. But the regime's tenure of office was comparatively brief; and with the *coup d'état* which brought General Manuel Odría to power, the dominant thrust of public policy lay in a dismantling of the economic controls which had been born during the Depression and wartime eras. Thereafter, the growth of industry, while aided now and then by tariff measures, continued to respond to the "normal" stimuli which had encouraged it all along: public investment outlays with their multiplier effects, export expansion with its effects on income levels, population growth, urbanization, the establishment of local assembly operations, and so on. Undoubtedly at least a portion of the new investment in manufacturing was made, however, to take advantage of the liberal import and foreign exchange policies then prevailing, as well as in anticipation of the possibility that import-substitution policies might be pressed more vigorously in the future. It should also be noted that the 1950's witnessed a most remarkable boom in the fishing industry which had already begun to develop in the preceding decade — and also in the ancillary industries supplying the fishing activities.

Aggregate Measures of Economic Growth and Change

According to Peruvian income and product accounts, the 1950 to 1965 period was one of rapid and reasonably sustained growth in the economy (except for a recession in 1956-1957). Although some degree of inflation was present, particularly towards the end of the period, the Peruvian gross national product increased in real terms at an average annual rate of 5.6 percent.[14] Population growth was high and, unfortunately, rising throughout this decade and a half, but the aggregate performance was nevertheless sufficient to give a 3 percent rate of growth in the average annual increase in real per capita gross national product.[15]

Behind this record lay a high rate of capital formation — gross investment averaged 24 percent of GNP during 1950-1965 — and structural shifts in production as well as a generally favorable export situation. From the last of these sources of expansion, foreign exchange earnings grew at an average annual rate of 8.9 percent for the 15 years following 1950, thanks in part to particularly rapid increases in fishing products, iron, and coffee.[16] From 1950 to 1964 the output of the fishing industry grew at an average annual rate of 19.5 percent, while that of the agricultural sector (including tree crops) grew at a rate of only 3.8 percent. Other sectors of production ranged between the two; e.g., manufacturing and mining averaged about 7.8 percent annually while electrical power averaged 8.8 percent. By 1965 the GNP stood at approximately $3.3 billion while the per capita gross product was in the neighborhood of $279.[17]

Table 2-1 presents an overview of the structural changes which occurred in the Peruvian economy between 1950 and 1964.[18]

Fishing

In a relatively few years fishing grew to become one of Peru's largest industries; by 1964 Peru was the world leader in its catch of fish. While tinned fish figured importantly in the initial development of the industry in the forties, fish meal became by far the most important of the products of the industry during the fifties. In recent years, there has been some research effort to adapt this product for human consumption, but thus far little progress has been made. Whereas fish are usually abundant off the coast of Peru because of the plankton-rich Humboldt current which comes up the coast from the south, they tend to disappear (apparently moving farther out to sea) from time to time when *El Niño,* another current, pushes down from the north. Recently the effects of switches in these currents, with some possibility of over-fishing, has led to a decline in the anchovy catch, which represents some 98 percent of the annual haul. In early 1966 the government introduced a short closed season for commercial fishing, having previously also intervened to lend support to the formation of an export combine. In 1969 it appeared likely that an even greater role was being contemplated for government involvement in the industry, although the exact nature of the new policies was not yet fully determined.

Agriculture

Agriculture constitutes one of the chief problems in Peruvian development. Its role, however, is vital to the economy inasmuch as expanded agricultural output is needed to feed a rapidly increasing population, to furnish raw materials for the manufacturing sector, to increase exports, to save the foreign exchange spent on food imports, and to raise the income levels of the large portion of the labor force employed in the rural sector.

Along the coast, a fairly modern type of agricultural exploitation is common, but in the impoverished interior — where, unfortunately, a large part of the population lives — the situation is much less favorable.[19] There, environmental problems (e.g., rugged mountains, arid regions, dense jungles, low-quality soils, etc.) have combined with cultural factors (such as illiteracy and the persistence of indigenous languages and ways of life), social organizational problems (unproductive land tenure arrangements), and overcrowding to produce especially difficult problems for raising output and incomes. As of the moment, only a beginning has been made in devising and implementing the kinds of complex programs necessary for incorporating the farmers of the interior more effectively into the national economic structure. In 1969, however, the military government promulgated a new agrarian reform law which seemed to signal a more serious

Table 2-1

Real Gross National Product by Industrial Sector, 1950–64 (Millions of *soles*[1] at 1963 prices)

	1950	1955	1960	1964
Agriculture and tree crops	8,790	11,190	13,386	14,909
Fishing	160	333	1,041	1,949
Mining	1,768	2,667	4,585	5,135
Manufacturing	5,286	7,681	10,642	15,181
Construction	2,000	3,218	2,671	3,589
Electric power, gas, water	218	252	480	709
Housing	3,404	3,784	4,345	4,920
Government	3,432	4,187	5,046	7,336
Other (commerce, transport, services, finance)	13,898	18,753	21,979	31,124
GNP	38,956	52,065	64,175	84,852

[1]Exchange rate: 27 *soles* = $1.00.

effort to reorganize and modernize the agricultural sector, although implementation of the new approach began not in the highlands but with the expropriation of the wasted sugar properties.

Mining

Although only 2 percent of the employed workers are in mining,[20] minerals output accounted for approximately 6 percent of the Peruvian GNP in 1964 and represented a major source of foreign exchange. Since the early fifties in particular, the Peruvian government has encouraged investment in this sector, and foreign capital, together with smaller amounts of domestic capital, has responded to the considerable investment potential of the field. Large, primarily United States-owned mining companies presently extract great quantities of copper, lead, zinc, iron ore, gold, and silver. The mines also produce molybdenum, tungsten, manganese, and varite. Petroleum, Peru's second most valuable mineral product after copper, is pumped in quantities sufficient to cover most of the country's increasing needs, although the exportable surplus of the petroleum fields has dwindled appreciably since 1957. Deposits of various minerals are worked in many parts of the *sierra*, but the petroleum fields are located mainly in northwestern Peru. Some exploration, however, continues in the Amazonian basin area. With the installation of a military government following the deposition of President Belaunde, one foreign-owned petroleum company was expropriated and by 1969 there were strong indications that more nationalistic policies would eventually be applied to the mining sector.

Manufacturing

Manufacturing production has been growing more rapidly than the economy as a whole, and the approximately 14 percent of the labor force employed in that field now produces an output of greater value than the 50 percent of the work force employed in agriculture.

Production has centered on consumer nondurable goods, although both consumer durables and capital goods are being produced locally to a greater and greater extent, as indicated in Table 2-2.[21]

The fact that domestic production of consumer nondurable goods has not increased its share of the market may be partially explained by the fact that this industry group is relatively mature and fairly competitive. New investment has apparently preferred to seek the less competitive, less developed industries. Production of intermediate goods has increased locally, but because industry overall has grown so rapidly, there has been no reduction in the need for imports.

The food, beverage, and clothing industries in Peru account for roughly 50

Table 2-2

**Relative Participation of Net National
Production and Imports among Major
Classes of Goods[1]**

	Percentage of Total Production	
Type of Good	*1958*	*1963*
Consumer nondurables		
Local production	68.8	67.9
Imports	31.2	32.1
Consumer durables		
Local production	12.6	17.4
Imports	87.4	82.6
Capital goods		
Local production	8.7	15.9
Imports	91.3	84.1
Intermediate goods		
Local production	53.6	52.4
Imports	46.4	47.6

[1]Net national production is defined as "net
of imported inputs."

percent of total national production. Table 2-3 gives an indication of the performance of the ten fastest-growing industries over the 1958-1963 period.

Industry is heavily concentrated in the Lima-Callao area. Almost all capital goods are produced there. Variations in the aggregate value of production per inhabitant for some of the major areas of Peru show a tremendous difference in the level of industrialization.

The Comisión de Industrias, of the Instituto de Planificación, summarizes major problem areas of industry in this way:

1. Forty-five percent of the industrial production consists of the elementary trans-formation of raw materials of mining and agriculture.

2. The gross national production of final industrial goods accounts for 69 percent of the market. That this participation is reduced 50 percent if imported inputs are discounted reveals a high dependence on foreign supply.

3. The overall growth of the sector (1958-1963) was not accompanied by a substantive growth of basic industry. This limits the future possibilities of expansion and of import substitution.

4. Industry shows a low capacity for absorbing labor. Due to its limited volume, it absorbed only 9.6 percent of the annual increase of the labor force between 1958 and 1963.

5. Industrial production is centralized to a degree of 59 percent in the Lima-Callao area. Of the production generated in the rest of the country, nearly 69 percent consists of the semielaboration of raw materials destined for export.

6. Ninety-eight and one-half percent of the industrial production is in the hands of the private sector, characterized by a high concentration in few businesses. Fifty percent of the gross value of industrial production is generated by only 155 firms.[22]

The Foreign Trade Sector

Like most underdeveloped countries, Peru is highly dependent on its external sector, which generally represents between 20 and 25 percent of its GNP. Since Peru has insufficient production facilities to meet internal demand, especially for capital goods, export earnings play a vital role in the economy. And, given the relatively high import content of investment expenditures, it is clear that the generally good performance of Peruvian exports in recent years has been closely related, in a facilitating way, to the remarkably high capital formation rate which Peru maintained between 1950 and 1965. At the same time, however, it is evident that the operation of a good many industries already in existence depends upon a continuing supply of various imported inputs. As would be expected, the import trend is toward more capital goods, raw materials, and intermediary products, but to relatively fewer consumer goods — this despite Peru's inability to feed its people as revealed by the fact that food products, in raw or processed form, accounted for more than 15 percent of imports in 1965.[23]

For a number of reasons, therefore, Peru is fortunate that its rather diversified set of exports has grown as much as it has over the past years: from

Table 2-3

Growth Rates of the Ten Fastest Growing Industries During the 1958–1963
Period

Industry	Average Annual Growth Rate 1958–1963 (Percentage)
Non-electrical machinery	31.8
Electrical machinery	28.4
Transport equipment	22.2
Simple metals	20.0
Printing	19.6
Chemicals	12.4
Furniture	12.0
Paper	11.8
Shoes and clothing	11.4
Beverages	11.3

Source: *Diagnóstico*, p. 12.

Table 2-4

Aggregate Value of Industrial Output
by Region

Area	Soles per Capita per Year (1963)
Lima-Callao	4,340
Central	1,040
North	893
Northcentral	710
South	492
Southcentral	180
Northeast	137
Southeast	103

Source: *Diagnóstico*, p. 12.

$193.6 million in 1950 to $667.3 million in 1965.[24] While imports, more often than not, have exceeded exports, the balance has been financed through substantial inflows of private investment capital and loans from the World Bank, the Export-Import Bank of Washington, and other lending agencies.[25] Thus for the most part (excepting, chiefly, the 1957-58 period), Peru was able to maintain a strong position in its exchange reserves. The impact of the recent nationalistic policies of the government may alter this situation.

The United States is by far the most important single customer for Peru's exports, having purchased 31 percent of the total exports in 1964.[26] Another 44 percent went to Western European countries. Exports to other Latin American countries were not very important, accounting for approximately 10 percent of the total.

The breakdown of 1964 imports is very similar to that for exports. Again the United States emerges as the most important trading partner, supplying 41 percent of Peru's total imports. Western Europe contributed 34 percent of the total, and other Latin American countries supplied approximately 12 percent.

Peru's good fortune in having a more diversified export base than many of its neighbors is a situation that offers some stability to the economy. Leading exports in 1964 are shown in Table 2-6.

Labor, Employment, and Productivity

Over half the economically active population of Peru is engaged in agricultural activity and mining. This conforms to the general pattern of Latin America, but contrasts sharply with the United States where manufacturing engages a far higher percentage of the labor force. Most of Peru's employable population, however, are poorly trained. SENATI (National Service of Apprenticeship and Industrial Labor) estimates that more than half of the industrial labor force is unskilled as indicated in Table 2-8.[27]

SENATI's estimates of deficiencies (difference between number needed and number available) of professionals-technicians and white-collar workers are 60.5 and 20 percent, respectively.[28] In early 1966, SENATI opened a technical training center financed by a 1 percent payroll tax on employers. Similar training programs to raise skills (and hence productivity) are in effect under other sponsorship. Altogether, however, the various programs fall far short of national needs in this area.

Unemployment

No reliable unemployment statistics for Peru are available, but the government estimates that unemployment is somewhere between 5 and 10 percent of the labor force. The true problem is greater than this estimate might indicate, because Peru suffers from considerable underemployment. In downtown Lima,

Table 2-5

Structure of Inputs of Peruvian Industry (Imported Inputs as Percentage of Total Inputs)

Industry Group	Percentage		
	1958	1961	1963
Consumer goods industries	20.2	26.2	23.2
Intermediate goods industries	18.5	21.2	21.4
Capital goods industries	69.0	73.8	79.0

Source: *Diagnóstico*, p. 29.

Table 2-6

Peru's Principal Exports, 1964

Commodity	Percent of Total Exports	Cumulative Percentage
Fishmeal	20.0	20.0
Copper	15.4	35.4
Cotton	13.3	48.7
Sugar	9.5	58.2
Silver	6.8	65.0
Zinc	5.8	70.8
Iron ore	5.8	76.6
Coffee	5.5	82.1
Lead	4.9	87.0

Source: U.S. Department of Commerce, OBR 65–46, p. 18

Table 2-7

Economically Active Population by Sector

	Percentage		
Sector	Peru 1961	Latin America 1960	U. S. 1961
Agriculture	50.0	47.2	7.4
Mining	2.1	.9	.9
Manufacturing	12.8	14.3	21.9
Construction	3.1	4.1	3.8
Other	32.0	33.5	66.0
Total	100.0	100.0	100.0

Sources: U. S. Department of Commerce, OBR 65–46, p. 14 (Peru); Alberto Baltra Cortes, *Crecimiento económico de América Latina* (Santiago, Chile: 1964), p. 117 (Latin America); and *The Annual Report of the Council of Economic Advisors* (Washington: 1964), pp. 230, 237.

Table 2-8

Labor Force by Type of Employee

Type of Employee	Percentage of Total Labor Force
Professionals, technicians	2.1
White–collar workers	14.9
Skilled and semi–skilled labor	31.5
Unskilled labor	51.5
Total	100.0

for example, there is a profusion of street peddlers selling only pencils, purses, lottery tickets, small sheets of polyethylene, or other very inexpensive items. Technically these people are employed, but certainly both from the standpoint of their earnings and productivity they are underemployed.

Wages

By United States standards, wages are extremely low. A 1963 survey in the Lima-Callao area showed that the average base wage of daily paid workers was $2.01 a day, and the average salary of white-collar workers $126.41 per month.[29] Wages are generally lower in the provinces. Agricultural wages in 1962 ranged from $.56 to $1.68 a day.[30] The average manufacturing work week in Peru in 1963 was 47 hours, compared to 40.4 hours in the United States.[31]

Fringe Benefits

A sizable share of labor and white-collar earnings comes in the form of fringe benefits, paid for the most part by the employer. In 1962 the cost of such items as termination pay, vacations, retirement pensions, profit-sharing bonuses, payments to the health and social welfare fund, life insurance, service bonuses, cost-of-living bonuses, workmen's compensation, and related benefits, came to 60.4 percent of the basic wage for laborers and 50.6 percent of the basic salary for white-collar workers.[32]

Productivity

Output per worker in Peru is generally low due to factors such as inadequate training, poor health standards, deficient diet, depressed living conditions, and low capital ratios in most industries. The gross product produced per worker in all of manufacturing equalled 196,200 soles (approximately $7,300) in 1963. Due primarily to high efficiency in the mining industry,[33] productivity in the export industries (584,000 soles per worker) was much higher than in the industries producing for domestic consumption (166,200 soles per worker). As shown in Table 2-9, productivity has been increasing in Peru, especially in the more mature consumer goods industry.

Table 2-9

**Rates of Growth in Productivity by
Industrial Classification (1958–1963)**

	Annual Rates of Growth (Percent)		
Industry	Labor Force	Output	Productivity
Consumer Goods	4.1	9.7	5.4
Intermediate Goods	5.1	6.5	1.3
Capital Goods	21.3	23.4	1.7
Total Industry	6.1	9.6	3.3

Source: *Diagnóstico*, p. 40.

Government and Business

Attitudes Toward Business

The Peruvian government is committed to rapid economic development,[34] and for the 20 years after 1948 gave strong indications that private investment should play a vital role in this growth. Accordingly, over the years it enacted legislation designed to attract private investment through tax incentives and other liberal provisions. Legislation such as the Mining Code, the Petroleum Code, the Electrical Utilities Law, and the Industrial Promotion Law were among the positive efforts made to attract private capital. Following the *coup d'état* of 1968, however, it appears that the government's attitude toward the private sector has become much more qualified.

The Industrial Promotion Law (No. 13270, November 30, 1959) offers several benefits for industries engaged in the manufacture of articles considered as basic.[35] These industries are entitled to such benefits as:

1. Exemption from all import duties on machinery equipment that is new, essential, and not competitive with local products.
2. The right to purchase or lease State land.
3. Exemption from all taxes except the stamp tax (if the industry is new) for a three- to ten-year period depending upon the location of the investment.
4. The right to invest from 30 to 100 percent of profits tax-free.
5. The right to adjust depreciation to major fluctuations in the currency (as measured against the United States dollar).
6. The right to use accelerated depreciation.
7. Exemptions from some indirect taxes for a fifteen-year period.

Industries engaged in the manufacture of articles not considered as basic may also receive similar benefits to a more limited degree.

Because industrialization is so concentrated in the Lima-Callao area, the government is especially eager to develop industry in other parts of the country. Thus benefits become progressively higher as investors settle in the coastal zone outside Lima-Callao, the *sierra*, and the *selva*.

It is also the formally declared national policy that there shall be no industrial or commercial monopolies (Article 16 of the Constitution). Unfortunately, such a policy is probably not economically feasible in some Peruvian industries, because the small market will not support several efficient, large-scale manufacturers. In other instances, the concentration of venture capital and other factors tend to limit the entry of competitors into a field. In reality, therefore, there are presently many local monopolies and some virtual monopolies on a national scale. While satisfactory empirical evidence is lacking, it is often said that collusive agreements (informal or otherwise) occasionally blunt the force of competition in a number of multifirm industries. During the interviews for the study covered in this book, the interviewers heard several references to industry meetings at which such things as prices and market areas are discussed. These meetings are advertised openly and are found in both consumer and industrial goods industries. One respondent made the point that although some firms will enter agreements, they will not conform to the terms of the agreements. In other words, collusive practices are acceptable to some firms as long as they, themselves, do not have to give up anything.

Government and Taxation

Any government must, of course, collect revenues to conduct its business. Unfortunately the Peruvian taxpayer does not always seem to pay his share of government expenses (cheating on personal income tax is said to be common, and many taxpayers simply do not pay the taxes they owe).[36] Because policing individual taxpayers is difficult, the government looks for most of its revenues from businesses, which are more easily scrutinized. Import-export duties and business taxes therefore provide the government with the bulk of its income.

Trade or Business Profits Tax: Taxable income is defined as being the difference between gross receipts and the total of expenses, charges, and losses which are necessarily incurred in the trade or business, excluding capital gains, proceeds from sales of trademarks and patents, income from foreign sources, dividends received, and certain rental income. The tax rate begins at 7 percent on the first 10,000 soles and rises progressively to 37 percent on profits over 5,000,000 soles. Because the tax is progressive, businesses sometimes find it expedient to subdivide artificially into several smaller businesses, each showing a lower absolute profit.

Special Business Income Taxes: Special tax schedules are applied to such business income as 1) interest, the rate being based on the full amount of interest received; 2) real estate income, with a rate of 7 percent after deductions; and 3) capital gains, taxed at a progressive rate of from 7 to 15 percent.

Surtax: Individuals and corporations are subject to a surtax based upon after-tax income. The tax schedule is complicated, with different rates applying to different types of income, but the basic schedule runs from zero on the first 30,000 soles up to 30 percent on income over 100,000 soles.

Stamp Taxes: These taxes are essentially documentary in nature, their incidence depending largely upon the type of document involved. Almost all documents bearing an acknowledgment of payment or obligation to pay a sum of money are subject to the tax. The rate is 5 percent on sales, 1 percent on salaries and wages, 1 percent of professional fees and 2 percent on real estate rentals.

Sales Tax: The sales tax is particularly interesting because it affects marketing directly. It is imposed each time a sale is recorded. Thus it is payable when the manufacturer sells to the wholesaler, the wholesaler to the retailer, and the retailer to the consumer. The tax encourages companies to sell on consignment (to eliminate a sale), shorten their channels (to eliminate a middleman), and to integrate vertically.

Other Taxes: Businesses are obligated to pay several other taxes, including: unemployment tax; registration taxes; business franchise taxes; foreign insurance taxes; a labor-training tax (SENATI); a tax for the Fund of Health and Social Welfare; and a social security tax. Special taxes have also been imposed upon specific industries (e.g. outdoor advertising and the beer industry).

Although the Peruvian government is committed to encouraging private investment, we feel that the complicated tax structure is injurious, because it encourages businessmen to resort to tax avoidance and evasion rather than to concentrate on operating more efficiently. The amount of taxes upon business does not matter so much (the consumer may well pay them in the long run), but the form that they take is confusing and interferes with efficiency. The government, however, having recognized the need for tax reform, has been studying the problem in recent years.

Government and Social Legislation

A substantial portion of a business's labor expense is the result of social legislation. Two of the more important pieces of such legislation in Peru are those which govern severance pay and retirement benefits.

Severance pay is especially high in Peru: basically it equals one month's pay for each year of service for both laborers and white-collar workers. Apparently it is extremely difficult for an employer to fire a worker without having to pay this amount. But as one might expect, a variety of subterfuges appear to have been devised to moderate the effects of this legislation on the firm.

Current legislation requires that the employer pay a pension to all male employees after 30 years' service. This income (which provides for all employees hired prior to July 12, 1962) must equal an employee's full salary during his last year of work. Somewhat reduced payments are obligatory for men after 25 years' service; a similar plan is in force for women. Employees hired after July 1962 are covered under a government pension plan, and the employer has no responsibility for their pension, aside from regular contributions to the social security funds. As with the severance pay obligations, it appears that many companies have sought methods of escaping legal requirements for retirement payments.

Government and Trade Policy

"Peru's trade policy is designed chiefly to stimulate national economic development and regional economic integration, to raise revenue for operating the Government, and to encourage international trade."[37] These policies are mainly achieved by regulating the level of customs duties and charges rather than by applying exchange restrictions or trade quotas.

Duties are generally high on luxury goods and on certain products that compete with locally produced goods. Equipment and goods considered essential to Peru's economic development are generally "dutied" at a low rate. Duties are usually expressed by a charge based upon weight or volume plus an ad valorem rate. Aside from the tariff itself, there are other import-connected taxes, such as a 1 percent charge for improvement of the port of Callao. These taxes, each fairly small in itself, mount up. An an example of this, imports of agricultural machinery are considered to be essential to Peru's development and therefore subject to only a token tariff. However, the miscellaneous taxes imposed with the importation of farm tractors brings the total charge to approximately 10 percent.[c]

The government is also committed to promoting the Latin American Free Trade Association (LAFTA, or ALALC in its Spanish form), an economic integration scheme initiated in 1960. The authors' impressions, gained during informal discussions, indicate that Peruvian businessmen have a relatively uniform attitude toward LAFTA at present. They agree the idea is a good one, and that sooner or (more probably) later it will become a reality. However, they feel that Mexico, Brazil, and Argentina are so far ahead of Peru that these countries would reap the benefits of a free trade agreement, whereas industry in Peru and the other less-developed countries would suffer. Thus they see a need for special concessions to the latter nations, including their own.

In March 1966, member countries of LAFTA met in Panama to discuss the problems of further integration. Reflecting the viewpoint mentioned above,

[c]This statement was made by the sales manager of a firm that imports and sells farm tractors. The interview was held in April 1966.

Peru's delegation presented a formal declaration requesting concessions. The delegates generally indicated that Peru supported further integration, but specifically mentioned that the less-developed countries should get special assistance, should not be forced into reciprocity agreements, and should not be forced to do anything that would endanger domestic economic and social development.[38] The latter proposal, if interpreted broadly, could make true integration an impossibility, and recent LAFTA negotiations on further trade liberalization have indicated a growing resistance on the part of many members to the granting of additional concessions.

It was interesting that during our talks with Peruvian businessmen not one manufacturer mentioned the positive aspect of economic integration, i.e. that it would open up other markets within Latin America for him. Discussions invariably assumed a defensive nature, reflecting perhaps a lack of competitive spirit in Peruvian industry. Interviewees showed almost no concern for the high prices that the Peruvian consumer must pay; instead, manufacturers were worried about the likely prospect of being put out of business by more efficient manufacturers in other Latin American countries.

In summary, although the free trade area concept appears to be accepted in a general sense by both Peruvian government and business, industry is basically opposed to making specific changes in trade policy which would reduce the hitherto protected positions of many businesses.

Government and Price Controls

As is common in Latin America, the government takes a direct role in regulating marketing by controlling prices of several commodities, primarily those that are basic to the needs of the consumer (such as flour, rice, produce, meat, drugs, and rent). Where rents are concerned, controlled prices are so unrealistic as to discriminate widely between renters who have been in one place for a long time and renters seeking new houses or apartments. (Rent is controlled by forbidding landlords to raise rent while a person is occupying the property.) This also discourages landlords from making improvements on existing buildings. It is not unusual to hear stories in Lima of landlords who attempt to *give* houses or apartments to the people who are renting them. Apparently the rental agreement was started long ago and at present the taxes and other expenses are more than the rent payment. The tenants naturally refuse the gift. These stories may or may not be true, but they do indicate the position in which some landlords have found themselves.

One of the most frequently used transportation methods, particularly for the poorer people in Lima as well as in the *departamentos,* is the *collectivo,* a kind of communal taxi which plies a regular route and collects a fare which is set by the government depending upon the zones of origin and destination. The Lima to San Isidro route, a trip of perhaps five miles, takes about one-half hour. On a round trip, a *collectivo* owner can make a maximum of about 25 soles, less than a dollar even before the recent devaluation. Although the owner's expenses are rising, he cannot raise the fare. As a result, many car owners are simply living on their capital and when their car is too old to run they will not be able to replace it. The situation is made even worse because many amateurs use their private automobiles as *collectivos* and regular taxis on their off-duty hours.

Some of the prices that are subject to government control are listed as follows:[d]

Pharmaceuticals	Sugar
Kerosene, gasoline,	Rice
and other fuels	Milk
Transportation	Bread
Movies	Flour
Soft drinks	Coffee
Beans	Meat

The government's influence on prices extends beyond this list, because many companies hesitate to raise prices out of fear of government retaliation.

Government Businesses

Although the future is likely to bring some changes in government policy, the intervention of the state as a producing agent has not been of great significance in Peru thus far. The government controls only 1.6 percent of the gross national product.[39]

Probably the most important producing business of the government is the steel mill at Chimbote, an operation that has not been a success. After the imposition of protective tariffs on foreign steel, the government steel corporation (SOGESA) has taken to importing the foreign steel itself (it is cheaper to import than to produce) and then selling it at inflated prices to businessmen. The government tobacco monopoly is the second largest of the state-sector producers. This operation, too, has not been a success — production has declined in recent years. In 1965 the government decided to turn the monopoly back to private industry. Other government producers in order of size are in the fields of 1) military clothing; 2) petroleum refining; 3) military leather; 4) police footwear; 5) salt; and 6) concrete pipes for water and sanitation.

Aside from manufacturing, the government runs the Peruvian Steamship Corporation, operating between Callao and North American ports; the Airport and Commercial Aviation Corporation, running the airports; an airline serving the more remote regions of Peru; a chain of excellent tourist hotels; several banks which support development activities; the Corporation of Fertilizers, producing and selling fertilizers; several railroads; and several hydroelectric power plants.[40] The government in 1969 began to turn its attention to a reorganization of the enterprises of the public sector to convert them into more effective instruments for development.

[d]This list, obtained from the United States Embassy, Commercial Section, is not official and is incomplete. We were unable to locate a complete list.

3

The Peruvian Market Environment

Marketing behavior, like all other forms of human behavior, is linked inseparably with the environment in which it takes place. Variables such as social tradition, the political system, geography, population, and levels of education, shape marketing practices to a notable extent. Altogether, these and the factors which compose the marketing infrastructure set the parameters within which marketing strategy is operative. It is therefore distinctly relevant here to consider the conditions which, in Peru, provide the milieu for industrial marketing policies. The salient characteristic of this market environment is a pronounced fragmentation of a multifaceted sort.

Geographical Factors

Peru encompasses an area of 496,222 square miles, roughly three times the size of California. The third largest nation on the South American continent, Peru is physically a country of great geographical contrast, from barren deserts to snow-covered mountains to dense steamy jungles. These features represent the basic three-way geographical division of Peru.

The Costa

The coastal desert, which extends from Ecuador to Chile, includes 11 percent of Peru's total land area. This area is usually divided by Peruvians into the *costa baja* (up to 850 feet above sea level) and the *costa alta* (between 850 and 6,500 feet). The former includes dry, flat plains, sometimes with sand dunes, and the latter is comprised of dry foothills and mountains, intricately carved by erosion. Both sections have one thing in common — they receive little or no rain.[1] In fact, the Lima weather station reports an average of one inch of rain annually, and in one place on the coastal desert to the south, no rainfall has been recorded in this century.

Despite the seeming inhospitality of the land, this section of Peru is the most densely populated and developed, and per capita income levels here are higher than elsewhere in the country. This is possible only because of the coastal rivers which carry water down from the mountains to provide irrigation for commercial agriculture as well as water and power for the coastal cities. The coast's sandy soil is highly fertile when supplied with water, and relatively lush river valleys are found up and down the coast (Figure 3-1). Unfortunately, the discharge of the rivers varies widely from month to month and from year to year.[2]

The government, realizing the importance of water to coastal development, is studying the possibility of rerouting the flow of some of the streams and rivers that now send their water down the mountains to the Amazon basin where it is not needed. An expansion of irrigated acreage on the coast has figured importantly in various development programs which have been devised in recent years. These programs, together with other plans for developing the large hydroelectric power potential of the sierran rivers (primarily to increase the supply of low-cost power to the coastal cities), should insure that the coastal markets will continue to play a dominant role in the Peruvian economy for years to come. The redistributive effects of the agrarian reform which began to be applied to coastal properties in 1969 should also do much to broaden the market for many items which are important to popular consumption patterns.

The Sierra

A second principal geographic area of Peru is the *sierra,* which comprises all the Andean highlands and valleys over 6,500 feet. Its average altitude is about 13,000 feet.[3] This area includes three great Andean mountain ranges: the *Cordillera Occidental* (West), the *Cordillera Central* (Central), and the *Cordillera Oriental* (East). The mountains, scattered valleys and plateaus of the sierra comprise 26 percent of Peru's area.[4]

The high valleys, especially between the Cordillera Occidental and the Cordillera Central, are used for agriculture and ranching, water being available from the rivers and moderate rainfall. But mountains transversing the area break the region up and make physical distribution of the output difficult. Furthermore, soil and climatic conditions interact with cultural and economic factors to depress the general level of agricultural productivity (and hence the incomes) in this region. For the most part the farming methods are quite primitive. The agricultural importance of the sierra is also greatly diminished by the difficult problem of transporting rural products over the western ranges to the coastal areas of more dense population, while the same conditions, with the high transport costs they imply, create problems for distributing coastal output to the scattered local markets of the sierra.

To the south around Lake Titicaca lies an immense high plain known as the *Altiplano.* Vegetation is sparse, consisting primarily of a rugged, tufted grass

Figure 3-1 Rivers and Mountain Ranges of Peru.

suitable for the grazing of llamas and alpacas. Living conditions here are difficult, and the Indians inhabiting this cold, wind-swept plain are among the poorest in Peru.

The Selva

The remaining 63 percent of Peru's land area lies east of the Andes and extends to the Amazon basin.[5] It includes a subtropical forest reaching up the eastern Andean slopes to a height of 11,000 feet (known as *ceja de la montaña,* or "eyebrow of the mountain") and the jungle proper (the *selva*).

Because rainfall is excessive in the selva (up to 193 inches annually), man's greatest problem there is to restrain the jungle growth and clear the land.[6] Once the land is cleared, the heavy rainfall quickly leaches the soil, discouraging the development of agriculture on a commercial basis. A shifting, subsistence-type cultivation does, however, provide a livelihood for some of the population of the region. Meanwhile, the LeTourneau Company has invested in a project in the region to demonstrate its agricultural potential. After clearing the land with large earth-moving equipment, they have planted grass and begun grazing cattle. They are now flying beef cattle daily to Lima.[7] The general commercial feasibility of the undertaking, however, has not as yet been altogether established.

The selva is at present undeveloped and sparsely settled. The lush vegetation hints at greater resource potential, but the difficult terrain within the area and the forbidding mountains between jungle and coast makes any development plan tremendously expensive. Relatively more promising, especially in terms of future commercial development, are the higher slopes of the ceja de la montaña, though even here the settlement and development problems are formidable.

The Peruvian selva abounds with rivers flowing off the eastern Andean slopes and joining together to feed the Amazon. Major tributary rivers of the Amazon are the Apurimac, the Ucayali, and the Marañon. Besides the possible future utility of some of these as sources of power, in some instances they provide a means of transport in a region in which alternative means of moving about are quite limited.

Demography

Population statistics can be used to describe a country in many different ways. Here they have been organized in a manner that reveals some of the major problems facing Peru as it seeks economic development.

Table 3-1

Distribution of Peru's Population by Age Group

Age Group	Percentage of Total Population
0–9	32
10–19	21
20–29	16
30–39	12
40–49	8
50–59	5
60 and over	6
	100

Source: República Peruana, *VI Censo nacional de población*, Tomo II (Lima: 1965), Cuadro 30, p. 46.

Rapid Rate of Population Growth

In the last 20 years Peru has experienced one of the highest rates of population growth in the world. Expanding from roughly 6,200,000 in 1940 to 10,400,000 in 1961, Peru's population now has an annual growth rate of almost 3 percent.[8] The problem of raising gross national production faster than population growth is thus extremely difficult.[9] Related to this problem is the fact that today more than 50 percent of the Peruvians are under 20 years of age.

The preponderance of these younger age groups places a burden on the older groups who must support those too young to work.

In the United States and Japan respectively, 40.5 percent and 45.8 percent of the population falls within the 15-64 age bracket, which is roughly equivalent to the economically active group in the United States.[10] The Peruvian census classified as economically active those who are in the country's labor force and who hold or have held remunerative employment. It shows that in 1961 only 31.5 percent of Peru's populace was economically active.

Table 3-2

**Native Language of Population of Five
Years and Over**

Native Language	Urban Population (Percentage)	Rural Population (Percentage)	Total Population (Percentage)
Spanish	76	45	60
Quechua, Aymara, or Aboriginal	22	54	39
Other	2	1	1
	100	100	100

Source: República Peruana, *VI Censo
nacional de población*, Tomo III, Cuadro
49 (Lima: 1965), p. 4.

A Varied Population

In Peru, as in many other countries of the world, a person's status is somewhat associated with his degree of "whiteness," although the actual distinctions must be made more on the basis of cultural (or "life style") than on racial lines. Peru's 1940 census revealed that 53 percent of the population was *mestizo* (a mixture of Indian and white) or white, while 46 percent was Indian.[11] Because respondents placed themselves into a particular category, and because higher social status is accorded the white and *mestizo* groups, it is likely that a higher percentage is actually Indian. The more relevant distinction is those who are culturally defined as Indians. These represent almost half of the population, adhere in varying degree to indigenous ways of life, and are only marginally (at best) integrated into the national economy and society.

Language is an attendant problem for marketers. Although Spanish is the national language and 80 percent of the population now speaks it, it is not the native language for many Peruvians and their facility in it is limited.[12] The native tongue of 39 percent of the population is Quechua or Aymara. Moreover, many of these men and women do not read or write. As a result, linguistic barriers are substantial to general marketing communication as well as to the transmission of information on such matters as new production techniques, particularly among the adult population.

Some 27 percent of the national population lives on the coast, another 65 percent lives in the sierra, and the remaining 8 percent in the eastern portion of the country. It is in the latter two areas that linguistic and cultural diversity are most pronounced. On the coast, the processes of assimilation have occurred to a much greater degree.

Migration to the Cities

In 1961, 47 percent of the population lived in urban areas and 53 percent in rural areas. A comparison with the 1940 census figures shows a strong migration to the cities, particularly those of the coast, although urbanization remains at a level far below that in the United States.

Whereas the overall population increased by 61 percent, the major cities were experiencing a much more rapid growth, as Indians came down from the mountains to the industrializing areas in an effort to better their economic status. As a result of this migration Peru's city governments were unable to keep pace with the population growth, and today the cities are surrounded by extensive slum areas called *barriadas*. The migration is continuing, and there is little hope that the government will be able to keep up with the surging demand for such basic services as electricity, water, and sewers. Since migration appears to be associated with at least a partial commitment to a nonindigenous life style and since it also brings the migrants into much closer proximity to the domestic manufacturing centers, the process of migration has been one factor accounting for the growth of the internal market even though the discretionary income of most of the migrants is scanty.

Level of Education

Illiteracy in Peru is far lower today than it was 20 years ago, but educating its populace remains one of the nation's biggest problems. A rise in the education level of the population is, of course, essential to increasing productivity. Illiteracy, as would be expected, is much higher in the rural areas than in urban centers — a factor which increases the difficulty of absorbing productively the rural migrants into the industrial economy.

More difficult to measure but just as important in evaluating the "quality" of the people is the type of training they have had. Table 3-6 gives an indication of the level of education attained by Peruvians as of the 1961 census. Almost 46 percent of the population had no formal education, and fewer than 1 percent had any university education. Although the levels of education are discouragingly low, the younger generations seem to be getting more education than those which preceded them.

The situation is actually worse than it may appear from Table 3-6, however, because the general quality of education is very low, especially in rural areas and low-income urban districts where, from the standpoint of promoting assimilation, it is most needed. Teaching techniques followed in many of the primary and secondary schools are decades out of date. Lessons are often taught by rote,

Table 3-3

**Breakdown of Population by Urban
and Rural Classifications**

	Peru 1940 (Percentage)	*Peru 1961* (Percentage)	*United States 1960* (Percentage)
Urban	35	47	70
Rural	65	53	30
	100	100	100

Source: Robinson, p. 107 and *The 1963
World Almanac and Book of Facts*, Harry
Hansen, ed. (New York: 1963), p. 252.

Table 3-4

**Population Changes of Some Major
Peruvian Cities, 1940–1961**

City	*Percentage Change in Population (1940–1961)*
Lima	230
Chiclayo	176
Trujillo	170
Arequipa	158
Callao	132

Source: Robinson, p. 108.

Table 3-5

**Literacy Rates of the Population of
Fifteen Years and Over** (Percentage)

	Literate	*Illiterate*
Urban 1961	82	18
Rural 1961	41	59
Total 1940	40	60
Total 1961	61	39

Source: Robinson, p. 85 and *VI Censo,*
Tomo III, Cuadro 57, p. 53.

Table 3-6

**Level of Education Attained by
Peruvians Over Four Years of Age**
(Percentage)

Level of Education	*20–24-Year-Old Group*	*30 Years and Over Group*	*Total Population Over 4 Years of Age*
No education	30.6	44.0	45.8
Some primary	51.2	41.3	43.0
Some secondary (general)	11.9	6.9	7.6
Some secondary (technical or normal)	2.8	1.2	1.1
Some university	1.8	1.5	.9

Source: *VI Censo,* Tomo III, Cuadro 67,
p. 246.

and there is little stimulation for creative thinking except in the very best schools which are extremely expensive.

Universities, which have access to better qualified teachers, are handicapped by the poor quality of the secondary school training, frequent student strikes, the economic obstacles which prevent students from engaging in full-time study, a lack of standards, and wholly inadequate library, classroom, and laboratory facilities. Outmoded curricula and teaching methods present a further problem in a good many fields of study. The notoriously low faculty pay forces many of the professors to work full time outside the university. Not surprisingly, the possibilities for engaging in academic research tend to be rather limited, and the quality of professional training is often impaired. Only in the 1960's has some progress been made in establishing modern business curricula, and even this has been confined entirely to universities in Lima. Consequently the supply of specialized business and technical skills is far from abundant, considering the needs of the country in its present stage of development.

Cultural Differences

The broad divisions of a country presented by its geographical characteristics and economic structure have less tangible counterparts in the environmental area of culturally formed attitudes, values, and social relationships. Given the lack of widespread empirical research on these matters in Peru, the dangers of overgeneralization are apparent. Yet because of the way in which these cultural differences bear on the complexion of the market environment in Peru, it is important to note some of the more significant variations in cultural traits which anthropological and sociological studies have found. One should remember, however, that the evidence on which such assertions are made is rather limited. For this reason the value of these observations is more suggestive than conclusive.

Indigenous Subcultures

In the eastern regions of Peru the rather sparsely distributed indigenous population consists in large part of Indians whose level of cultural development has scarcely transcended the primitive nomadic stage — in which hunting and fishing, with some mixture of shifting subsistence cultivation, form the basis of their livelihood. Around the river port of Iquitos and a few other centers of settlement which have evolved in part through migration from other regions of the country, one finds a more commercial pattern of the organization of resources and a relatively more modern style of social organization in general — these together with some modification in attitudes, tastes, and values. These segments count for comparatively little in the total national market, for reasons of both numbers and aggregate purchasing power (per capita income levels in eastern Peru are exceedingly low).

Of far greater importance (at least potentially) is the much more numerous indigenous population of the sierra. In this region, Indian families who have managed to retain some land over the centuries tend to be grouped into independent communities; the remainder live in dependent communities which have been engulfed at one point or another in the country's history, by the expansion of private estates. These estates are generally owned by nonindigenous landholders, many of whom reside elsewhere – in provincial capitals, in Lima or even in some instances abroad. In both sorts of communities, the basis of livelihood rests heavily on low-productivity farming (with some raising of livestock), small-scale trading activities (with most permanent shops resembling limited-range general stores), and home crafts (with or without village specialization). Often there are small but permanent open-air markets which, during periodic fairs and the more important religious festivals or *fiestas*, draw both traders and customers from considerably wider regions than the one served by day-by-day market activity.[13]

While variations are to be found from region to region, and even from community to community, in general the type and style of social organization which prevails is characteristic of most peasant and nonliterate societies.[14] Interpersonal associational patterns have their major basis in kinship groups, including ceremonial kinship linkages established in a complex system of *compadrazgo* (the designation of sponsors or godparents on ritual occasions), but *cofradías* (confraternities) and other organizations often serve as focal points for the conduct of religious *fiestas*. In addition, community civic structures often exist – particularly in the independent indigenous communities – to handle affairs of common interest, and communal work teams seem to be rather widely employed for the construction of public projects (e.g., roads, schools, churches, and the like). Reciprocal labor exchange appears to be a fairly customary technique for mobilizing labor toward such private ends as harvesting and house construction. Economic defense associations – formed, for instance, to defend the peasants' land claims – are by no means unknown.

Religion might be expected to constitute the basis of the most comprehensive type of social organization, since the Peruvian Indians are nominally Catholic. But the formal constitutional apparatus which North Americans associate with denominational membership is not often much in evidence. Instead, the religious beliefs and practices of the indigenous population contain a heavy infusion of non-Christian elements, including folk magic; and it is through participation in *fiestas* and various folk rituals rather than participation in more "European" forms of religious life that much of the populace is linked with the religious structure.

As for attitudes and values, the indigenous population tends to be quite parochial and restricted, with an experientially justified suspicion of the outsider. Conventional norms define and control many aspects of life such as the type of clothing, diet, medical practices, household equipment and entertainment. Age and sex tend to weigh heavily, but not exclusively, in the assignment of occupational roles – though ordinarily children have to assume work responsibilities at an early age. In general, a high social value is assigned to hard physical labor; idleness is considered sinful, and frugality is deemed virtuous (as well as a practical necessity).

Nuñez del Prado's study of the Indians of the Cuzco area records the following personality traits, which seem to be fairly prevalent in the highland indigenous subculture:

The Inca-speaking native of the Cuzco area behaves in two different ways, depending on whom he is dealing with. With mestizos, he is suspicious, silent, withdrawn, and nearly inaccessible; he offers a passive and systematic resistance. He is humble, fearful, and inattentive; reticent and evasive in his answers, indecisive in his attitudes. He suppresses and hides his emotions and rarely reveals his disagreement even when he finds himself in fundamental opposition. He is obsequious at times, but this attitude implies that he wants something very specific, that he expects an almost immediate reward. With other natives he is open, communicative, fond of practical jokes, he makes a display of his industry and is ready and willing to cooperate; he shows his feelings and states his opinions without reserve. He is fond of fiestas and enjoys himself in them. When he is drunk, he is impulsive and courageous in a fight; he bears grudges, is vengeful, astute, and often mocking. He is sober and moderate in his sex life, frugal in eating, and tranquil in daily affairs.

As a general observation, we can say that he is extremely conservative; he allows no sudden changes and is openly resistive to traits, techniques and practices different from those to which he is accustomed, at least until he has a chance to convince himself personally and objectively of the advantages he might gain from an innovation. Even so, he vacillates for a long time before deciding to accept the new practice. He has lived in a closed circle in which tradition and custom are his basic schools, and it is a nearly static circle which gives him no opportunity to grasp other possibilities or take initiative in unfamiliar matters. His accumulated knowledge is limited to the circumscribed round of relationships in his community, and his world is limited to the community, the estate, or the nearest town where he usually trades. . . . It is logical to think that initiative requires a favorable experience and innovation a previous tradition of change; as long as these conditions are not found, it is natural for us as outsiders to regard the native communities as 'asleep' or 'backward.' Most of the native's activities consist of repeating routine behavior.[15]

The foregoing remarks should not, however, be construed to indicate that the indigenous subcultures of the Peruvian highlands are properly viewed as closed and static systems. On the contrary, there is considerable evidence which suggests that they are open to change and to contacts with the larger social system of the nation at a number of points.

Through the local and regional markets, for example, the indigenous segment of the economy interacts (admittedly to a limited degree) with the world beyond the sierras. And in certain regions, innovations in economic organization such as credit cooperatives have been introduced with notable success. Other local change-inducing influences have emanated from the mines (with their employment opportunities for learning new skills and attitudes) and schools — as well as from more recent agents of change like the national community development program known as *Promoción Popular.* Moreover, it must be remembered that in the larger provincial towns, and even in some of the smaller ones, the Indian population lives close to and interacts in varying ways with the mestizo segment. From these several situations of interaction there has emerged an intermediate socio-cultural stratum known as *chólo,* a term commonly employed in Peru to designate those persons in the lower portions of the social structure who are in the process of losing their cultural identity as Indians but who have not yet been fully assimilated into the patterns of life characteristic of the mestizo society.

A final major source of cultural interpenetration — one which is of growing importance — is migration from the sierra to the coast, a move which sometimes involves a "step" process that includes an intervening stop in some provincial urban center. Without going into the matter in all its obvious complexity, one may generally summarize the migration phenomenon as consisting of an initially permanent move to the coast, and for others of an original temporary move (e.g., to work as seasonal labor on the plantations or temporarily in the cities) which may develop into a permanent shift of residence. Among those who have made such moves, many visit their home villages frequently, despite the expense of travel.

When the Indian moves to the city, the cultural shock of a different environment is partially absorbed by his membership in a club of migrants from his native community.[16] He also has contact with his former community in the wholesale market, which "is a social and communication center for many *serranos* (mountain people), both Indian and non-Indian. Close contact is maintained with the town of origin through . . . the truck drivers . . . . The market area features mountain music, mountain food, cheap hotels catering to mountain visitors, and it is close to a district where many serranos live . . . ."[17]

Mangin points out that within the barriada (slum), where the migrant Indian lives, "there is a feeling of separateness from the city . . . . There is a relatively high degree of integration and 'belongingness,' and considerable pride in achievement and satisfaction with home ownership."[18]

Criollo or Mestizo Subculture

The cultural outlook of the mestizo segment of the population has been termed *"criollo."*[a] O. G. Simmons says that the criollo type of personality may be characterized by:

a quick and brilliant mentality, a facile creative talent, and a profound sense of humor . . . . *Viveza* (shrewdness), *ingenio* (ingenuity), and *picardia* (roguishness) are qualities consistently attributed to the *mestizo* who is thought to be very *criollo,* as is the ability to *palabrear,* to be very good at verbal suasion . . . . Outwitting or overcoming an opponent through astute trickery . . . is an example of the criollo talent at work . . . .[19]

Expression of the criollo outlook usually shows itself in leisure-time activities. Where it does concern work, Simmons says:

[a]For present purposes, the mestizo-criollo subculture may be taken as including, in addition to racially mixed persons, assimilated Indians as well as persons whose ancestry includes no Indian forebears.

It prescribes techniques for getting around work or at least making it as palatable as possible. The mestizo is not averse to work, and can work hard and long when there is no other alternative, but he is far from feeling the ethical obligation to his occupation that Weber summed up in his concept of a 'calling.'[20]

The criollo outlook is thought to be derived from the behavior of the Peruvian upper classes after the break with Spain. Although these groups were influenced by the Spanish, they also wanted to differentiate themselves as being Peruvian, so they cultivated certain facets of their behavior as being typically "criollo."[21] Today, supposedly, the slowly rising mestizo middle class seeks to emulate its former leaders.

It must be recognized, however, that what is here called the criollo subculture is complex and varies somewhat according to region and socioeconomic position. At one end of the subcultural continuum, particularly in the smaller highland towns, the life style of the criollo category shades into cholo and even indigenous categories, with which a good many culture traits may be held in common. At the other end of the continuum, especially in the Lima-Callao area, it would be impossible to draw any sharp line of differentiation between those following criollo ways of life and those who live in the more cosmopolitan and modern urban subculture. With these problems in mind, however, it may be useful to include in the criollo category most of the non-Indian (culturally, not racially, viewed) people who live in the provincial towns and cities as well as many, if not most, of the lower and lower middle-class inhabitants of the larger urban communities of the country.

Among this group, the occupational structure is far more varied than it is within the indigenous subculture, including — in addition to those engaged in farming, ranching, land-renting, and artisan trades — criollos who earn their livelihood from commerce, the professions, blue-collar and white-collar jobs in the private sector, government employment, and the like. Generally speaking the average level of formal education tends to be higher than it is among the Indians; the criollo involvement in national and regional political processes is greater; and criollos are ordinarily more likely than Indians to participate in social clubs and (at least so far as concerns the women) formal religious activities. While many criollos may be able to speak some Indian language, their principal language is Spanish, and their dress is European, usually rather conservative. Food preferences customarily include some emphasis on traditional Peruvian foods, just as their social interaction and entertainment patterns which built largely on family and close friendship ties tend to adhere to conventional or traditional Peruvian customs.

For the most part, the criollo woman's role is that of a subordinate. Even lower middle-class criollo families often try to employ at least one domestic servant. Tempered occasionally by paternalism, the criollo attitude towards the Indian is one of deprecation. There is some evidence that power-oriented types of relationships and status preoccupations rather than achievement-oriented behavior figure rather prominently in the personality structure of the criollo segment. The criollo outlook may be characterized as essentially a provincial one.

Urban-Cosmopolitan Subculture

Centering in the elite groups of Lima, but with increasing emulation by those occupying lower socioeconomic positions in Lima and elsewhere, is a third general life style which takes many of its cultural patterns from abroad. As Simmons has put it, these members of the social elite look upon themselves as:

the heirs of the Spanish tradition in Peruvian culture, as the guardians and observers of that tradition, and as those who have accomplished whatever has been done for Peru .... To their Hispanicism they have assimilated much of the cosmopolitan way of life of New York and Paris.[22]

Thus, the upper-class Peruvians are ready to consider innovation as attested to by their acceptance of supermarkets, martinis, and hot-water showers in place of open markets, *pisco sours,* and cold-water bathing, and for reaching them the marketing practices employed in advanced countries are generally appropriate.[23] Thanks largely to such factors as urbanization, increased purchasing power among the middle classes (and, to some extent, among organized industrial workers), education and the spread of mass communications media, the preferences of this group in material consumption have tended to be copied — so far as income permits — in less elevated portions of the social structure, even where social interaction patterns have remained at least partially imbedded in older, more traditional cultural forms. Over the longer term future, it seems certain that the other subcultures will be increasingly displaced by the influences emanating from this urban-cosmopolitan segment of the national social system. But for the present, cultural heterogeneity is a factor which both fragments the national market and creates difficult challenges for the design of effective marketing policies.

Political System

Constitution and Voting

The constitution in force today, the fifteenth that Peru has had since it declared its independence, was adopted in 1933. It shows clear influence of its American and French counterparts. The list of national, social, and individual guarantees is extensive, but under certain circumstances and within limits, constitutional guarantees may be suspended. Even in ordinary times there is often a certain disparity between the provisions of the constitution (and the legal codes in general) and those which are practiced in reality. As in many other countries, personal favors and informal payments may be used, on occasion, to lend flexibility to law and public administration. In common with most other Latin American countries, there has also been an historic tendency for the aims of legislation and public policy to exceed the actual capacity of the administrative machinery in the area of implementation and enforcement.

Consequently the transactional environment of business activities is sometimes affected with elements of risk and uncertainty which are of political origin, and at times, political and legal skills may be more valuable to a firm's operations than business and technical skills.

A citizen must be literate in order to vote in Peru, a requirement that bars a great portion of the Indian population from participating in governing public policy. Eligible voters — every literate citizen between twenty (eighteen for married persons) and sixty years — are obligated to vote. The voter who fails to satisfy this obligation cannot, theoretically, apply for a government concession or sign a valid contract. At the same time, however, one should keep in mind that there has not always been, even in recent years, a direct relationship between voter preferences as manifested in electoral processes and the selection of political leaders. "Disguised disenfranchisement" is no less a feature of the less developed society than "disguised unemployment."

Government Organization

Formally, at least, the president is selected by a majority vote of the electorate, and, true to Latin American custom, has quite extensive powers, including a certain latitude for rule by presidential decrees. Indeed, the various divisions of the executive branch of government exercise a considerable discretionary authority over economic matters as well as other affairs. The presidential term of office is six years, and the president may not succeed himself. On occasion, however, the tenure of the presidents in office has been shortened by *coups,* and chief executives have sometimes been brought to power by nonelectoral means. This is what occurred in 1962 and again in 1968.

The legislature consists of a Congress of Senate (45 members) and a Chamber of Deputies (140 members). Their terms run concurrently with that of the president. Congress must approve the president's choice of ministers, may approve the president's proposed policy, and may censure ministers or even appoint investigating committees. While congressional power is generally less than in the United States, a Peruvian Congress controlled by parties hostile to the president can nevertheless block the enactment and implementation of much of a chief executive's program.

Peru is divided into twenty-three *departamentos* which are in turn divided into *provincios,* which are further broken down into *distritos* (see Figure 3-2). The districts are then subdivided into municipalities or townships. The president appoints a prefect to govern the departments. The provinces in turn are governed by subprefects, the districts by governors, and the towns by lieutenant governors or mayors. For decades, the Minister of Government and Police had complete authority over the prefects, who in turn controlled the subprefects, and so forth down the line through the municipal level.

In an attempt to decentralize and democratize the government, the Belaunde administration instituted a reform which provided for election of officials at the

Figure 3-2 Political Departments of Peru.

various subnational governmental levels, but in spite of these changes, the Spanish tradition of authoritarian, centralized, and bureaucratic rule is still the norm. "Almost all responsibility resides in the central government, and ultimately with the President. Everything is initiated or decided in Lima . . . ."[24] The balance of voting power lies on the coast, because literacy rates are highest there. The numbers of registered voters indicate that in 1963 the department of Lima contained 37 percent of the eligible voters, whereas the coastal departments altogether had 69 percent.[25] Thus centralization of government is reinforced as politicians seek the favor of the most important voting blocs in the urban electorate, and the geographical distribution of social investment is affected accordingly. In addition, at least the tacit acquiescence of the military is essential to continuity of rule by the party in power.[26] Somewhat paradoxically, despite the tradition of strongly centralized rule, little has been done over the years to consolidate the country into a unified socioeconomic system, the business dimension of which is an integrated national market.

Political Parties

At the time of this study, the president of Peru was Fernando Belaunde Terry, an architect of great personal magnetism who developed, during the 1950's, a broadly based political movement known as Acción Popular. Moderately nationalistic and center-left reformist in orientation, the Acción Popular party won a plurality in the national elections of 1963, in coalition with the much smaller Christian Democratic party, but failed to capture control of the Congress. The dominant position in the legislature was assumed by an opposition coalition consisting of a personalistic party led by General Manuel Odría (a former dictator and president) and the large Peruvian APRA party — the latter a formerly revolutionary but presently reformist party which has stated objectives quite similar to those of Acción Popular. Despite the apparent similarities between APRA and Acción Popular-Christian Democratic platforms, however, the 1963 elections led to a governmental impasse which seriously impeded for several years the taking of effective action to deal with critical national problems. In 1967 the Christian Democratic party split into rival factions and ultimately left the ruling coalition. In 1968, as has been noted, the government of President Belaunde was overthrown by the military who also seem dedicated to the objectives of national development and social reform, though attained by means more accelerated than the civilian political system had permitted.

In addition to the foregoing parties, there are a number of smaller political parties and groupings ranging from the extreme left to the far right. While the political future of the country is quite uncertain, it seems probable that future governments will tend to adopt more nationalistic and interventionist policies than have prevailed hitherto and will likely also place a greater emphasis on internally oriented development policies (as contrasted with export-oriented policies), including agrarian reform and state-fostered industrialization.

4

Marketing Infrastructure

Within the constraints set by the environmental factors described in Chapter 3, marketing practices of manufacturers are also influenced by what we are here calling marketing infrastructure: i.e., transportation and communications, wholesaling, retailing, marketing research facilities, professional societies concerned with marketing and accounting facilities and practices. With the exception of communications facilities (which are discussed in Chapter 9), these aspects of marketing infrastructure are considered below.

Transportation and Communications

Highways

"Because the Andes Mountains bisect Peru from north to south, setting up a barrier to transportation which can be surmounted only with difficulty and expense, transportation in Peru has tended to be regional and local except by sea and air."[1]

Table 4-1 classifies Peru's highways by type of surface as of about mid-1964. Inasmuch as nearly 40 percent of Peru's roads are classed as "unimproved" or "rough" — hardly more than trails in some cases — transportation other than between the major coastal cities becomes an enormous problem. The Pan-American Highway, running the length of the country along the coast, makes up most of the 12 percent of Peru's roads that are classified as asphalt. This highway would be considered a secondary road in the United States.

Peru's road-building plan calls for the construction of nearly 2,000 miles of new roads, the reconstruction of nearly 4,000 miles of existing ones, and increased maintenance on nearly 15,000 miles of the highway system. In addition to construction by contracting with private firms, the government of Peru is using engineering units of the Peruvian Army to speed its highway construction program in the selva.

Many people, including former President Belaunde, believe the economic future of Peru is closely linked with the development of the selva, which includes two-thirds of the land area but less than 10 percent of the people. As a result of this belief, much of the highway construction effort is going into connecting the jungle regions with each other and with the coastal cities, particularly Lima. There is even a road plan which would connect Lima and Brasilia, the Federal District of Brazil, by way of La Paz, Bolivia.[2] Realization of this plan, if indeed it is ever implemented, lies far in the future, however.

In the sierra, various problems afflict road-building and maintenance efforts. Here, as in the selva, it is expensive to move in the necessary construction equipment and supplies. Roads are constantly damaged by landslides and the abrasive undercutting of mountain rivers; at times their surfaces crack under the stresses exerted by daily variations in temperature of up to 70 degrees Fahrenheit. Existing roads often follow zig-zag courses along the valleys which run lengthwise between the mountain ranges, and bridging requirements are high. On the coastal desert, sand drifts across the roads and must constantly be cleared. In the selva this sand is replaced by jungle vegetation which, together with torrential rainfall and frequent landslides, often renders the roads impassable for extended periods.

Table 4-1

Highways in Peru by Type

Type of Surface	Miles of Highways	Percent of System
Asphalt	2,444	12
Gravel	4,903	24
Graded & Drained	5,203	26
Unimproved	7,765	38
Total	20,315	100

Railways

One glance at Figure 4-1 will indicate the general nature of the Peruvian railway infrastructure which consists of several separate lines in different parts of the country, and has never been integrated to form a national system. Built chiefly to carry ore from the mines to the coast and (especially with many narrow-gauge lines) to move sugar to points of embarcation, the railway facilities link only a very few of the leading cities. Considering that even on these latter lines the nature of the intervening terrain depresses the amount of traffic generated en

Figure 4-1   Railroads of Peru.

route, it does not appear that any major amplification of the railway systems would be economic for the foreseeable future.

A traveler in Peru is able to see clearly the railway problem by taking the Central Railway (Ferrocarril Central del Peru) to Huancayo. Originating in the port of Callao, the line climbs the mountain by a series of switchbacks, to a height of some 15,700 feet above sea level at the continental divide. To reach La Oroya, the main base-metal smelting and refining center in Peru, the rail line crosses sixty-one bridges, passes through sixty-five tunnels and encounters twenty-one switchbacks. The costs of operation and maintenance are necessarily high. As Figure 4-1 shows, other lines go from Huancayo to Huancavelica and from La Oroya to Cerro de Pasco and beyond, but for the most part these are private and unscheduled.

Although other rail lines in Peru are not as spectacular as the Central Railway, the problems encountered are much the same. The other main railway, the Southern Peruvian Railway *(Ferrocarriles del Sur del Peru)*, runs from the Pacific Ocean ports of Matarani and Mollendo, via Arequipa and Puno, to Cuzco. Twice weekly there is a connection at Puno with the Lake Titicaca steamer service to La Paz, Bolivia.

At present the major railways are in the process of modernization, chiefly involving the replacement of steam locomotives with diesel electrics. Considering the problems of the country cited above, rail service is generally reliable and efficiently managed.[3]

Water Transportation

In the jungle, until roads are completed, passengers and goods must be moved by river. Because the rivers descend so rapidly, however, this is a hazardous and expensive matter. The center of the jungle river system such as it is, is Iquitos, on the Amazon. From Iquitos, river steamers also move down river to the Atlantic Ocean where they connect with ocean steamers to other parts of the world.

Peru's best ocean port is Callao, through which some three-quarters of its imports and one-third of its exports pass. At many of the other smaller ports on the coast, small "lighters" must be used to load and unload ocean freighters. Other ports are being improved, but the progress is slow. Coastwise shipping service is available but is, for many purposes, less satisfactory than truck transport or air transport.

Air Transportation

Air transport has been used in Peru for over three decades, and in some areas is the only means of transportation. A number of international carriers operate between Lima and foreign cities. An ultramodern airport terminal was built near

Lima in the mid-1960's and should be large enough to accommodate the increased traffic brought about by Peru's continued economic development.

The capital cities of most of the departamentos are served by the domestic airlines, although many of the provincial airports have unpaved runways. In the selva region, regular flying schedules cannot always be maintained because the rainy season at times prohibits flying for week-long periods. There are three main domestic airlines, of which Compania de Aviacion Fawcett S. A. is the largest. The Peruvian Air Force provides much of the air transportation in the sierra and selva.

Wholesaling

Because importers in Peru often act as distributors or wholesalers (and also sometimes as retailers), and because some nonimporting wholesalers are also engaged in retailing, it is difficult to characterize wholesaling with any degree of certainty. According to the 1963 Economic Census, however, there were 2,153 wholesaling firms in Peru, each of which employed fewer than five persons, and 1,430 wholesaling firms, each of which employed five or more persons.[4] Of the former type, many of which appear to have only one or two employees, 1,989 firms are located in the Lima-Callao area. Of the larger wholesalers (i.e., those with five or more employees), 960 are located in the Lima-Callao region. The census, however, includes without differentiation firms which do both wholesaling and retailing and those engaged only in wholesaling. Furthermore, it overstates by an unascertained degree the actual number of distinct firms, since a good many of the larger firms appear to have been listed several times under different product categories. Multiple listings also arise from listing separately the branch offices of firms. Thus some of the larger firms appear several times both in the "under five employees" category as well as in the "five or more employees" category. Many of the smaller wholesalers listed in the census would seem to be individuals with stalls in the markets who sell to other operators of market stalls or to street vendors.

The 1963 census classifies the wholesalers by product group and number of employees and gives the address of each, but provides no other information. Until the publication of the census results in 1967, even this imperfect and limited statistical information on wholesaling channels was lacking.

The actions and practices of Peruvian wholesalers (*distribuidores* or *mayoristas*) are almost indescribably complex and varied, but a few principles will be set forth here. Most of the data in this section come from two sources: 1) interviews with wholesalers, and 2) material gathered by the classes of Dr. Konrad Fischer Rossi of the *Escuela de Administracion de Negocios para Graduados* (ESAN).[5]

Many of the manufacturers interviewed plan, when possible, to bypass wholesalers and sell directly. Manufacturers seem to have a general lack of knowledge of just what functions a wholesaler performs. There is probably a general lack of services on the part of the wholesalers — and his margin of profit is a generous one.

Much merchandise, particularly food, is sold through local wholesale markets (*mercados mayoristas*) often organized by the municipalities. The stalls themselves are operated by individuals. In this type of business, much like the farmers' markets of the United States, the retailer travels to the market and carries his purchases back to his store for resale.

Other wholesaling is done by combination import-distributor houses. Most of these houses — Wiese, Berckemeyer, Ferreyros, Cosmana, and IMACO to name a few — maintain offices in the departamentos and some do retailing in these outlying offices. In general the distributors interviewed indicated that their sales are distributed approximately in this ratio: Lima and suburbs 60 percent, and other departamentos 40 percent. Some of the more important wholesaling houses own substantial, if not controlling, interests in mining, manufacturing, or agricultural operations, whose products they may distribute.

Wholesalers generally do little advertising except when forced to by a particular distribution contract or when the manufacturer (usually from the United States) has a cooperative advertising arrangement. The primary method of choosing customers is on the basis of credit rating. The wholesale gross profit margins for several goods are shown in Table 4-2.

Retailing

Retailing in Peru takes a variety of forms. The large stores, of which there are very few, consist of department stores such as Sears and Oeschle and a discount department store opened by La Scala; variety stores such as Monterrey and Tia's; and supermarkets. In addition there are a number of other retail chains — particularly in such fields as home furnishings, shoes, and textiles — some of which are owned jointly with manufacturing facilities. Vastly more numerous are the independent and usually quite small retailers having one to three employees — often a father-son or husband-wife combination — not unlike the "mom and pop" stores found in the United States. According to the 1963 census, Peru contained only 2,363 retail firms with five or more employees each. In terms of numbers of "establishments," however, the largest group by far consists of the small peddlers or street merchants, called either *minoristas estacionarios* or *minoristas ambulantes* depending upon whether they have an established place of business (a customary location) or move from place to place (with or without pushcarts or similar vehicles). Besides these types of retail outlets, there are company-operated or company-sponsored commissaries which, in various mining settlements and plantation communities, supply the resident labor force with a range of simple consumer products; most of the companies operating such stores purchase stocks through buying offices located in Lima.

Table 4-2

Selected Wholesale Gross Profit Margins

Type of Good	Gross Margin (Percent of Selling Price)
Steel pipes—lap welded	18
Steel pipes—seamless	29
Shirts	29
Underwear	29
Tea—raw materials	15-18
Potatoes	23
Bananas	34
Oranges	56
Fresh beef	24
Fresh fish	34-67

The Large Store

Sears Roebuck del Peru S. A. has been in Lima for nearly twenty years. At present the company operates three stores, one in the middle of the downtown business section, one near a shopping center in a wealthier Lima suburb, and one recently opened in another Lima suburb, which specializes in hard goods. During this period the company has established itself as the style leader of Peru (at least for that segment of the market it serves), and sells on a fixed-price basis. In contrast some of the smaller retailers expect haggling over prices.

As of 1966, about 50 percent of Sears' sales were on credit, up from 45 percent in 1965. In spite of the fact that Sears does not require a downpayment (competitors require from 7 to 15 percent down), its bad-debt write-off is slightly less than in the United States. Sears apparently initiated the widespread use of consumer credit in Lima, but now most of the larger retailers have some credit facilities. Sears has normally budgeted 2.2 percent of its sales for advertising, with a high emphasis on newspaper advertising. Sales have reportedly increased from 25 to 30 percent annually for the past several years.[6]

Layout of goods in the Peru Sears stores is almost identical to that of stores in the United States. Those in Peru are, however, priced higher and are of lower quality. Currently about 75 percent of the goods sold by Sears in Peru are made there. This percentage has been constantly increasing.

Unlike most retailers in Peru — and in the United States for that matter — Sears gives its sales clerks constant training. Sales clerks get about one and one-half days' training when starting on the job, and have regular (at least weekly) training meetings thereafter. Although Sears undoubtedly has the best service facilities of any retailer in Peru, service is still a problem. Since the company does not stock all parts for its merchandise, it is often necessary to wait for some time for replacements to be shipped from the United States.

The discount department store opened by La Scala in mid-1967 is located about ten blocks from downtown Lima in the lower-middle-class section of Brena. "Scala Gigante," as it is called, is one of the largest stores in the Spanish-speaking world. It has more than five miles of display racks and cases and reportedly can accommodate 10,000 people at one time. The store has thirty cash registers which are tied into electronic data-processing equipment. Another such discount department store is scheduled for the upper-middle-class section of Miraflores.

The only United States type of shopping center in the country is owned by TODOS S. A., a subsidiary of a North American firm that is also involved in constructing middle-class homes in the Lima suburb of Monterrico. The main store of the center is a food supermarket also called TODOS (meaning "all") and is operated by the company along with two other stores in Lima. These are excellent stores and would compare very favorably, except for higher prices, with supermarkets in the United States.

TODOS reportedly has a high gross profit margin for all imported and many domestic items in order to compensate for the low margin on government-controlled items. Overall gross profit is said to be less than 20 percent of sales, while net profit is said to be 2 percent. After several years of experience TODOS developed a system of buying produce directly from the farmer, after planting but before harvesting. This evolved from the lack of standardization and grading in Peru and the requirements of TODOS' customers, mostly upper and upper-middle-class Peruvians and foreigners, for better quality merchandise. TODOS, therefore, buys fields, arranges for their harvesting, grades the merchandise and trucks it to its outlets. The lowest grade merchandise is sold in the local markets.

In 1966 TODOS was planning to set up "superettes" with local store owners in other Lima suburbs. Also planned was a large mechanized warehouse to be built before the end of 1966 to service all of the TODOS stores. In addition to the three TODOS stores, there are ten supermarkets operated by Super Markets S. A. These are not quite of the quality of TODOS.

A government agency (the *Corporacion Nacional de Abastecimientos del Peru* or CONAP), was planning a series of "supermarkets" in the poorer suburbs and the barriadas of Lima by 1966. This is the slum area which is filled with squatters' huts. One of the objectives of the plan was to develop more efficient middlemen.[7] Reasonably modern retail practices are utilized in most of the other larger stores and chains in the Lima-Callao metropolitan area.

The Small Store

The smaller stores go by many names: *bodegas* (dry grocery stores); *boticas* (drug stores without prescriptions); *ferreterias* (hardware stores, much like those in the United States); *carnicerias* (butcher shops); *chinos* (many of the small shopkeepers are Orientals); and so on. A good many of these small shops are found in the central business districts of the towns and cities, but they are also dispersed throughout secondary business zones and residential areas. In addition there are markets in which vending is carried on from stalls in most towns and cities. These stores have small stocks and commonly obtain their goods on consignment or some other form of credit. They often purchase from a wholesaler only when they have a definite sale, and then in very small lots, e.g., one or two bottles of a patent medicine. The stores are generally laid out in a fashion similar to the small rural stores of several decades ago in the United States, and many of them, especially in the provinces, have no signs announcing their presence. The smaller hard goods stores sell on credit, but their installment contracts may be handled by a bank or finance company. Advertising, special promotions, and reduced-price sales are not used much by most of the smaller shops. Pricing practices vary, with a mixture of relatively firm prices or prices reached by customer negotiation.

To the outsider this may seem like inefficient retailing, but with inexpensive labor and the general lack of adequate transportation facilities, the small shop provides a definite service to the public. Prices in the small stores are higher than those of supermarkets and other large stores, perhaps as much as 10 to 20 percent. But the fact that these stores keep very long hours and are open on

Sundays and holidays, along with a long-established tradition of buying from this type of outlet, apparently keeps the price differentials from being a deterrent to much of the buying public. A part of the price differential, of course, may represent the charge for consumer credit when this is provided.

Ambulantes and Others

Many of the *ambulantes* (peddlers) use a pushcart or type of three-wheeled foot-powered cycle with a basket measuring perhaps four by six feet attached in front. Others move about by foot, carrying their merchandise on their backs, while still others display their few wares on the sidewalks or on the ground by the side of the streets. Some of this last group change their location from time to time, while others tend to remain in a fixed location. These peddlers sell everything from fresh fruit and vegetables to new and used clothing and shoes. Haggling to determine price is normal.

Many of these peddlers make up a part of what has been called "disguised unemployment." Inasmuch as the net profit from a business such as this is often no more than S/ 20 per day (approximately 75 cents in 1966), it is evident that the human resources devoted to this type of selling are far from being fully employed. Nevertheless, this substitution of labor for capital serves an economic function for the consumers as well as for those who derive a meager livelihood from the activity.

The Feria

In the departamentos other than Lima, the *feria,* or fair, is an important means of commerce. Indian and mestizo peasants — traveling by train, truck, foot or donkey — come into the city (usually a provincial capital) from miles around to sell their agricultural or craft items and to buy their own requirements. Some of the commerce takes the form of bartering, but for the most part money exchange is used. Articles offered for sale are both new and used, ranging from hardware to clothing, foodstuffs to medicine, craft items, and the like. Vendors of manufactured items as well as handcrafted goods congregate for these occasions, and a certain amount of wholesaling as well as retailing business is commonly transacted. Aside from the trading function, the feria constitutes one of the major social events in the Indians' otherwise rather drab existence.[8] Not the least important aspect of these events is their role as a major link in the communications system of outlying regions. Considering the widespread illiteracy and limited telecommunications facilities, direct personal communication is the chief means of transmitting information about prices, products, services, consumer preferences, and events of general interest.

Professional Societies Concerned with Marketing

The Peruvian business community suffers from a relative lack of professionalization in business careers and business education, although these latter shortcomings have been accepted as challenges in recent years by voluntary professional associations. There are two major professional societies in Peru concerned with marketing and extension of education in the business field. The Instituto Peruano de Administracion de Empresas (IPAE) is somewhat comparable to the American Management Association in the United States and has an extensive program of publications and seminars on various business topics. The Asociacion de Dirigentes de Ventas del Peru (ADV) is more comparable to a combination of two United States organizations — the Sales and Marketing Executives' Club, with which it is affiliated, and the American Marketing Association. The ADV holds monthly meetings with from 100 to 200 members in attendance and also conducts well-attended evening classes in basic marketing, sales management, and similar subjects.

Accounting Facilities and Practices

Ultimately, of course, the adequacy of decisions taken in marketing management is measured in economic results for which there are empirical measures in the area of accountancy. As presently practiced by many firms, however, accounting analysis does not always provide either the empirical data on which decisions may be taken or a framework for evaluating decisions already made.

Records Required

Registered concerns in Peru are required by law to keep the following bound statutory books in Spanish: inventory and balances book, journal, and a general ledger. These books must be registered with the judicial authorities, and if the capital of the concern exceeds S/ 100,000 or if its gross annual income exceeds S/ 500,000, they must also be registered with the taxation authorities.[9] The structure of the accounts is also prescribed by law and is not necessarily the form most suitable for managerial decisions. In some instances, in fact, the legal accounting requirements may actually restrict the choices in business policy in an undesirable way. For instance, firms are legally barred from creating a reserve for bad debts; in order to write off bad debts firms must prove to the government's satisfaction that they have taken all the necessary legal steps to collect the sums owed them. The credit standing of the buyer thus becomes one of the most important factors in a sale and the development of a wider use of credit sales transactions has been inhibited.

Despite these legal restrictions, however, indications are that particularly small and medium-sized firms are able to revise sales and income figures at the end of the year in order to reduce tax indemnities — although the quality of their business decisions are not necessarily enhanced as a consequence.

Neither the auditing and certification of financial statements by independent public accounting firms nor the public disclosure of corporate financial statements is required by Peruvian law — and it goes without saying that neither practice is customary in the absence of legal compulsion. This is true even with firms whose shares are listed and traded on the Lima Stock Exchange, and it is rare that securities are marketed to the public by means of an offering prospectus (the contents of which, in any case, are not regulated by law).

Financial Statements

The examination of financial statements in Peru emphasizes the balance sheet, and the statement of profit-and-loss tends to become a byproduct. The latter frequently does not disclose cost of sales, selling and general expenses, and related items, but rather classifies these costs under headings such as salaries and wages, materials cost, depreciation and the like.[10]

Cost accounting is very little advanced in Peru, especially in a form useful for managerial decision-making. One of the questions in the survey, for example, asked for a classification of company costs into certain areas, including marketing costs. Although some of the firms were able to give fairly exact answers, many found it necessary to estimate the answers and others had no knowledge of their costs. Many of the firms which did not know their cost distribution acknowledged, however, that this is a type of information they would like to know. While in some instances interviewees may simply have been concealing information, supplementary inquiries convinced us that in most cases the respondents were truly ignorant of the kinds of cost information being sought.

All this implies strongly that the financial analyst's work is often impossible to carry out effectively in Peru and that the task of marketing management is substantially handicapped. Operating with current financial information is clearly a risky business.

5

Research Design and Sample Characteristics

In 1966, under the sponsorship of the Ford Foundation, the authors made a field study of marketing in Peru. The empirical results of this research as well as the general impressions formed during its completion provide the bulk of the next several chapters. Because the foundations of meaningful research lie in the formulation of a design that carefully outlines objectives and the methodology for accomplishing them, this chapter provides important background to the reader, allowing him some judgments as to the quality of the research. In addition, the characteristics of the sample are discussed in some detail to provide perspective to the reader as he evaluates the findings.

Research Design

Objectives of the Study

The objectives of this study, together with several working hypotheses, have been presented. These objectives, paraphrased briefly, are:

1. To describe the domestic marketing strategies and practices of manufacturers in Peru.
2. To examine the relationships between these strategies and practices and the socioeconomic environment, which in many ways parallels that of other developing nations.
3. To explore the relationship between these strategies and practices and six specific variables: nationality of ownership; type of management; sales volume (size of firm); value of the typical purchase; industry type; and degree of competition.
4. To investigate some of the implications of marketing for economic development.

The data for achieving these objectives was based on personal interviews of marketing executives or general managers of business firms operating domestically within Peru.

The Research Instrument

The research instrument was a questionnaire containing seventy-four questions which related to marketing organization, marketing research, product planning, distribution channels, advertising, personal selling, physical distribution, pricing, and basic company characteristics. Questions were phrased as neutrally as possible, and in particularly sensitive areas (e.g. profits, margins), respondents were asked to place their companies in fairly broad classifications.

The questionnaire, which had been originally prepared in English, was translated by one of Peru's leading marketing experts, a man who was familiar with both English and Spanish terminology in the field. The field investigators, by studying the translated questionnaire, soon became familiar with Peruvian marketing terminology.

The major limitation of the questionnaire was its length. The breadth of the study precluded going into great depth in any particular area, with the exception of those interviews where respondents were willing to spend several hours with the investigator. There was no apparent way to overcome this problem, which was inherent in the objectives of the study.

Sampling Procedures

To assure that the data collected would be meaningful, the sample was limited to ten major industries, allowing us to interview approximately ten companies in each industry. The industries included in the sample were chosen for their relevance to Peru's *internal* development. Most of the important manufacturers in Peru were represented. Suppliers to the export industries were included, exporters were not.

The industrial classifications used were based on market rather than production similarities (for example, the kind of customer served was considered to be a more important characteristic for grouping than the physical composition of the product). The ten industry groups chosen were:

> Food and beverages
> Textiles, clothing, and footwear
> Automotive products
> Pharmaceuticals
> Household durables
> Products for office use
> Construction products
> Products for agricultural use
> Products for the fishing and mining industries
> Other industrial products

The first five industries produce consumer goods and the last five manufacture industrial goods.

Because no complete list of firms existed at the time of the study, many sources were utilized.[1] A list of 185 companies was developed using a quota sampling procedure. During the course of the study the interviewers contacted approximately 130 of these firms. Ten refused interviews, and because of schedule and time limitations it was not possible to interview another ten. This study, then, is based upon 110 completed semistructured interviews and upon 45 unstructured interviews with other persons involved with marketing in Peru. The interviews with manufacturers were held largely with presidents and sales managers.

Interviewing

A letter of introduction was presented to the respondent or to his secretary at the first contact. This letter briefly explained the study and its sponsorship, and solicited the cooperation of the respondent.

In Lima, interviews required at least two and as many as eight visits to a firm. In the *departamentos* (comparable to our states) outside of Lima, an average of less than two visits was required, perhaps because firms realized that the interviewers would be in each city only two or three days. Executives may also have accorded more importance to the visit because they see university researchers much less often than do executives in Lima. In both the departamentos and Lima, telephoning difficulties proved to be a formidable barrier.

Approximately 50 percent of the interviews were held in Spanish, 20 percent in a mixture of Spanish and English (called Spanenglish by one of the respondents), and the balance in English. Few problems with respondent rapport were encountered.

Sample Characteristics

To study the influence of environmental and product variables on the marketing strategies and practices actually used in Peru, the researchers classified respondents according to key variables. Although the breadth of the study precluded the detail essential to the precise determination of any single variable's influence on firm's strategy, cross-tabulations of strategy with these key variables enabled the authors to suggest some probable relationships. This part of the research can be considered basically exploratory.

The six variables hypothesized as having the greatest potential influence on marketing strategy are discussed below.

Nationality of Ownership

The basic hypothesis underlying the tabulation of results by nationality of ownership was that most foreign-owned firms, being from the more developed countries, would use a more advanced marketing technology and would be more aggressive in their marketing. Peruvian firms, accustomed to little competition and a situation where demand often exceeds supply[a] (even at high prices) would have less incentive to develop their marketing technology.

To determine nationality of ownership, respondents were asked to indicate the approximate percentage of the firm owned by Peruvian, European, North American, and other owners. Because many firms were owned jointly, we decided to classify a firm as Peruvian if over 50 percent of the capital was Peruvian, and foreign if over 50 percent of the capital came from outside Peru.[b] Classification of ownership is shown in Table 5-1.

Foreign capital played a significant role in the ten industries surveyed. The number of firms in each category of ownership appeared to be large enough to offer significant comparisons.

Type of Management

The tabulation by type of management was an attempt to show differences in behavior between the owner-managed firm and the professionally managed one. It was hypothesized that the owner-managed firm would have a marketing technology less developed than that of the professionally managed firm, inasmuch as owner-managers held their positions by right of ownership rather than by ability alone. The "family firm," in which the top management positions were occupied by the members of a family group, was included in the owner-manager class. Certainly, some of the owner-managed firms were headed by very capable owner-managers, many of whom surrounded themselves with professional managers.[c] Nevertheless it was clear that managers who were hired on the basis of ability would, in the aggregate, incorporate a more advanced marketing technology for their operations and would market more aggressively.

The type of management was determined by asking if the owners of the firm were active in managing it. If the response was "yes," the interviewers assumed

---

[a]The phrase "where demand exceeds supply" may offend some economists who would correctly note that, in theory, price adjusts to equate demand and supply. In practice, frictions in the market often prevent prices from adjusting to changes in demand or supply. In Peru, as in many developing countries, tariffs and import quotas are often established to encourage local production. Even with consumption that is restricted because of high prices, the total of local production and imports may not be adequate to satisfy demand at a given level of price. Therefore, we use the phrase "demand exceeds supply" to indicate that production resources are scarce relative to demand.

[b]A potential weakness of this basis for classification is the possible separating of ownership and control. For instance, actual foreign control over policy making could be possible even when local investors own more than half of the stock.

[c]Indeed, relatives could very well be professionally trained managers.

Table 5-1

Ownership of Sample Firms

Classification	Number of Firms
Peruvian–owned	65
Foreign–owned	45
Total Firms	110

Table 5-2

Management of Sample Firms

Classification	Number of Firms
Owner–managed	65
Professionally–managed	45
Total Firms	110

Table 5-3

Size of Sample Firms

Classification	Annual Sales Hundred—thousands of soles[1]	Number of Firms
Small	0–26.8	45
Medium	26.8–150	33
Large	Over 150	23
No answer		9
Total Firms		110

[1]At the time of the survey, the currency exchange rate was 26.8 soles to a dollar. The categories in terms of dollar sales were approximately 0–$1,000,000; $1,000,001–$5,500,000; and over $5,500,000. The exchange rate was changed in 1967 to more than 42 soles to a dollar.

that the role was important and that the firm was basically owner-managed. A "no" response indicated professional management.

The owner-manager apparently plays an important role in Peruvian industry. The large number of owner-managed firms in the sample was especially significant because the sample consisted of the largest firms in Peru. The similar numerical breakdowns of firms in the nationality of ownership classifications (Table 5-1) and the type of ownership classifications (Table 5-2) are purely coincidental. Several foreign-owned firms were owner-managed and many Peruvian-owned firms were professionally managed.

Size of Firm

Firm size was considered a key variable because the large firm would have greater potential for specialization than would the small firm. The authors hypothesized that large firms would have a more advanced marketing technology and would market more aggressively.

Although most business firms in Peru are very small (five or less employees), our interest lay in the population of larger, more economically significant firms which probably are more important in the country's long-run economic development. Because the study was concerned primarily with marketing, we chose to measure firm size with the marketing output measure of annual sales.

The size classifications were adapted to fit the Peruvian market. Firms were classified as large if the sales of the product or product group being studied were over $5,500,000. The number of firms in each category were adequate for comparative purposes.

Degree of Competition

The previous three variables were relatively simple to measure, although admittedly the classifications used had some weaknesses. The degree of competition, however, was not so easily quantified. The number of competitors was known, but several competitors did not necessarily mean heavy competition (e.g., the industry sometimes had made a pricing agreement). Competition is based more on performance than on structure. It was decided that a *competitive index* should be established, based upon both the number of competitors and the respondents' evaluations of price competition (made on a five point scale). Elements of nonprice competition were not included in the index.

Points for the competitive index were awarded as follows:

Number of Competitors	Points	Rating of Price Competition		Points
0	0	1	Light	1
1	1	2		2
2–3	2	3	Moderate	3
4–5	3	4		4
6–10	4	5	Heavy	5
Over 10	5			

The *index* was arrived at by adding the point scores for each firm for the two variables included. The resulting *index* could thus vary from 1 to 10. The point scores of the *index* are shown in Table 5-4

The frequency distribution was somewhat bell-shaped, with each of the three classifications containing enough firms to be useful in making comparisons. It was hypothesized that heavy competition would stimulate marketing aggressiveness and the development of marketing technology. The competitive index may exaggerate the true amount of competition somewhat, because respondents were likely to have been biased toward overstatement of the amount of competition they face.

Value of the Typical Purchase

It was desirable to determine the influence of the product and the market on marketing strategy. Following the product-market classification system developed by Udell[2] the value of the typical purchase was selected as one product-market variable. For consumer goods, the buyer was the ultimate consumer (not the middleman); for industrial goods, the buyer was the firm making the purchase. Respondents were asked the approximate value of the typical purchase (of a particular product) made by their customers. Almost all responses were estimates since few firms had actually studied this question. The respondents had a general idea of the value of the typical purchase, and we felt that variations from actuality most often fell within the fairly broad ranges used for classification.

We hypothesized that firms selling products with a low value of purchase would be more concerned with volume and would therefore have developed their marketing technology further and would market more aggressively than firms making fewer sales of higher value.

Unfortunately, the *moderate* and *very high* categories contained so few firms that comparisons could be misleading. The reader should consider this possible weakness in evaluating the analyses involving the value of typical purchase.

Table 5-4

Degree of Competition for Sample Firms

Classification	Index Points	Number of Firms
Heavy competition	8–10	25
Moderate competition	4–7	45
Light competition	1–3	30
No answer		10
Total Firms		110

Table 5-5

Value of Typical Purchase for Product of Sample Firms

Classification	Average Value of Purchase (soles)[1]	Number of Firms
Low purchase value	0–200	36
Moderate purchase value	201–2500	15
High purchase value	2501–25,000	30
Very high purchase value	25,000 and over	10
No answer		19
Total Firms		110

[1]At the time of the survey, one sole equalled $.037; in 1967, a change in the official exchange rate altered this to around $.024.

Table 5-6

Industries Represented by Sample Firms

Consumer Goods	Number of Firms
Products for automobiles	10
Food and beverage	17
Textiles, clothing, footwear	12
Pharmaceutical	9
Household durables	9
Total consumer goods firms	57
Industrial Goods	
Products for office use	9
Products for construction	10
Products for agriculture	8
Products for fishing and mining	12
Other industrial products	14
Total industrial goods firms	53
Total Firms	110

Type of Industry

Survey results were tabulated by industry (ten broad industry categories) and by type of industry (consumer-industrial). The consumer-industrial compilation was expected to show variations in marketing strategy because of basic product and market differences (for example, many customers versus few customers). It was hypothesized that consumer goods producers would have a more advanced marketing technology and would market more aggressively than would industrial goods producers.

Industries represented by sample firms are presented in Table 5-6.

The number of firms in the consumer-industrial categories appeared to be adequate for comparative purposes. Although some firms in the consumer goods category sold to industrial firms (for example, automobile battery producers served both consumers and manufacturers), the category used represented the major focus of the firms' business activities. The number of firms in each industry did not appear large enough for very many industry-by-industry statistical comparisons.

**Other Characteristics of
Firms Interviewed**

Location

Manufacturing in Peru centers in the Lima-Callao area, where 65 percent of gross production takes place and 71 percent of the manufacturing labor force is employed (both figures are based upon firms of five persons or more).[6] The sample was composed of 84 percent Lima-Callao firms and 16 percent provincial firms. Thus the sample concentration in the major metropolitan area was greater than actual overall industrial concentration. Because the industry classifications used in this study did not coincide with those used by the *Peruvian Census,* we could not make a "ten industry" comparison with the sample for concentration in the Lima-Callao area. However, because industries within our sample were unusually concentrated in the central metropolitan area (pharamaceuticals, for example), the sample probably conformed roughly with the actuality.

Size

Firms interviewed were classified by size on the basis of both sales volume and number of employees. The former has already been discussed. By design, the sample consisted of the larger-than-average firms. The percentage breakdown of respondent firms according to number of employees is shown in Table 5-7.

Because the upper range of the frequency distribution was open, it was not possible to compute an average without making an assumption about the midpoint of the upper range. The interviewers, based on their interview

Table 5-7

Size of Sample Firms

Number of Employees	Percent of Total Firms
50 or less	19
51 to 100	14
101 to 300	31
301 to 500	14
Over 500	17
No answer	5
	100

Table 5-8

Common Ownership Links of Sample Firms

	Percentage of Respondents				
Response	Total	Peruvian	Foreign	Consumer Goods	Industrial Goods
No	55	81	16	61	47
Yes, privately–owned	42	14	82	39	47
Yes, government–owned	3	5	– –	– –	6
	100	100	100	100	100

experiences, estimated the midpoint of this range to be 750 employees. Using this estimate, Peruvian firms were slightly larger than their foreign-owned counterparts (281 employees as compared with 269). On the other hand, computations of sales volume showed Peruvian-owned firms to be smaller.

Consumer products firms were larger in terms of employees and smaller in terms of sales volume than industrial products companies were. Peruvian-owned and consumer goods firms may have had lower capital ratios and may have been producing less with more labor than the foreign-owned and industrial goods firms.

Common Ownership

Each respondent was asked whether the firm belonged in whole or in part to another firm or group of firms. The general intent of this question was to obtain an indication of the concentration of industrial power through links of common ownership between or among different businesses. During informal discussions the researchers often heard the statement that forty families control the industrial power of Peru. The potential influence on marketing of an industry structure dominated by forty industrial families would, of course, be tremendous. Buying decisions would undoubtedly be strongly influenced by the consideration of purchasing within the "family." Instead of a free market in which product value and service would determine success, one would find a structure within which contacts with the "right" individuals in the family group itself would be more crucial.

Aware of the potential influence on marketing of concentrated industrial power, and yet not having the resources to study this question in depth, we simply asked, "Does the firm belong, in whole or in part, to another firm or group of firms?" If the response was "Yes," respondents were asked to identify the type of firm or group of firms.

Responses indicated that foreign-owned firms were generally owned by foreign businesses rather than individuals. Occasionally a foreigner had come to Peru to invest his own capital in a business, but this was clearly the exception. The high percentage of ownership links in foreign-owned firms did not indicate a power concentration *within* Peru, but simply showed that many of these firms were extensions of businesses rather far removed from the local scene.

Only 16 percent of the Peruvian-owned firms showed ownership links with other firms. This figure may have been understated, however, because respondents may either have wanted to hide the common ownership relationships or else did not know of them. Results, in general, suggested that the concentration of industrial power was not a highly influential factor among firms sampled.[d]

Common ownership links between industrial goods producers appeared to be more common than among consumer goods producers. The researchers' observations substantiated this, as several of the industrial goods firms

[d]Francois Bourricaud might argue with this statement. From his extensive study of the Peruvian oligarchy, he concludes that a relatively few families maintain control of the Peruvian economy through their large land holdings and subsequent power in the agricultural sector, their key positions in the blanks and other financial institutions which enable them to control credit, their political influence, their mining holdings,

Table 5-9

Age of Sample Firms

| Years in Business | Percentage of Respondents | | | | |
	Total	Peruvian	Foreign	Consumer Goods	Industrial Goods
5 or less	14	9	21	9	9
6 – 10	20	19	21	13	28
11 – 20	25	26	25	20	30
21 – 50	32	34	28	42	21
Over 50	9	12	5	16	2
	100	100	100	100	100

interviewed had been established by a parent firm to improve an inadequate supply situation. Generally, the objective of the sibling firm was not to build up industrial power, but to service the requirements of the parent organization.

Age

Another introductory question was asked to determine the age of the firms in the sample. Results are shown in Table 5-9.

The age patterns of business firms in the sample were consistent with the researchers' expectations. Exemplifying the increasing interest of foreign investors in Peru in recent years, foreign-owned firms tended to be younger than Peruvian-owned firms. Industrial goods producers were much younger than consumer goods producers. This pattern fits with normal theory of economic development, which states that the capital goods industry becomes important in a developing economy only after the consumer goods industry is relatively well developed. This is really no more than common sense. Until industry has developed to a certain threshold level, there simply is no adequate market to support the production of industrial goods.

Following the methodology that has been presented and interviewing the group of firms that has been described, we obtained the data that is presented in the next several chapters.

---

and their ownership of many industrial enterprises. He does point out, however, that the oligarchy is least powerful in the industrial sector and that growth of this sector constitutes one threat to their power. Francois Bourricaud, "Structure and Function of the Peruvian Oligarchy," *Studies in Comparative International Development,* II, 2, Political Sociology, Original Series 016 (St. Louis: 1966).

Section II: Marketing Strategies and Practices of Manufacturers in Peru

Without a knowledge of existing marketing practices and problems in a developing nation, it is impossible to determine marketing's actual or potential role in that country. Although some of the following description has direct application only to Peruvian manufacturers, the attendant implications should be useful in evaluating the role of the marketing concept and marketing practices in many of the other developing nations of South America, and perhaps in those of other parts of the world.

The following chapters attempt to evaluate hypotheses concerning the impact of the owners' nationality (Peruvian or foreign); the type of management (owner or nonowner); the size of the firm; the kind of industry (consumer or industrial); the degree of competition; the value of typical purchase, and the nature of the economic, political, and social environment. Precise measures of all of these independent variables and their influences on marketing management and the developmental process were predictably difficult to obtain. On the other hand, far too many data were gathered to be presented in this report. Therefore, each of the following chapters presents a summary of the data and analyses which we used to derive the findings of this study.

**Marketing Organizations
in Peru**

To obtain an overview of the marketing operations of Peruvian manufacturers, the interviews began with a discussion of the marketing organizations of the 110 manufacturers comprising the sample.

The Interview Technique

Respondents were asked to draw a table of organization for their marketing operations, indicating the number of people involved in performing each function. The purpose of this question was twofold: 1) to determine the scope of the firms' marketing activities, and 2) to obtain an indication of the extent to which the marketing organization had been developed in each of the firms.

Seventeen possible marketing functions were suggested to the respondents as they described their tables of organization. The rationale for suggesting specific functions was based on an apprehension that respondents might otherwise fail to recognize many of the functions as marketing activities. The question did, in fact, prove to be educational; in some instances respondents expressed surprise and interest that marketing embraced so many activities. Undoubtedly, presenting the specific functions resulted in some overstatement of the respondents' marketing activities.

Main Responsibility for Marketing

Responses to the organization question were difficult to tabulate, because there were almost as many different tables of organization as there were respondents. One method used was to classify responses according to which individual in the firm held principal responsibility for marketing. The manager who held major responsibility for marketing had to be actively involved in marketing management. In other words, a general manager who simply approved or disapproved the marketing plan would *not* hold the main responsibility for marketing activity.

The lack of marketing specialization can be seen in Table 6-1; in 55 percent of the firms, marketing responsibility had not been delegated to a marketing specialist. The chief executive usually spent a majority of his time on production, personnel, and financial problems; marketing received relatively little of his attention. This lack of specialization is particularly significant because the sample was taken from a group of relatively large firms. The smaller firms of Peru (which predominate) are even less specialized.

Table 6-1

**Manager Having the Major Responsi-
bility for Marketing**

	Percentage of Responses				
Responsible Individual	All Firms	Peruvian– Owned	Foreign– Owned	Consumer Goods	Industrial Goods
Chief executive	55	63	45	38	71
Sales or marketing manager	40	33	50	56	27
Others within the firm	5	4	5	6	2
	100	100	100	100	100

Lack of marketing specialization is prevalent in most developing (and some more developed) countries. As Sherbini has pointed out:

Generally speaking, the tendency in the early life of new manufacturing concerns is to place primary emphasis on staffing the production, financial, and general administrative departments of the firm. All thinking about sales is generally deferred to the point of actual production. [1]

A study by the Northern Wisconsin Development Center also reveals an inadequate marketing orientation.[2] The typical owner or manager of a small manufacturing firm in northern Wisconsin is not marketing oriented. His training or experience usually has been in some production capacity prior to going into business for himself. Thus he has had little previous contact with marketing or some of the other basic functional areas of management.

Because of this limited contact with marketing he is inclined to interpret the term narrowly, often as a substitute for the word "sales." While he recognizes that something has to happen between manufacture and ultimate use of the product, he does not fully understand the economic utilities of form, time, place and possession which comprise total marketing performance.

Our research revealed that Peruvian-owned firms had considerably less specialized marketing management than those owned by foreigners. This reflects the importation of marketing technology by the latter. Yet, only slightly over half of the foreign-owned firms have the marketing responsibility vested in someone other than the firm's chief executive.

Industrial goods producers specialized less in marketing than their consumer goods counterparts. This may be explained by the fact that industrial goods producers often have only a few potential customers, and that sales are often made on a personal, manager-engineer to manager-engineer basis. Also, fairly frequent common ownership links between industrial goods producers and their customers somewhat eliminate the need for an aggressive marketing activity.

A 1964 study of Brazilian consumer goods manufacturers tended to corroborate the data in Table 6-1. In "two-thirds of the companies surveyed, sales policies were established by the production department rather than by the sales organization."[3]

Stages of Development of Marketing Organization

A second tabulation of the firms' marketing organizations utilized an adaptation of Stanton's concept of the evolution of marketing management.[4] We added a preliminary stage of marketing organization to the four stages used by Stanton. The five stages which are used in this study are defined in this way:

Stage 1 — The *gerente* or president is responsible for most of the marketing functions in addition to his other responsibilities; in most cases, marketing problems receive little attention relative to production and financial problems.

Stage 2 — The sales manager is responsible for the field sales force; most other marketing activities are spread throughout the firm.

Stage 3 — Most marketing activity is grouped under one marketing executive, who is usually called the sales manager.

Stage 4 — Marketing management is fully integrated, often under a vice-president of marketing or a marketing manager. Activities such as inventory control, transportation, warehousing, and product planning are the responsibility of the chief marketing executive.

Stage 5 — The marketing concept becomes the basic orientation for the entire firm. All short-term company policies are highly conditioned by their marketing implications. This stage cannot be represented on an organization chart. It is reached when attitudes of all company executives reflect the marketing concept.

The five stages of marketing organization development are derived from the historical experience of the United States. Only in recent years have marketing organizations in the United States begun to evolve into stages 4 and 5. The evolution closely parallels the increasing importance of marketing as a determinant of a firm's success as businesses compete more vigorously for their shares of the market. In the United States, the recognition of the role of marketing and the need for integrating it into the firm's operations have been aided by marketing education. The relative lack of such education in Peru suggests that organizations there develop more slowly, despite a need for more advanced marketing management.

While the results of classifying respondent firms into the five stages are somewhat parallel to those of the previous tabulation, they provide a more precise picture of marketing organization and therefore are a better indication of the importance accorded to marketing in the firm. As Table 6-2 indicates, we judged one-third of the firms to be in stage 1, with all marketing functions supervised by the president of the firm. Only 39 percent of the firms were in stage 3 or beyond, where the responsibility for most marketing activities are assigned to one executive other than the president. In only 3 percent of the firms had the marketing concept been accepted by the firms' management.

Marketing organizations of Peruvian-owned firms were less sophisticated than those of firms owned by foreigners. The difference is significant, since only 29 percent of the Peruvian-owned companies had reached stage 3 or beyond, whereas 53 percent of foreign-owned firms had reached that level of development.

The industrial goods producers generally lagged behind consumer goods producers in the development of their marketing organizations. This may be due to very concentrated markets for industrial goods which, initially at least, call for a few intimate personal contacts rather than robust marketing programs. Another important factor is undoubtedly the relative youth of this group of industries. The initial organization of several industrial goods producers, according to respondents, was based primarily on the observation of a glaring need for a certain product or product line unavailable in Peru at the time except through importation. The government, anxious to build up a capital goods industry, granted tariff protection, and new firms were established. Because of markets previously developed by importers, no great marketing problems were immediately evident. In other words, an economic factor — market demand — was combined with a political factor — tariff protection — to create profitable business opportunities. The resulting new firms are often so protected that a strong marketing program and the adoption of the marketing concept are not considered essential to success.

Many industrial goods producers established on this basis are now beginning to find that they have problems. One example is a firm supplying the fishing industry. Its sales boomed as the industry underwent a heavy capitalization program. Now, however, most of the companies processing fish products are well-supplied with basic machinery, so demand for that machinery has declined. Replacement orders cannot be expected for some time; the machinery manufacturer is therefore undertaking an expanded marketing program to broaden its product line and markets.

The stage approach to marketing development is fruitful enough to merit cross-tabulation with some of the other important variables, specifically the type of management and the size of company.

Expectations were that firms under the direction of professional managers would have reached a more advanced stage of marketing organization than those

Table 6-2

**Stages of Development of Marketing
Organziation in Peru**

Stage of Development	Percentage of Respondents				
	All Firms	Peruvian– Owned	Foreign– Owned	Consumer Goods	Industrial Goods
1	34	44	20	21	49
2	27	27	27	25	29
3	31	27	36	48	12
4	5	– –	11	6	4
5	3	2	6	– –	6
	100	100	100	100	100

Stage of Development	Percentage of Respondents				
	Owner– Managed	Non–Owner– Managed	Small Firm	Medium Firm	Large Firm
1	43	23	47	16	30
2	32	20	23	38	22
3	22	43	30	28	40
4	3	7	– –	12	4
5	– –	7	– –	6	4
	100	100	100	100	100

managed by owners. This proved to be true because 57 percent of the professionally managed firms had reached stage 3 or beyond, whereas only 25 percent of the owner-managed firms were in this situation. However, inter-relationships with other variables such as nationality of ownership and size may account for some of this difference.

The larger firms, better able to support specialization of management functions, could be expected to show a higher level of development of their marketing organizations. As shown in Table 6-2, none of the small firms interviewed had reached stage 4 and only 30 percent were in stage 3. In contrast, 46 percent of the medium-sized and 48 percent of the large firms were in stage 3 or beyond. Actually, the medium-sized group, with an above-average represent-ation of foreign-owned firms, shows the most advanced organization, with 18 percent of the firms in stages 4 and 5.

It appears that the development of the marketing organization is influenced by the size of firm, type of industry (consumer or industrial), nature of ownership (domestic or foreign) and type of management (owner or nonowner). In addition, the development of marketing organizations has not progressed very far in Peru.

In about one-third of the companies interviewed, marketing activity has been grouped primarily under one marketing executive, most often the *jefe de ventas* (sales manager). The ability of this executive to conceptualize the need for a fuller integration of marketing activity and to convince others of the merits of the idea will determine more than anything else the speed at which the marketing organization reaches maturity within the firm. It should not be inferred that any one stage of marketing organization is optimal. The marketing organization should best meet the needs of the firm (which are dependent on its social, political, and economic environment and the resources available to it). Thus, the optimal stage of marketing organization may vary widely from firm to firm. However, the marketing organization should evolve from stage 1 toward stage 5 as marketing becomes more critical to success. The firm should be looking to future needs rather than evaluating its organization on the basis of the past. As will be shown, current marketing problems and practices in Peru call for a more advanced marketing organization than that now employed by many firms.

The Individual Marketing Functions

The seventeen particular marketing functions set forth in the questionnaire were tabulated on the basis of who held primary responsibility for these functions. Results show that a marketing executive, sales manager, or member of the sales staff had primary responsibility for 42 percent of the specific marketing functions. Others within the firm (accounting manager, administrative manager, or production manager) were responsible for 33 percent of the functions, and the chief executive was responsible for the remaining 25 percent.

Credit and price policies were usually kept in the province of the chief executive. Sales management, sales promotion, sales forecasting, marketing research, advertising, selection of marketing personnel, product planning, salesmen training, customer service, and marketing budgeting were most often performed by the marketing manager, sales manager, or a member of the sales staff. Other personnel usually were responsible for billing, warehousing, collections, transportation, and statistical sales control.

Because of the questionnaire's length and because specific questions related to individual functions followed, the interviewers did not attempt to probe very deeply into any of the individual functions. It is likely that the effect of suggesting functions to the respondents and the failure to determine levels of activity (many firms perform certain marketing functions only in an extremely elementary sense) means that the actual marketing activity of the firms was not as complete as responses indicate. Nonetheless, even with the strong likelihood of overstatement, only 46 percent of the firms interviewed claimed to be engaged in any kind of training for their salesmen. Only 53 percent mentioned any marketing research activities; just 62 percent said that they were performing customer service activities, developing forecasts, and preparing marketing budgets. Only 59 percent of the firms had a person responsible for advertising, even in a coordinating capacity with an agency.

The organization of the marketing activity varied widely from firm to firm. Figure 6-1 presents a diagram of the marketing organization of an automotive products producer and distributor at an elementary stage of development (stage 2).

In this firm, the general manager is not directly responsible for any marketing activities, but he definitely controls decisions made at the level below him. While the production manager supervises warehousing and marketing research, the accounting manager handles billing, statistical sales control, and collections. Responsibility for forecasting, budgeting, and transportation belongs to the sales manager. Other marketing activities become the responsibility of a management committee which includes all four managers shown in the diagram. The committee's list of responsibilities includes sales promotion, advertising, customer service, and sales management — activities that logically would fall within the domain of the sales manager.

Another firm, this one in the food and beverage industry, shows a more developed organization (stage 4). This firm has specialized the marketing function to a considerable degree. It has adopted the product management concept; has a special department for advertising, including four employees used for product testing; has a sales department that includes a distribution section; has a marketing research department; and has formed a special marketing department for a product line that differs significantly from the company's usual products. The *sub-gerente commercial* who heads this marketing organization can truly be called a marketing manager. The firm is diagrammed in Figure 6-2.

In connection with the food industry, it is appropriate to mention the role of the International Basic Economy Corporation (IBEC) in promoting sound

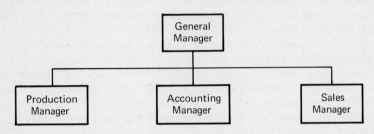

Figure 6-1   Primitive Marketing Organization.

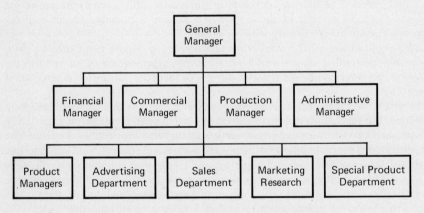

Figure 6-2   Advanced Marketing Organization.

business practices, including marketing, in a number of developing countries. "IBEC will use appropriate techniques for the *profitable* development and management of operations in food production and distribution, construction and financial services, as well as the timely divestment of these ventures, giving priority to the developing nations."[5] This method of setting up businesses and then turning them over to local management has benefitted Peru in three instances: the development of TODOS, a supermarket company; the construction and operation of COPESA, a shopping center company; and the construction of more than 1,000 moderate-cost homes in the Lima suburb of Salamanca de Monterrico. In the last example, a local contractor actually did the construction. IBEC helped with planning, financing, and marketing the project.

A number of mistakes were made in each of these projects, IBEC readily admits. The important point, however, is IBEC's demonstration that massive projects greatly needed by the population can be undertaken at a profit to the firms undertaking them.

Summary and Evaluation

The widely varied tables of organization found among the sample firms preclude the drawing of an "average" firm. Any such average would be misleading. The marketing organizations of manufacturers in Peru may be characterized as only recently recognizing that several marketing functions are performed more effectively if they are organized under the supervision of one man. Very few firms would rate marketing activity as important to the firm's success as production itself. In a great many firms, especially the smaller ones, the president or general manager is the marketing manager because he does not visualize marketing as important enough to warrant a specialist.

Although it is clear that such environmental factors as market size and degree of competition have a major influence on marketing organizations, we believe that the development of specialists in production and finance indicates that the time for marketing specialists in Peru and other developing nations is now. However, until businessmen recognize the importance of marketing it is unlikely that much effort will be made to establish more advanced marketing organizations. Educational efforts concerning the role of marketing and the training of marketing specialists are essential to the future development of industry in Peru and other developing countries. Unfortunately, most such educational efforts are currently concentrated in the more developed nations of the world.

7

Marketing Research in Peruvian Industry

Marketing research is the application of the scientific method to marketing problems in order to reduce uncertainty and improve the quality of business decisions. The implementation of the marketing concept requires that management determine the needs and desires of the firm's intended markets. The extent of marketing research is an indicator of both the adoption of the marketing concept and the quality of management. A *normative* model of marketing behavior would show research as playing a critical role in the management of the business enterprise.

Initially, marketing research may be used to define markets and characterize purchase motivations. This information is useful in establishing objectives and providing guidance for business planning. Prior to a product's introduction, marketing research can be used to evaluate a product and its proposed marketing program. During and after introduction of the product, marketing research is used to evaluate and explain results. In other words, it provides a flow of information to management. With this information, the product and its marketing program can be adjusted to meet changing needs of the market.

Experience in the United States has shown that larger firms, better able to support a marketing research staff, were the first to use marketing research effectively. As benefits of the research became evident, other firms began their own research efforts. Thus, at any given time, United States industry has been composed of many firms using marketing research in varying degrees.

The use of marketing research in developing countries is not great. Harper W. Boyd, et. al., have reported on discussions with 40 teachers of marketing from 18 developing countries.[1] The consensus among the 40 was that marketing research is not widely used in these countries and will not be so for some time. Major reasons seem to be:

(1) The attitudes toward marketing — business and government administrators tend to view marketing as a mechanistic process involving transportation, storage, and exchange.
(2) Governments typically do not encourage competition; thus the need for data to get ahead of competitors is viewed as small.
(3) Firms are small and management talent to undertake research is limited.
(4) Marketing, including marketing research, is a relatively low status occupation.
(5) Technical problems are many, and include:
    (a) Difficult probability sampling, due to out-of-date maps, un-

numbered dwelling units, several primary family units inhabiting one dwelling, language variations within a country, and inadequate transportation to outlying areas.

(b) Expensive and sometimes impossible data collection. Telephone service is poor and infrequent, mail service is uncertain, people in certain cultures do not wish to talk with or answer questions from strangers.

(c) Considerable errors in responses and non-responses because of servants protecting the homeowner from the interviewer and because of the large number of taboo subjects. In some countries, any interviewer is suspected to be a tax department investigator.

Commercial Marketing
Research Facilities

One indication of the use of marketing research is the extent and size of commercial marketing research firms in a country. In general, commercial research facilities are lacking in Peru. In addition, those facilities which are available seem to be neglected by business. It was a common statement among interviewees in manufacturing firms that there were "no agencies able to carry out a research project." A common statement from research agencies, however, was that "there is no market for marketing research in Peru."

Only four marketing and advertising research firms were identified in Peru. The largest of these employed only eight people and the owner worked parttime. At least two were one-man firms with one or more clerical employees. Publicidad Mercurio S.A., which is primarily an advertising agency, publishes a detailed monthly list of estimated advertising expenditures by brand and media, even to the radio and television station or newspaper used. Some larger advertisers used this service, but reportedly business was not sufficient to yield a profit for the publisher.

So far as can be ascertained, the first formal marketing research study done in Peru was, curiously, on the market for diamonds in 1944. Research has grown considerably since then, but research information and facilities are still small by most standards. A reported 80 to 90 percent of the commercial marketing research is sponsored by organizations with foreign capital — La Fabril, Proctor and Gamble, and Gillette, for example.

Table 7-1

Marketing Research by Peruvian Firms

	Percentage of Respondents				
Classification	All Firms	Peruvian– Owned	Foreign– Owned	Consumer Goods	Industrial Goods
Research	62	51	78	67	57
No research	38	49	22	33	43
	100	100	100	100	100

	Percentage of Respondents				
	Owner– Managed	Non–Owner– Managed	Small Firm	Medium Firm	Large Firm
Research	49	70	74	55	71
No research	51	30	26	45	29
	100	100	100	100	100

Utilization of Marketing Research

Although the researchers asked the interviewees whether their firms engaged in marketing research, no definite criteria were used to establish whether a company was actually involved in research activity. Because of this, many companies may have stated that they were engaged in marketing research, even though they should not be considered as actively engaged in such activities. Indirect checks, however (e.g. determining what research activities were carried on and who held responsibility for them) helped to establish the level of marketing research activity.

As shown in Table 7-1, 62 percent of the total firms interviewed claimed that they engaged in marketing research. This certainly overstates the amount of research activity, because many of these firms conducted only superficial investigations. Often the general manager assumed main responsibility for marketing research, in addition to his many other responsibilities.

A higher proportion of the foreign-owned firms were engaged in marketing research than the Peruvian-owned firms (78 percent as opposed to 51 percent). More consumer goods than industrial goods producers conducted marketing research activities. This is probably because the former are typically selling to broad markets that are distant and because of the middlemen which separate them from the ultimate consumer. On the other hand, an industrial goods producer with only two or three major customers may have sufficient information from frequent personal contacts with the customers. However, some industrial goods producers are now finding that their initial markets are becoming saturated and that replacement demand is not adequate to keep their plants operating at full capacity. A previous application of marketing research to delineate new marketing opportunities might have alleviated many of the current problems of lack of demand.

Firm size was positively correlated with the use of marketing research in Peru, as it is in the United States. The smaller firms did the least research. A higher proportion of the firms headed by professional managers were engaged in marketing research than were owner-managed firms. This was due in part to the larger size and heavy foreign ownership of the firms with professional managers.

It is interesting that the industry with the largest percentage of firms claiming to perform marketing research produced products for construction, probably because many of the products currently being used by contractors are new to Peru. Therefore, firms must do research to determine market potentials and obtain other necessary information. The food and beverages industry was also a relatively heavy user of marketing research.

In summary, size and nationality of ownership had the greatest influence on Peruvian manufacturers' use of marketing research. Differences between the levels of these factors were large enough to be attributed to more than intercorrelations. Type of industry and type of management also had some influence on the firms' use of research.

Types of Research Activities

Businesses engaging in marketing research activity were asked to specify what kinds of research were performed. Interviewers made no attempt to define the research areas beyond naming them unless the respondent asked for clarification. Such requests were not frequent. Hindsight suggests that definitions would have been helpful, in spite of the time it would have added to the interview. As the questionnaire was presented, respondents were not forced to use any criteria for deciding whether they could legitimately claim to engage in any given type of research. Thus, a firm that had *once* asked its salesmen to submit a report of buyer opinions about a product could claim to engage in consumer surveys.

The net result of this questionnaire weakness is that the use of the various types of marketing research in Peru is likely to be overstated.

If one looks at the presence of various types of marketing studies, the results indicate that manufacturing firms in Peru are well on the way to accepting the need for marketing research. On balance the impression is that such research is rather widely practiced in Peru. *Qualitative* adjustment of the results, however, shows that most of the research being carried on is extremely primitive and that results of the research may be as misleading as helpful.

Table 7-2

Marketing Research by Type of Activity

Research Activity	Percentage of Respondents						
	All Firms	Peruvian–Owned	Foreign–Owned	Consumer Goods	Indus-trial Goods	Owner Managed	Non–Owner–Managed
Sales analyses	57	48	71	61	53	48	71
Market analyses	53	41	69	60	45	48	60
Product tests	44	37	53	56	30	23	51
Consumer surveys	38	26	55	49	26	32	47
Advertising research	24	9	44	32	15	18	31
Packaging tests	14	6	24	18	9	11	18
Psychological tests	6	1	13	9	4	6	7

Research Activity	Percentage of Respondents					
	Small Firm	Medium Firm	Large Firm	Heavy Comp.	Moderate Comp.	Light Comp.
Sales analyses	44	67	78	80	60	47
Market analyses	36	64	78	68	56	47
Product tests	31	39	57	68	40	43
Consumer surveys	29	42	57	52	36	40
Advertising research	13	27	43	40	16	27
Packaging tests	4	24	22	20	16	10
Psychological tests	--	12	13	16	2	7

Sales Analyses

It is surprising that only 57 percent of the firms interviewed conducted sales analyses, an extremely basic and essential activity. Without sales analysis, a business firm truly is operating blindly. When sales are rising and production capacity is fully utilized, management may not see a need for such research activity. But profits realized under these circumstances are precarious, and the firm is extremely vulnerable to the growth of competitors attracted by the firm's marketing success. Sales analyses by type of customer, product salesmen, and sales area should be a normal activity for any firm, small or large.

Sales analyses in Peru were most often performed by the general manager, although the sales manager was sometimes given this responsibility. Only 13 percent of the firms interviewed had a special department performing sales analyses. When the chief executive himself conducts the analysis, the depth is not likely to be great; when a special department does the work, the analysis is more likely to be reasonably sophisticated, unless the investigation is conducted by a clerk with little direction or knowhow.

Nationality of ownership appeared to be a major variable determining factor in sales analysis activity. Seventy-one percent of the foreign-owned firms, as opposed to 48 percent of the Peruvian-owned firms, conducted sales analyses.

Consumer goods producers were a bit more likely to conduct sales analyses than were industrial goods producers. We suggest that this is due to the lengthy and more complicated distribution network for consumer goods which requires study to understand what is going on in the marketplace. The industrial goods producer feels less need for such information because he is closer to his customers who are likely to be few and often in direct contact with him.

Firm size was directly correlated with the conduct of sales analyses. The larger firms apparently felt better able to support the staff needed for such research. However, less than half of the large firms had one man working fulltime on this activity. Firms headed by professional managers, presumably because of the manager's greater familiarity with management and marketing technology were more likely to conduct sales analyses than owner-managed firms (71 percent as compared with 48 percent).

The level of competition also appeared to be directly correlated with sales analysis activity. Competitive pressures increase the incentive for sales analyses. Assuming the analysis is well done and that strategy is adjusted on the basis of it, competition improves marketing efficiency. This usually is to the benefit of the firm, the economy, and the consumer.

Market Analyses

Market analyses differ from sales analyses primarily in that the latter are oriented toward the study of the firm's past and current sales, and the former toward the estimation of market potential and future sales.

Almost as many firms (53 percent) conducted market analyses as sales analyses (57 percent). This is encouraging. Every firm should make an analysis of the market prior to entry into a business, but there is the danger that a firm might make a one-time study and settle back to run the business on the basis of results of this original research. Fortunately, the fairly high incidence of this type of research suggests that many firms are continuing this research, both for new product introductions and for the updating and improvement of current products and marketing strategies. Most market analyses are, however, performed by the chief executive, suggesting that such studies are superficial. In only about one-fourth of the respondent firms were market analyses performed by a special department. Another 16 percent of the respondents used an advertising agency or outside research agency for this type of research.

Foreign-owned firms engaged in market analyses far more often than the Peruvian-owned firms. The greater marketing awareness and technology of the foreign-owned firm explains part of this variance. Some of the difference may also be explainable on the basis of prior market knowledge. Peru is a small market, and Peruvians who have grown up in the country may feel that they are close enough to the market to understand and evaluate it without formal research. They may feel that their personal experience is adequate to guide strategy decisions. Often, of course, they will be wrong and experience alone will not be an adequate guide. The managers of foreign-owned firms, who are often unfamiliar with the Peruvian environment, may feel unprepared to evaluate the market without formal research. Thus the foreigner's lack of experience could prove to be an asset, because he is fairly free from bias and therefore has to depend upon facts for his decision-making.

A hypothetical example of the value of unbiased market analysis follows. In the traditional segmentation of the consumer market in Peru, five consumer groups, based on income levels, are labelled A, B, C, D, and E. Many companies producing for the consumer market make a semiautomatic judgment that only the upper level groups, A and B, contain potential customers. These groups are relatively small, so the manufacturers decide that production must be limited and that a high price must be charged.

A foreign-owned company entering the Peruvian market receives the same initial information. The manager, familiar with the concept of social class in his native country, decides that he wants more information. He discovers that there are three basic social classes in Peru; the upper class oriented to modern and international values; the middle class deriving its values from *"criollismo,"* and the *cholo* and Indian lower classes, whose values differ widely according to their basic tribal group and degree of assimilation to European values and norms. Furthermore, he discovers that the lower class, by far the largest single group, includes many people who aspire to the middle class, and, therefore, associate with *"criollismo."* His product is then designed, priced, and promoted to appeal to the *criollo* or the lower class. The foreign owner's market is broad enough to support mass production, and he develops a profitable market overlooked by his more traditional competitor. This example is hypothetical, but not unrealistic. Since markets have been found among the lower income groups of Peru, the example shows the potential advantages of a careful market analysis, which considers both economic and social variables affecting buyer behavior.

Consumer-oriented firms were more likely to conduct market analyses than industrial goods producers (60 percent as compared with 45 percent), probably for reasons similar to their greater interest in sales analyses. An important consideration may be the fact that consumer markets are considerably more widespread throughout Peru than are industrial markets, which tend to be concentrated in the Lima-Callao area. Less is likely to be known about distant markets, such as the Arequipa area, than about familiar local markets.

Size appeared to be directly correlated with the performance of market analyses, as it was with all the types of research activity. In addition to the greater staff and financial capabilities of the larger firm, the investments to be made in new markets are typically greater. The spending of $10,000 for information on which to base a $1,000,000 investment decision is more easily justified than buying $10,000 of information to evaluate a $50,000 investment.

Firms led by professional managers were more likely to engage in market analyses than owner-managed firms (60 percent as opposed to 48 percent). In addition to the greater marketing technology of the professional manager, the intercorrelations of size and nationality of management variables explain the variance between the two groups.

The level of competition and the use of market analyses appeared to be directly correlated, although not quite so closely as in the case of sales analyses. The intercorrelation of other comparison variables with competition may explain why this variable showed a strong influence on the use of both sales and market analyses.

Other Research Activities

The other marketing research activities studied followed the same general pattern established for market and sales analyses, although they were performed less frequently. Only 6 percent of the firms conducted psychological tests related to marketing, and only 14 percent engaged in packaging tests. Foreign-owned firms showed an especially heavy dependence upon consumer surveys relative to their Peruvian-owned counterparts. Owner-managed firms showed an exceptionally infrequent use of product tests (usually interpreted by respondents to mean quality-control tests).

A related type of marketing research, not discussed with manufacturers, concerns information on farm prices. This is needed by farmers, particularly those far away from the central markets in Lima and Callao. The Officina de Estudios Económicos of SIPA has gathered market price data for several years. These data are broadcast daily on Radio Nacional, Radio Agricultura, and Radio Continente. This step in the right direction has two shortcomings: Radio Nacional, owned by the government, has power enough to reach outside the Lima-Callao area, but only broadcasts 15 minutes each day starting at noon. More morning broadcasts are needed. The other two stations do not have enough power to reach far outside of Lima. A call has been made for more extensive gathering and wider broadcasting of farm prices around several of Peru's other major cities.[2]

Summary and Evaluation

Although marketing research in Peru is not sophisticated, many firms are attempting to utilize it as a guide to their marketing planning. The *quantity* of research ostensibly performed is perhaps greater than what one might expect, but responses undoubtedly overstate the amount of research actually done. The *quality,* because of such factors as poor secondary data, a lack of marketing education, and facilities, is generally poor.

Marketing research was most often performed by foreign-owned, professionally-managed, and large-sized firms. Producers of consumer goods and firms facing strong competition were also among those conducting the most research. Size and nationality of ownership appeared to have the greatest influence among the preceding factors. Because size was least likely to be influenced by possible intercorrelations with the other variables, the impact of size on the utilization of marketing research was especially clear. The strong influence of size and nationality of ownership indicates the importance of resources and technology to marketing research efforts.

8 Product and Service Management in Peru

A product is that which the customer receives when he makes a purchase. It is a bundle of satisfactions, produced by nature and industry, for sale in the marketplace. As such, the product usually has physical, psychological, and sociological dimensions, each of which contributes to the value of the product to the customer.

In no dimension of marketing strategy is the marketing concept more obvious than in the management of products. In addition to being both the genesis of the firm's entire marketing program and the vehicle through which sales and profits are realized, the product is the firm's social justification for being. Through the product, or service, the customer receives the satisfaction which he is seeking and the firm renders a service to society. To maximize the profits of the enterprise, and to be of maximum social service, the product must meet the needs and desires of its intended consumers.[a]

Product Planning and Development

Product planning and development is essentially the adjustment of production to the demand of potential customers. Although the wishes of the customer should be the controlling influence in product development, the purpose is to create a product which will satisfy the customer *and* sell at a profit. The better the product offered at a given price, the easier other aspects of the marketing process will be.

Product development may take three forms: 1) creation of a new product; 2) improvement of an existing product; and 3) development of new uses for an existing product. Most product development activities center on the improvement of existing products to better serve the needs and desires of consumers. In Peru and other developing societies, one would expect product management activities to concentrate on the adaption of products originated elsewhere to the markets of Peru. For example, the large and fancy stove with clocks, timers, multiple burners, and many other features which appeal to the middle-class market in the United States would not be appropriate to the typical Peruvian homemaker. A much simpler device, more economical to purchase and use, would be substantially more appropriate. The marketing concept would suggest that stoves and other products should be altered according to the specific needs and desires of the Peruvian market consumer.

[a]The assumption that profits are directly related to the application of the marketing concept presumes a competitive market.

Responsibility for Product Planning

Product planning is the evaluation and selection of a firm's products to insure that they fulfill the current and potential needs of the market and the firm. Product planning in Peru is most often the responsibility of the sales manager or the chief executive. In Peruvian-owned firms, the chief executive plays the dominant role, and in the foreign-owned firms, the sales manager usually assumes responsibility for product planning.

Eighty percent of the respondents claimed to be engaged in product planning activities, to one degree or another. This percentage did not vary significantly between foreign-owned and Peruvian-owned firms.

Of the seventeen marketing functions presented to respondents, product planning ranked fourth in frequency of occurrence among the Peruvian-owned firms and seventh among all the firms. Product planning is clearly a relatively well recognized and common managerial activity in Peru.

Although extensive information on this important function were not obtained, observation indicated that most product management activities were highly unsophisticated. In many cases, product planning amounted to no more than a general manager's decision to add another product when the sales of an existing product started to decline rapidly. Only the larger consumer goods producers seemed to have a fair grasp of the full scope of product planning. Interestingly, the foreign-owned firms were often more careless about decisions to add products than the Peruvian-owned firms. The fact that their overseas owners often provide fully developed products and may insist on their introduction (or at least apply pressure for introduction) probably explains this behavior.

Innovation and Imitation in Peru

Innovation is the introduction of a new way of doing things. It may consist of a new way of marketing a product, a new production method, a new custom, or a new device. At this point, our inquiry is limited to the introduction of a new product to the marketplace of Peru.

Few if any new products are developed in Peru because of the limited amount of basic research performed there. However, a product is an innovation to the consumer if it previously has not been available to him. Therefore, in a developing nation, a firm may be an innovator by adapting and introducing to the local economy a product developed elsewhere.

To obtain a measure of the "imitative-innovative" activities of Peruvian firms, respondents were asked to indicate how many new products they had introduced to the market over various periods of time. The wording of the question caused some confusion. For example, what is the definition of "new"? Does a minor change in a present product make it a new product? How much of a change is necessary for the product to qualify as being "new"? A product that is new to one firm would be old to another which has been producing it for many years; or the firm's new product may be old to the consumer, who has been purchasing it as an import. Therefore, the number of new products introduced by a firm is only a very rough measure of its product imitation-innovation activities and undoubtedly overstates the actual amount of innovation which has taken place.

Eighty-eight percent of the respondents said that they had introduced a new product at some time in their past. This percentage did not vary much on the basis of either nationality of ownership or type of industry. Of the firms introducing new products, 13 percent claimed that they were continually introducing new products. Another 23 percent had added a new product within the last two years.

The preceding percentages did not vary considerably when classified according to the analysis variables. However, Peruvian-owned firms and consumer goods producers had introduced more new products recently than foreign-owned firms and industrial goods producers. Managers of small firms tended to claim that they were continually introducing new products, and professionally managed firms tended to have more recent new product introductions. Firms experiencing a substantial amount of competition appeared to have a few more new products than those with less competition, while firms selling products of very high value were less likely to have made recent introductions.

The overall conclusion to be derived is that the managers of most firms, regardless of classification used, claim to be quite active in the introduction of new products. It was quite apparent that these new products did not originate in Peru, but were adaptations of products previously developed in other countries. This type of product innovation is essentially a matter of import substitution. By introducing products largely developed elsewhere, Peruvian manufacturers avoid most of the costs and risks of product research and development.

Incentives for Product Introductions

Because innovation through product introduction plays an important role in economic development, the researchers were interested in finding out what has influenced the introduction of new products. Once these influences are determined, public policy may be adjusted to encourage a more rapid rate of introduction.

The most important consideration in a proposed new product introduction is demand, and the respondents almost universally reported that they felt this was most important in evaluating their new product introduction proposals. However, the potential demand for new products in Peru is limited because the nation is small in terms of total population and a large portion of the population has very little discretionary income. At present, the greatest opportunity is for new products which more economically serve the nondiscretionary needs of the consumer market[1] and for industrial goods which enable Peruvian producers to lower their production costs and selling prices.

A redistribution of income would greatly increase market potential for most Peruvian industries. For example, the affluent mass market in the United States is a major factor in the prosperity of its industries. The encouragement of a Latin American common market would also increase the market potential for Peruvian producers. Peruvian manufacturers tend to fear economic integration because of the competition of larger producers in Argentina, Brazil, and Mexico. However, if the Peruvians could compete, they would benefit greatly from integration because they would gain access to larger markets than would the producers located in the bigger countries. If one looks at economic integration as an exchange of market potentials, the smaller countries are certainly receiving more than they are giving up.

A redistribution of income, which would increase the purchasing power and standard of living of the masses, would also reward the wealthy because they own most of the industry in Peru. Therefore, they would benefit from the growth of consumption and economic activity. A more even distribution of income does not pose, in the long run, an economic threat to the wealthy class. Instead, it is a major key to the future prosperity of the nation and the future economic situation of all classes in the Peruvian society.

Public Incentives for
Product Development

There are at least four publicly controlled influences which encourage new product introductions: 1) *special legislation* (other than tariffs) to promote and protect national and foreign capital investment in Peru; 2) *tariff policies* including high import duties to protect local industry and low tariffs to minimize the cost of parts and materials which must be purchased abroad; 3) *government investment* programs (for example, in highways and schools) which generate demand; and 4) *licensing* requirements which protect existing firms.

Special legislation was important to a number of companies. More than one-fourth of the firms interviewed mentioned this as being the most important of the publicly controlled influences affecting the introduction of new products. Foreign-owned and consumer goods firms felt that this was somewhat more important than did the Peruvian-owned and industrial goods manufacturers. These results imply that legislation, such as Peru's Industrial Promotion Law, has

Table 8-1

**Publicly Controlled Influences on New
Product Introduction**

Influence	Percentage of Firms Introducing New Products				
	Total	*Peruvian*	*Foreign*	*Consumer*	*Industrial*
Special legislation	28	25	32	33	24
Tariff policies	21	20	22	20	22
Government investment	7	7	5	7	7
Licensing, etcetera	5	– –	14	7	4
Others	5	4	8	9	2
No influence	34	44	19	23	41
	100	100	100	100	100

encouraged investment and thus made more new products available to the Peruvian consumer.

Tariff policies were also reported to be important, although to a lesser degree. Slightly more than one-fifth of the firms who had introduced new products felt that this was the most important publicly controlled consideration. Tariffs were mentioned with similar frequency by each classification of firms. Having heard a great amount of "protectionistic" talk among businessmen, we had expected that tariff policy would be considered more important by the respondents. It is possible that tariff protection tends to be taken for granted by a number of firms because high import duties have become rather commonplace in recent years. Of those firms who did mention tariffs as influencing new product introductions, some were considering the value of the *low* tariffs on parts and materials which they purchase, rather than protection from imports.

Other considerations, such as government investment programs and licensing or other arrangements with other firms were evidently not so important, except in the construction industry where government investment creates demand directly. None of the respondents mentioned the potential indirect effect of increased government investment insofar as it might improve the *quality* as well as the size of the market by providing a better distribution system, raising the education level of consumers, or providing jobs and incomes for consumers. The authors were surprised that businessmen were not more aware of these important potential long-run benefits to Peruvian industry.

While demand remains the most essential criterion for new product introduction, special legislation, tariffs, and government investment play a significant role in providing an incentive for new product introductions in Peru. For example, Peru's Industrial Promotion Law and a protective tariff encouraged the establishment of a plywood manufacturing plant in the jungled selva region.

Problems of New Product Introduction

Perhaps the most interesting question regarding product planning concerned major problems encountered in the process of introducing new products. Although the question was open-ended, answers tended to cluster around certain themes. However, there was no single outstanding theme, indicating that problems vary widely.

Only 17 percent of the respondent firms felt that they had no major problems associated with new product introductions. Foreign-owned firms and consumer goods producers were less likely to feel that they had no major problems in this area. The differences in the responses of the various types of producers were quite marked. This is especially noteworthy because intercorrelations between type of ownership and type of industry would tend to decrease the differences within each category.

The slowness of consumers to adopt new ideas was a real problem. Foreign-owned firms found it to be more severe than did Peruvian-owned firms. This may be due to a higher ratio of inappropriate products introduced by foreign-owned firms or because the managers, having operated in a more developed market, were accustomed to a consumer population that was willing to accept change readily. However, we believe that an inadequate study of consumer needs and the resultant introduction of inappropriate products is often the major problem, rather than overly traditional consumers.

The tradition-bound consumer complaint was particularly prevalent among respondents in the construction materials industry. The complaint was probably justified because of a lack of construction and product standardization. For example, producers of metal household windows were forced to build to the building contractors' specifications. This adds to the cost, because of the very short production runs, and also adds to the time required to build a home or apartment building.

Competition, which should stimulate new product introductions, created problems for some firms. It is more often a problem for consumer goods producers than industrial goods producers. The authors were surprised to find that foreign-owned firms (24 percent) found competition a greater problem than did Peruvian-owned firms (11 percent). One would expect that firms accustomed to markets in the more developed countries would find the Peruvian market less competitive. Two hypotheses might explain the strong awareness of competition by foreign-owned firms. First, many of these firms may have entered the market after a rather hasty and incomplete study of the environment and with the preconceived notion that Latin-American businessmen were inefficient and would not provide much competition. However, once the foreign-owned firm actually began doing business in Peru, it may have discovered that it had underestimated the competition. Measured against the original and false preconception, competition indeed seemed strong. A second explanation may lie in the failure of the foreigner to adapt to local business practices. This hypothesis was corroborated by one interviewee who suggested that the most effective combination of investors would be a foreigner (who would be well-trained in modern business techniques) and a native Peruvian (who would know how to avoid the numerous idiosyncrasies of Peruvian law and would have the personal contacts to get things done).

Thirteen percent of the "new product introducers" stated that introductions were expensive and difficult. Some mentioned the unavailability of media for specific customer groups as one reason for the expense and difficulty.

Lack of market information is a real problem. Many of the sources of secondary information available in developed countries such as the United States are nonexistent in Peru. Thus, the gathering of market information can be both difficult and expensive. Consumer goods producers most often recognize the need for more market data; industrial goods producers said they thought they had enough market information. The lack of market information in foreign markets has often led businessmen to (1) take the position that consumer needs and motivations are universal, (2) rely on deeply ingrained stereotyped impressions of a foreign culture, or (3) depend on the opinions of domestic businessmen on the assumption that they know their markets.[2] Any of these approaches may lead to gross misjudgments concerning a market.

The view that it is difficult to sell quality goods in a price-conscious market indicates a failure of firms to realize that they should produce to meet market needs. *If* the Peruvian consumer prefers a poorer quality, less expensive product, the company's product mix is simply misdirected.

Government price controls were a problem in the consumer goods field. In some instances, such as with telephone rates, price controls are quite obviously based on political rather than economic considerations.

Summary and Evaluation

Product management is not strong in Peru. Responsibility generally rests with a top executive, who does not have enough time to thoroughly evaluate present and future products. Consumer goods producers and foreign-owned firms appear to be significantly more aware of the many facets of product management, and it is apparent that most firms are adding products to their line fairly regularly.

Original product research and development is rarely conducted in Peru. A partner in a major business consulting firm, when asked if he knew of *any* firms in Peru that were conducting research and product development, answered after considerable reflection that he could not think of one! He noted that nearly all new products are simply copies of foreign-made products, sometimes on a

Table 8-2

Problems of New Product Introduction

Problem	Percentage of Firms Introducing New Products[1]				
	Total	Peruvian	Foreign	Consumer	Industrial
Consumers are traditional, slow to adopt new ideas	17	14	22	17	17
Competition is very strong	16	11	24	20	13
New products are difficult or expensive to introduce	13	11	16	17	9
There is a lack of market information about style acceptance, demand changes, and so on	11	9	14	20	4
It is difficult to sell quality in a price market	9	11	5	7	11
Government controls prices	9	7	11	15	2
There are no major problems	17	22	11	9	26

[1]Columns may not add to 100 due to multiple answers.

licensed basis and sometimes just copied. In large measure this may be appropriate behavior for Peruvian industry. As Levitt has pointed out, the vast majority of new product introductions, even in a developed economy, are *imitations* rather than true *innovations.* He suggests that a firm attempting to innovate continually rather than imitate is in fact attempting the impossible, and will spend itself out of business.[3] Given the comparatively small size of business firms in Peru and their technological lag, it seems appropriate that these firms should concentrate on imitation at this stage of their development. In this way, Peruvian industry can take advantage of modern technology relatively quickly and inexpensively. Given the present stage of the country's development, industry should emphasize the imitation and adaption of existing products to the specific needs of the Peruvian markets. Although many firms are active imitators, much more effort is needed to properly adapt products to the needs and desires of Peruvian buyers.

Service

The "product" is frequently more than just a physical entity. It may include installation, instructions on product use, a warrantee, and numerous other product-related elements. Because products are purchased for the productivity and satisfaction which they yield, and because the services connected with the physical product are often critical to buyer satisfaction and productivity, these services constitute a major portion of the product and represent an important part of marketing. Indeed, services are often the chief element distinguishing the products of one manufacturer from those of another.

The need of Peruvians for service is especially great for several reasons. First, the level of education in Peru is generally low. This means that many buyers require training before they can use products effectively. This is especially true of products such as fertilizer, and even soap. A second factor influencing the need for service is the fact that many consumers cannot afford to repurchase the product if it fails. As a consequence, repair services are frequently needed. For example, automobiles which would have long ago been discarded in the United States are still being driven in Peru. Prolonged use is also common for television sets and other household appliances, as well as industrial equipment.

Product service constitutes a difficult managerial problem for Peruvian industry because of the scarcity of well-trained service personnel and the geographical dispersion of the population. Much of the population lives in areas that are relatively inaccessible to service outlets. Distances are great and transportation facilities are highly inadequate throughout most of the rural regions of the nation. This, of course, makes the provision of service both difficult and expensive.

In the following analysis, service has been classified into two principal categories, presale and postsale service. The former consists of those services directly related to making the sale; the latter pertains to service necessary to keep the product functioning and the customer satisfied.

Presale Service

Each respondent was asked whether his firm provides its customers with "engineering or technical services" prior to the sale. Almost two-thirds of the firms interviewed claimed that they provided presale service. In many cases, this meant that a technically qualified salesman performed such activities as studying a customer's needs and estimating his requirements. All of the drug companies felt that their salesmen (detailmen) performed service by educating the physician about the usefulness of the product. This raises the question as to when salesmanship ends and service begins. For purposes of this study, the researchers considered a firm to be offering presale service when the salesman or technical representative went beyond a presentation of the product and its advantages.

Foreign-owned firms were more likely to offer presale services than were Peruvian-owned firms (78 percent versus 53 percent). This is probably a reflection of foreign management's greater awareness of the importance of service in a purchase decision.

Industrial goods producers were substantially more frequent purveyors of service than were consumer goods manufacturers. This is to be expected in that a manufacturer faced with a decision to purchase a costly installation will generally require some rather detailed engineering information before making his buying decision. It is less obvious that the manufacturer of jelly will benefit by offering his retailers advice on how to keep the product from spoiling on the shelves. Within the consumer goods industries, manufacturers of food and beverages, textiles, clothing and footwear, and household durables were less often found to offer presale services than were manufacturers in other industries.

The most frequently performed presale services were estimation of the buyers needs, demonstrations of the product, and the offering of specialists to answer questions about the product. To obtain an indication of the extent of the service offered, we asked how many people were actively involved in presale service. Because this approach neglects the qualitative aspects of service, it is a less-than-perfect measure of service activity.

An arithmetic mean was computed for each type of respondent. Because almost all drug companies classified their salesmen as being servicemen, a separate tabulation was made, excluding the drug companies. If one believes that a typical detailman can be considered as highly involved in presale service, the first column of Table 8-4 may be used. If one believes that detailmen are primarily selling rather than servicing, the second column should be used.

The arithmetic mean for all firms indicates that an average of 6.3 employees are engaged in presale service work. When drug companies are taken out of the sample, this average drops to 4.9 people. One of the most substantial differences in the averages occurred between Peruvian-owned and foreign-owned firms. This

Table 8-3

Presale Service

Response	Percentage of Respondents				
	Total	*Peruvian*	*Foreign*	*Consumer*	*Industrial*
Service	63	53	78	47	81
No Service	37	47	22	53	19
	100	100	100	100	100

suggests that the familiarity of the management of foreign-owned firms with service practices in more developed countries has stimulated the use of service in Peru.

Predictably, consumer goods producers had fewer personnel in presale service activity than did industrial goods producers. Professionally managed companies used more personnel in their presale service activities than did the owner-managed firms. Because nationality of ownership was highly intercorrelated with the type of management, it was not possible to determine whether nationality of ownership or type of management was the more important factor in explaining the difference.

Although size apparently influenced the number of presale personnel, it was not so important as the previously mentioned variables. In fact, the high intercorrelation of size with nationality of ownership and type of management suggested that the influence of size may have been even less than Table 8-4 indicates. When drug companies are eliminated from the sample, medium-sized firms employ even fewer presale service personnel than the small firms do. Large companies, however, employ more presale service personnel than the small or medium-sized firms.

The influence of competition upon the number of presale service employees was not clear. Results are substantially different in the two columns because of the predominance of drug companies in the heavy competition group. Because intense competition was highly interrelated with foreign ownership, and to a lesser extent with professional management, this group's use of service personnel may have been exaggerated. If this was the case, high competition may actually have led to fewer service personnel being used. When drug companies were eliminated from the sample, heavy competition did seem to have resulted in fewer service employees.

The value of the typical purchase seemed to be inversely related to the number of presale service employees in column one. This is, of course, contrary to expectations. This apparent contradiction is explained by 1) the influence of the drug companies which had a large number of service personnel and are all found in the low purchase value category; and 2) the small number of firms in

Table 8-4

Number of Employees in Presale Service

	Average Number of Employees	
Classification	All Firms	All Firms Except Drug Companies
Total firms	6.3	4.9
Peruvian–owned	3.4	2.4
Foreign–owned	10.3	8.0
Consumer goods	5.8	3.1
Industrial goods	6.8	6.8
Small	5.4	4.2
Medium	7.0	3.4
Large	7.1	7.1
Owner–managed	3.8	3.5
Professionally–managed	9.8	6.6
Heavy competition	7.5	3.4
Moderate competition	6.1	5.5
Light competition	6.1	4.8
Very high purchase value	4.0	4.0 ⎫ 4.3
High purchase value	4.4	4.4 ⎭
Moderate purchase value	5.5	5.5 ⎫ 3.4
Low purchase value	6.8	2.1 ⎭
Automotive products		6.2
Food and beverages		2.6
Textiles, clothing, footwear		.9
Pharmaceutical		25.9
Household durables		.5
Office products		4.4
Construction–related products		8.6
Agriculture–related products		6.8
Products for fishing and mining		6.8
Other industrial products		7.2

Table 8-5

Postsale Service

	Percentage of Respondents				
Response	*Total*	*Peruvian*	*Foreign*	*Consumer*	*Industrial*
Service	54	45	67	42	69
No Service	45	55	33	58	31
	100	100	100	100	100

the moderate purchase value category which may mean a lack of statistical reliability. When drug companies were eliminated from the sample and when low-moderate purchase value categories were compared with the high-very high purchase value categories, it became apparent that the number of service personnel is directly related to value of typical purchase. Averages in this group of comparison variables were lower than most, because the nineteen firms that did not answer the value of purchase questions had an unusually high number of presale service employees (more than ten).

Postsale Service

The sale itself does not terminate the marketing process. Insofar as one of the firm's objectives should be customer satisfaction, many postsale activities may be needed. Such engineering or technical services as installation, repairs, user training, and suggestions as to additional product uses are valuable in establishing rapport with customers and building future sales. This type of activity also affords the firm an opportunity to gather useful market information.

Fewer firms provided postsale service than offered presale services (54 percent as against 63 percent), perhaps because presale services are often required to make the sale. After the sale, the customer has less leverage on the seller, especially if the seller lacks a customer orientation.

The relationships between the analysis variables and postsale service were somewhat similar to those between these variables and presale service. The one exception to this was the pharmaceutical industry. Whereas all drug firms interviewed claimed to provide presale service, only 44 percent claimed to provide postsale service.

Data on the number of employees engaged in postsale services is presented in Table 8-6. The average number of employees involved in postsale service is 6.2, similar to the average number performing presale service. The elimination of drug companies from the postsale sample does not have as much effect on results as it did in the presale sample.

Table 8-6

Number of Employees in Postsale Service

Classification	Average Number of Employees	
	All Firms	All Firms Except Drug Companies
Total firms	6.2	5.6
Peruvian–owned	3.3	3.4
Foreign–owned	10.2	9.1
Consumer goods	4.9	3.5
Industrial goods	7.8	7.8
Small	3.7	4.0
Medium	6.0	3.0
Large	7.1	7.1
Owner–managed	3.7	3.8
Professionally–managed	10.1	9.2
Heavy competition	9.9	7.0
Moderate competition	6.4	6.5
Light competition	3.1	3.3
Very high purchase value	9.7	9.7
High purchase value	6.4	6.4
Moderate purchase value	6.2	6.2
Low purchase value	3.7	1.0
Automotive products		5.8
Food and beverages		1.3
Textiles, clothing, footwear		1.5
Pharmaceutical		13.3
Household durables		7.3
Office products		9.6
Construction–related products		5.4
Agriculture–related products		7.6
Products for fishing and mining		9.6
Other industrial products		7.3

Variations in the number of postsale service employees were fairly substantial, with foreign-owned firms using almost three times as many service people as Peruvian-owned firms. Industrial goods producers, large firms, professionally managed firms, companies with heavy competition, and producers with high value products all employed substantially more postsale service personnel than their counterparts. The influence of firm size, type of industry, and degree of competition is apparently stronger in the case of postsale service than for presale service.

Responsibility for Customer Service

The sales manager or someone on his staff was responsible for customer service approximately half the time. In 15 percent of the firms, the chief executive assumed responsibility for customer service. Other executives were in charge of service in 34 percent of the firms interviewed. Peruvian-owned firms were most likely to assign the responsibility to someone outside the sales department, whereas foreign-owned firms saw customer service most often as a function of the sales manager or his staff.

Dealer Service

Most firms offer some type of nontechnical service to their middlemen, such as the extension of credit and the offering of promotional aids or cooperative advertising. The use of these services is discussed in the section about distribution channels.

Summary and Evaluation

Service would be considered an *essential* activity by almost all firms in a developed nation. In Peru, however, at least one-third of the manufacturers surveyed apparently did not offer any customer service. Service appears to be a definite area of weakness in marketing programs in Peru. That lack of service is due to 1) a lack of concern with customer satisfaction; 2) the difficulty of obtaining qualified personnel to perform the service; and 3) the seller'market prevailing in most industries due to high import duties and a lack of competition. As an example of the second problem, one firm selling a consumer durable good wanted to provide repair service. However, experience with its own service department showed that repairmen were irresponsible and poorly trained, and that customer complaints about service were frequent. Rather than accept the expense and responsibility for training its own men, the company reestablished the department as a separate company in order that a reputation for poor service would not affect company sales.

The greatest differences in service activity were associated with nationality of ownership and type of management. The foreign-owned and professionally managed firms apparently felt most strongly that good service is important in achieving success.

It is particularly noteworthy that several firms in the textiles, clothing, and footwear industries provided little or no presale or postsale service. In view of the fact that many of their goods are sold to "cutters" and other industrial buyers, one would expect the manufacturers to provide service.

Marketing Communications in Peru

Marketing communication is a process by which information pertaining to products and services is exchanged between producers, middlemen, and consumers. "The individual arrives at his belief about the value of a good (or service) on the basis of his perceptions, direct and indirect, of that good (or service), and his resulting judgment of the extent to which it will serve his needs."[1] Thus, marketing communication, by creating awareness of options (in products and services), and developing familiarity with characteristics of those options, lays the basis for valuation, and thereby enables economic exchange to take place.

"Promotion," which denotes communication directed from producers toward consumers, is a somewhat more limited term than marketing communication. Advertising is a form of promotion which presents a nonpersonal, openly sponsored, paid message regarding a product, service, or idea. Personal selling is salesman-to-prospect communication. Sales promotion involves marketing activities other than personal selling and advertising, which stimulate consumer purchasing and dealer effectivenesss (e.g., displays, shows, expositions and demonstrations).

Marketing Communications and Development

In a simple economy where labor is not highly specialized, producers and consumers usually communicate on a personal basis. This face-to-face communication is very effective, because producers are able to adapt their behavior to the needs and desires of individual customers. Feedback is immediate, and behavior can be easily altered.

However, as technology expands and labor becomes more specialized, producers and consumers become more widely separated. With mass production comes the need for mass marketing, including mass communications. While personal selling remains effective in numerous situations, economic efficiency requires the economies of mass communications.

The change from a predominately personal communications network to mass communications is complicated. In a developing country, the extreme socio-economic variations between market segments call for different communications systems. For instance, in Peru, the modern and traditional market sectors utilize communications networks that are basically different. "In the modern sector, emphasis is stronger on impersonal communication, the mass media, and on extracommunity communication — sources from outside the community. In the traditional sector, personal communication is more important. Here, emphasis is on intracommunity communication — sources in the local community — and egocentric communication — direct observation."[2] Clearly, mass marketing communications to reach consumers in villages such as Ticaco are entirely inappropriate:

Only the Guardia Civil troopers receive a newspaper regularly in Ticaco. Movies have been shown in the community only on rare occasions by the Health Department. The 43 radios are owned mostly by government employees and some store keepers. There is as yet no library to provide reading materials.[3]

In communities such as this, personal mobility is a primary communication medium affecting consumption patterns. Creating a communications infrastructure to link producers to the lower income groups may prove to be difficult. If consumers cannot read, the printed media are relatively unproductive for marketers. If, as in Peru, they are widely scattered in population pockets throughout a rugged and difficult terrain, the initial investment required to provide radio and television may be overwhelming. Furthermore, the low income rural population often does not have the means to purchase television and radio receivers, although the advent of the transistor radio has vastly increased the radio audience in Peru.

As long as demand is adequate to satisfy all producers and industry produces familiar products, as is likely when initial domestic production is directed toward import substitution, the mass media will receive little private economic support. The firms involved already sell all that they can produce, and the high costs of communications inefficiencies can readily be passed on to consumers. This structural situation is conducive to slow-paced economic development, because efficient media for mass communications can be an important stimulus to economic growth. They allow for the presentation of new ideas, products, and services into the economy, and facilitate the transfer of technology from developed to underdeveloped areas. These media also offer producers an efficient means of communicating information about products and services; in many instances, it is far less costly to deliver messages through advertisements carried by mass media than by personal selling.

Unfortunately, if a mass communications system does develop, it is often oriented to serving the needs of a minority of the population — the upper and middle income groups. Producers' immediate economic interests are often limited to these groups, because they have the bulk of the purchasing power. Thus, the natural development of communications media, in a country such as Peru, may accentuate the separation of the lower income majority from the middle and upper income minorities. The "dual economy" is encouraged rather than discouraged.

In addition to an efficient media structure, successful marketing communications require skills in using the media. Communicators must understand the forces that shape customer demand and must be able to translate this understanding into effective messages. Unfortunately, the communicators (marketers) in a developing economy are not likely to understand the language and motivations of the lower classes. Sophisticated research is infrequent and the normal social barriers inhibit effective intuitive judgment. Therefore, messages as well as media are likely to be most adapted to communication within the middle- and upper-class groups.

Given the potential importance of marketing communications for economic growth, it is desirable to evaluate the existing communications system as well as the manner in which it is used by the business community.

The Marketing Communications Infrastructure in Peru

A brief description of the existing institutions for economic communications is essential in evaluating the communications practices of businessmen in Peru. To a great extent, businessmen must operate within the constraints of the existing system, using the media that are available.

Advertising Agencies

In 1966, Peru had sixteen advertising agencies and several other firms that prepared cinema, outdoor, direct mail, and other types of marketing communications. All media expenditures grew between 1962 and 1966, but the greatest growth was shown by television. One agency manager estimated that 40 percent of all advertising in Peru goes through advertising agencies. The rest, presumably, is placed directly by advertisers.

As in the United States, agencies generally are paid a 15 percent commission on the advertising they place, with additional payment made for special services (such as marketing research) that might be rendered. Theoretically, the advertiser would pay the same amount for working through an agency as he would by going directly to the media, because the media offer agencies a 15 percent discount. However, media in Peru reportedly do not protect the advertising agencies very well. Companies dealing directly with media are often able to obtain substantial discounts. As a result, 75 percent of outdoor advertising in Peru is placed directly as is half of magazine advertising; on the other hand, 90 percent of television advertising is placed through an agency.[4] The soft rate structure is especially prevalent in the *departamentos* outside Lima.

Many agency people believe that they have not convinced business or government of the value of their services. In early 1966, the Asociacion Peruana de Agencias de Publicidad (APAP) and various media cosponsored a campaign entitled *Publicidad es Prosperidad* (Advertising is Prosperity). The objective of the campaign was to explain why advertising was important to Peru.

Advertising Media

The following data about communications media in Peru describe the situation as it was at the time of the study in 1966.

Television. Peru had 18 television stations (six of them in Lima), covering eighteen cities and towns with a combined population of nearly 3,700,000 people. A total of 242,000 television sets were installed in these cities.

As Table 9-1 shows, an estimated 32 percent of all homes in cities where television was available had sets. In the Lima-Callao area, where 87 percent of the television sets were located, the percentage of homes with sets was 42.

Higher income families were most likely to have television sets, although there was a surprising number of televisions in slum apartments. Table 9-2 indicates that television sets were found in most Peruvian homes with a monthly income of over $370, but also in three-quarters of the homes with monthly incomes from $74 to $370.

It is interesting to speculate how even 6 percent of the families with monthly incomes of less than $37 were able to have television sets. Among Peruvian families, several wage earners may live in one household. This is done to achieve "economies of scale" in rent and quantity food purchases; it may also be done to acquire some discretionary income for such things as radios, irons, blenders and television sets. In a survey conducted in Arequipa, 10 percent of the working class families interviewed owned television sets, whereas only one family had a telephone, and none had a refrigerator or hot-water heater.[5] Television has clearly achieved considerable success with consumers in the short time since its introduction. The major challenge facing Peruvian television is to attain an audience large enough to attract advertisers.

Radio. In 1966 there were 171 radio stations in Peru; 43 of these were located in the Lima-Callao area. It was estimated in the same year that over one and one-half million radio sets were in operation, many of them transistor sets.

One of the most serious problems of radio advertisers is their diverse audience. The Lima-Callao area, for example, has forty-three radio stations, no single station having a particularly strong following.

Table 9-1

Number of People, Homes and Television Sets in Selected Peruvian Cities

City	Number of People (000)	Number of Homes (000)	Number of TV Sets (000)	Percent of Homes with TV
Lima–Callao	2,420.5	501.3	210.5	42
Arequipa	200.6	40.1	13.2	33
Other Cities	1,084.4	216.7	18.2	8
Total	3,705.5	758.1	241.9	32

Source: J. Walter Thompson Peruana, *Perfil del Merado Peruano*, December 1966, p. 25.

Table 9-2

Homes in Lima–Callao with Television Sets by Income Class, 1966

Monthly Income	Number of Homes (000)	Number of Homes with TV (000)	Percent of Homes with TV
More than $370	34.1	31.4	95
$74 to $370	162.9	115.8	75
$37 to $74	266.6	57.9	25
Less than $37	77.7	5.4	6
Total	541.3	210.5	42

Source: J. W. Thompson Peruana, *Perfil del Merado Peruano*, December 1966, p. 26.

Newspapers. Peru has more than fifty newspapers with a total daily press run of some 900,000 copies. These varied between Lima's rather sophisticated *La Prensa* and *El Comercio* to crude examples from the smaller provincial capitals. Ten newspapers were printed in Lima, with a press run of 781,000 copies. Readership was estimated at about four persons per issue. The fragmentation problem is also a problem in newspapers, but to a lesser extent than in radio.

Magazines. There are reported to be well over 120 consumer, trade and institutional magazines sold in Peru, but only a few printed more than 10,000 copies. The seven most important — *Caretas, Vanidades, Buenhogar, El Mundo, Intima, Oiga,* and *Gente* — had a total circulation of 221,000. Readership was estimated at about four persons per issue.

Cinema. There are about 280 *cines* (movie houses) in Peru, 132 of these in the Lima-Callao area, with an estimated total annual attendance of about 273,000,000. In other words, on the average, the Peruvian citizen attended the movies more than twenty times per year. This may be due to the fact that, by almost any standards, movies are inexpensive in Peru, tickets running from as low as about nine cents to more than ninety cents. All *cines* in Peru have a five- to ten-minute period for advertising before the feature begins. Sometimes movie shorts are shown in which the advertising is of good quality. Frequently, however, poorly prepared slides are used. Such slides often show an unfortunate tendency to crowd all there is to say about a particular advertiser into ten seconds of film. The result is often a jumbled mess.

Outdoor. Outdoor advertising is important in Peru, although an 8 percent tax is charged by the government. The tendency for the poorer people to tear down metal advertising signs to use for the walls of their houses is also a deterrent. Outdoor advertising is nonetheless a popular media, and there are an estimated thirty firms providing it. One of these, Publicidad Ross S. A., was estimated to have 25 percent of all the outdoor advertising business in 1965.

Direct Mail. The postal system has equally serious problems. To post a letter, for example, it is usually necessary to go directly to the main post office or one of only a few branches. And, to be certain that a letter or package will not subsequently have its stamps removed (to be sold again) and the item destroyed, it is advisable to have the piece machine-cancelled. All post office branches, unfortunately, do not have this service. The mail is also very slow and somewhat expensive. The inefficient and undependable postal system limits the use of direct mail advertising in Peru. Firms using direct mail often utilize personal messengers, which is a rather expensive proposition.

Advertising and Sales Promotion

The Importance of Advertising to Businessmen. To evaluate the importance that Peruvian businessmen attach to advertising, one should consider both attitudes and behavior. If behavior correlates with attitudes, the validity of the latter is reinforced. Sometimes, however, attitudes and behavior will not correlate. Such a situation suggests either that businessmen have been inaccurate in expressing their attitudes or that constraints limiting behavior prevent them from doing what they would like to do. Measures of attitudes toward advertising and its usage are presented in Table 9-3.

Attitudes toward advertising in Peru were measured by asking respondents to evaluate its role in the success of their major product or product line on a five-point scale, ranging from "of great importance" (5) to "of little importance" (1). Respondents indicated that they felt advertising was closer to "of great importance" than to "of little importance." As expected, consumer goods producers considered advertising more important than did industrial goods producers. Advertising is often most efficient in selling in mass markets. On the other hand, personal selling is usually given relatively greater emphasis in industrial marketing, because the larger size of the purchases involved both require and can support the use of salesmen.

Larger firms placed more importance on advertising than smaller firms did. Large firms engaging in mass production have special pressure to sell their output in mass markets. They are also more likely to have the working capital necessary to invest in advertising campaigns. The manager of the small business may not have adequate capital to support media advertising. Faced with this situation, he may rationalize that advertising is not very important to him anyway. However, one textile manufacturer reported that he "saves" his advertising budget for about three years and then spends it all in a relatively extensive campaign.

Professionally managed firms considered advertising more important than did owner-managed firms. This may be partially explained by the correlation between firm size and type of management. It may also be true that owner-managers, who are probably less sophisticated businessmen than their "professional" counterparts, lack confidence in advertising. Advertising expenditures involve a very tangible input to achieve a less tangible output. Until better methods for measuring the effectiveness of advertising are developed, owner-managers, on the average, may hesitate to engage in advertising. Indeed, until such time, it cannot be said with any degree of authority that advertising would be a productive investment.

Firms with heavy competition rated advertising as somewhat more important than did firms with light competition. However, firms with moderate competition felt that advertising was most important. Factors other than competition appeared to be more closely related to the importance attributed to advertising. One possible inference is that the stimulation of *selective* demand is not a major problem for Peruvian business.

Within the consumer products industries, the household durables industry ranked far below the others in its estimation of the importance of advertising to sales success. This may be attributed to the relative smallness of the firms

Table 9-3

Respondents' Evaluations of Advertising's Importance to Product Success and Their Use of It

Classification	Average Point Score[1]	Percent Who Advertised in Past Year	Average Percentage of Sales Spent on Advertising[2]
Total firms	3.7	68	1.8
Peruvian–owned	3.7	60	1.6
Foreign–owned	3.8	80	2.1
Consumer goods	4.2	75	2.5
Industrial goods	3.2	60	1.0
Small	3.5	73	2.2
Medium	3.8	67	1.7
Large	4.1	70	1.3
Owner–managed	3.5	62	1.6
Professionally–managed	4.1	78	2.1
Heavy competition	3.7	64	2.0
Moderate competition	4.0	76	1.5
Light competition	3.2	63	2.1
Very high purchase value	2.9	70	.5
High purchase value	3.2	70	1.5
Moderate purchase value	4.4	67	1.9
Low purchase value	4.2	67	2.5
Automotive products	4.1	80	2.2
Food and beverages	4.6	71	2.4
Textiles, clothing, footwear	4.2	67	1.8
Pharmaceuticals	4.4	78	4.2
Household durables	3.4	89	2.1
Office products	3.0	67	1.7
Construction–related products	3.6	50	1.9
Agriculture–related products	3.6	62	0.8
Products for fishing and mining	3.5	67	0.7
Other industrial products	2.7	57	0.4

[1] Key: 5 = of great importance; 1 = of little importance

[2] Average of all respondents, including those not advertising.

interviewed in this industry, and to the relative newness of the products they currently manufacture. With the exception of radios, household durables are found relatively infrequently in Peru. At this point, the need exists for building primary demand in the product category.[a] Present marketing strategy might be to "skim the cream" before building primary demand. However, if the public is to be made aware of the benefits of household appliances, the producers must advertise. Only when the market has been built to a sufficient size will brand advertising be most productive.

Within the industrial products industries, the "other industrial products" group rated advertising lowest in importance. Members of this industry produce goods used to produce other goods. The survey sample included plastics, glass, steel tube, transformer, pump, and cardboard box manufacturers. The demand facing these manufacturers is dependent upon the demand for finished consumer goods. Customers are relatively few and can be reached easily with personal selling. Advertising media selectively reaching this industry's customers are scarce.

The competitive structure of these industries is often monopolistic or oligopolistic. The government's desire to encourage production of industrial goods has led to strong tariff protection for many of these manufacturers. All these factors point toward the lack of a need for advertising. For instance, the government-owned steel plant, SOGESA, is a monopoly. Import duties on steel are very high, forcing manufacturers to buy from SOGESA. Although advertising might be of some limited use, strong incentives for stimulating demand do not exist. Current market demand sometimes even exceeds production capacity, forcing SOGESA to import products and resell them.

The office products industry also ranked low in its estimation of the importance of advertising. Media constraints explain this situation. The few media available in the business field limit the possibilities for advertising products such as business forms and data-processing equipment, although some respondents mentioned the value of advertisements in United States publications, such as *Business Week*, which are read in Peru. A second indication of the importance granted advertising is the number of firms using it. The percentages of firms which advertised in the past year are shown in Table 9-3.

Foreign-owned firms, as compared to Peruvian-owned firms, were more likely to use advertising; consumer goods manufacturers were more likely to use advertising than industrial goods producers. Although attitudes suggested that larger firms would be more apt to use advertising, actual use indicated that size did not have a significant influence. Professionally managed firms advertised more than owner-managed firms; firms with moderate competition were the heaviest advertisers.

Average value of purchase surprisingly had almost no influence on actual behavior. The consumer goods firms, on both attitude and usage measures, were more positive toward advertising than their industrial goods counterparts. Yet the value of purchase, directly related to the consumer-industrial classification showed, if anything, that lower value goods are advertised slightly less. Many firms attempting to reach wide markets may be neglecting a very efficient tool for this purpose — advertising.

[a] The market for many appliances such as washers and dryers is, of course, held back due to the present adequate supply of domestic help. One has little need for a machine when a washerwoman does a good job by hand, and, incidentally, when the washerwoman does not know how to operate the machine. Those who cannot afford domestic help are likely to also be unable to afford appliances.

Nine of ten firms in the household durables industry advertised, despite the industry's low estimation of advertising. Apparently industry members recognize that they must increase primary demand for their output, but at the same time feel that other factors are more important in their immediate future. Also, some companies may be "following the leader."

The lowest incidence of advertising was found in the construction-related products industry. One respondent explained, "We can just keep up with current orders, much less look for additional business." As capacity and demand equalize in the industry, more of these firms can be expected to advertise.

Of the five firms in the food and beverages industry that did not advertise, some, curiously enough, were firms which produce beer. Brewers were substantial advertisers in Peru for many years — so much so that they attracted the attention of the tax authorities and the Peruvian Congress. Since 1949, five separate taxes have been levied on the industry, and advertising is felt to have been the factor bringing about the taxes. In 1965 the industry decided to suspend its advertising, although in 1966 a two-month campaign by the industry's trade association, the Comité de Fabricantes de Cerveza, extolled the virtues of drinking beer without stressing a particular brand.

The shares of market and advertising for the five firms in this industry are presented in Table 9-4 for the years 1962 through 1965. For 1963 and 1964, market share and advertising share are reported; the market share is not available for 1962; and there was no advertising in 1965. Despite substantial changes in the shares of advertising, there were no major changes in the market shares. This may be traced to the fact that most breweries sell a large portion of their beer in the geographic areas where their plants are located, enjoying a virtual monopoly in those areas. Another of the food and beverage industry firms that did not advertise gave three rather interesting, though not totally coherent, reasons for not advertising: 1) It is not needed; the product's sales rise 25 percent annually without advertising; 2) advertising would help only temporarily because too many families are poor; 3) if the product were consumed in Peru at the New York rate, the country would need 500 more factories of this size.

A summary cross-tabulation of attitudes toward advertising and use of advertising (Table 9-5) showed that even though a fairly strong correlation between the two measures existed, there were some exceptions. Most important, perhaps, was the fact that 11 firms, believing that advertising was from "somewhat important" to "very important," still did not advertise. (A few of these firms are in the beer industry.)

Simply asking respondents whether they use advertising did not provide a quantitative measure of the amount of advertising they do. The quantitative measure shown in Table 9-3 was the percentage of sales spent on advertising. The reader should recognize some of the weaknesses in this measure. If a company's total sales are high, it may have a large advertising budget, but the percentage of sales figure may be low. Conversely, a small firm may spend little on advertising, but as a percentage of sales the expenditures are likely to appear high. The

Table 9-4

Market Shares of Peruvian Beer Industry Versus Shares of Beer Advertising

Company	Share of Market 1963	1964	1965 (Percent)	Share of Advertising 1962	1963	1964 (Percent)
Backus and Johnston's Brewery del Peru	47	45	46	38	48	44
Cia. Nacional de Cerveza	34	34	34	50	46	37
Cia. Cervecera del Sur del Peru Ltda.	9	10	10	- -	- -	- -
Cia. Cervecera del Cuzco Ltda.	6	6	6	12	6	7
Soc. Cervecera de Trujillo Ltda.	4	5	4	- -	- -	12
TOTAL	100	100	100	100	100	100

Source: Material supplied by the Comite de Fabricantes de Cerveza.

Table 9-5

Correlation Between Attitudes and Usage

Attitude	Scale Point	Number of Respondents Advertise	Do Not Advertise
Very important	5	40	7
	4	15	1
Somewhat important	3	13	3
	2	3	1
Not very important	1	4	12
		75	24
Arithmetic Mean of Attitude Scores		4.01	1.88

expenditure *per sale,* another measure of how much advertising is done, may be very different from the percentage of sales statistic.

Faced with a large amount of information to gather, and the problem of asking answerable questions, we asked respondents what percentage of the product's sales were spent for advertising. Many answers were only estimates, because respondents did not actually have the information; others may have been estimates based on the total sales of the firm rather than on the specific product or product line being studied. We came to the conclusion that most firms in Peru did not maintain advertising expense records for particular products. Table 9-3 shows the percentage of sales spent on advertising, including responses by firms that did not advertise at all. Because actual sales figures were not available, averages could not be computed on total group sales. Thus, they are unweighted averages of the individual firms' percentages. Each firm was placed in a range of a frequency distribution, and midpoints of the ranges were used for averaging.

Firms in the ten-industry sample spent an average of 1.8 percent of sales on advertising. Foreign-owned firms spent a greater amount on advertising relative to sales than Peruvian-owned firms did. Consumer goods producers spent more on advertising relative to sales than industrial goods firms did. These findings are consistent with the attitude and usage measures previously discussed.

Tabulation by average value of purchase displayed significant variations in the percentage of sales spent on advertising. High value products utilized an average of only .5 percent of sales, and the low value products, 2.5 percent. Average value of purchase did not appear to influence the decision to use or not use advertising. However, once that decision was made, the actual amount spent as a percentage of sales declined with the increase in average value of purchase. The best explanation lies in the needs of the product — low value products generally are intended for mass markets, requiring more advertising expense. High value products are intended for narrow markets, and require only minimal advertising expense.

The pharmaceutical industry reported spending a considerably larger percentage of sales on advertising than any other industry. It appeared that actual expenditures were probably even higher. The marketing practices of the pharmaceutical industry more than any other seemed to parallel those in the more developed countries, reflecting the ownership by international manufacturers. The fact that their messages are aimed at physicians who are well-educated and who need good product information may explain this situation.

The industry producing products for agriculture reported spending less than one-half the average percentage of sales spent on advertising. In view of Peru's shortage of food, and the havoc which importing food raises with the balance of payments, this is disquieting. If farmers are to start using the fertilizers and machinery so necessary for increased production, they must be educated in their uses. Advertising could be of great help in this process.

Value of the typical purchase and firm size appeared to have the greatest influence on the percentage of sales spent on advertising. The apparent influence of the type of industry was probably due primarily to intercorrelations with value of the typical purchase. Nationality of ownership and type of management influenced the amount of advertising to a lesser extent, and some of this influence may have been due to intercorrelations with each other and firm size.

In summary, advertising is "somewhat important" to businessmen in Peru. Attitudes toward it and use of it are fairly well correlated. Characteristics of the product and its market appear to have the greatest influence on advertising, although management technology, as implied by the nationality and type of management, is also important. Competition did not seem to stimulate advertising.

Organization of Advertising in Peru

The manufacturer in Peru assumes prime responsibility for product advertising. In three-fourths of the companies interviewed, no one else did any product advertising. In some cases (13 percent) retailers advertised the product, and in others (12 percent) wholesalers advertised it. These figures may be slightly understated, because some manufacturers may have not been aware of middleman advertising. For example, one of the respondents reported no advertising for his firm, but when he was reminded by the interviewer that some advertising signs were seen in the city of Huancayo, he recalled that these were installed by the firm some years ago and are presently being maintained by middlemen.

Foreign-owned firms were more successful in getting middlemen to advertise than were Peruvian-owned firms. Consumer goods producers and companies in the food and beverages and products for agriculture industries also received more advertising help from their middlemen. In general, however, middlemen did not extensively advertise manufacturers' products.

Forty percent of the respondents offered cooperative advertising to their middlemen, yet only 25 percent indicated that middlemen advertise the product. The difference may be partially accounted for by the orientation of the questions. The first, about middlemen advertising, was limited to a single product or product category. The second, on cooperative advertising, related to the company as a whole. It may also be true that many middlemen do not want to take advantage of cooperative advertising. The offering of cooperative advertising was almost twice as common among foreign-owned firms (54 percent) and consumer goods producers (48 percent) as it was among Peruvian-owned firms (28 percent) and industrial goods producers (26 percent).

Within the manufacturing firm, advertising was most often the responsibility of the sales manager or his staff (63 percent of respondents), although 29 percent of the firms assigned this responsibility to the chief executive.

Advertising research, performed by 24 percent of the respondents, was almost always the responsibility of the advertising agency. Only a few companies had their own employees engaged in this activity.

Among foreign-owned firms with home offices overseas, the Peruvian office maintained prime responsibililty for budgeting. In 39 percent of these cases the home office played no role in setting the budget; in 57 percent of these firms the home office approved or disapproved the advertising budget. However, according to the interviewees, this approval was almost always semiautomatic. No changes were made unless the office in Peru deviated substantially from past years — these were usually approved if they were properly defended. Decentralization in the setting of advertising budgets is apparently a fact of life in Peru.

Use of Advertising Agencies

Management of advertising agencies complained that Peruvian business does not use the services of the advertising agency as often as it should. This may be a biased viewpoint in that the seller is essentially complaining that people do not buy enough of his services. Yet it does raise an important question about the degree of marketing specialization used by manufacturers in Peru. Table 9-6 indicates the use of advertising agencies by respondents.

Less than half of the advertisers in the sample used the services of an advertising agency. Because the sample was drawn from a population of Peru's larger manufacturers, the percentage of *all* firms using advertising agencies is undoubtedly much lower. Very few firms had their own advertising department. Among the 50 percent of respondent advertisers not using an agency, very little advertising work was performed by a qualified specialist.

Foreign-owned firms, although having access to central offices in Latin America and the United States for technical aid in advertising, still used agencies slightly more frequently than Peruvian-owned firms. It appears that a considerable disparity in advertising practices does exist between the Peruvian and foreign firms. The latter are more likely to advertise, to spend more on advertising, and to use specialists.

Consumer goods firms surpass industrial goods producers in using advertising agency services. The advertising campaigns of consumer goods firms tend to be more complete and require greater skill in preparation. Often the industrial goods manufacturer's advertising consists of no more than one or two advertisements in a few trade publications.

Agency services used by respondents are indicated in Table 9-7. Peruvian-owned firms were less inclined than foreign-owned firms to take advantage of agency services. Comparative percentages of use were: packaging preparation, 32 as against 10 percent; general marketing planning, 36 versus 15 percent; market research, 36 versus 20 percent; and advertising research, 59 versus 40 percent.

Table 9-6

Use of Advertising Agencies

		Percentage of Advertisers			
Response	Total Firms	Peruvian-Owned Firms	Foreign-Owned Firms	Consumer Goods Producers	Industrial Goods Producers
Use an agency	47	44	50	53	38
Do not use an agency	53	56	50	47	62
	100	100	100	100	100

Table 9-7

Advertising Agency Services Utilized by Respondents

Type of Service	Percentage of Agency Users Utilizing the Service
Prepare advertisements, layout, and copy	83
Place advertisements in media	79
Plan campaigns and media	74
Prepare point-of-sale materials	50
Perform advertising research	50
Conduct market research	29
Aid in general marketing planning	26
Prepare packaging (design, test)	21

Advertising Objectives

The establishment of distinct, well-defined objectives is an important part of an effective advertising program. Unless the firm understands what it wants to accomplish with the advertising, success is not likely. Table 9-8 indicates the objectives stated by survey respondents.

The columns in the table do not total 100 percent because some firms had multiple objectives and two firms had none. Few respondents were able to state their advertising objectives clearly. Although it is possible that firms did not want to divulge specific objectives, no respondent refused to answer the question. The responses to the question may have been overstated because the interviewers often pressed for answers. The interviewers' definite impressions were that advertisers in Peru spend their advertising money with only a vague idea of what they want to accomplish — rather like firms in other parts of the world.

The stated objectives were both vague and passive. Many respondents replied that they wanted to increase sales, and then looked askance at the interviewers as if the answer was so obvious that the question was foolish. Not one respondent mentioned advertising as a means to increased profits. Other objectives, such as announcing products and providing information, or maintaining brand awareness, ("to let the market know we are here") may imply passivity. Many businesses are in a position where little action is necessary to attain sales, but some would do well to attempt more forceful advertising. No specific, aggressive objectives were stated. Firms in Peru are not thinking in terms of increasing their market share in segment "X" or increasing profits by building volume in certain types of outlets.

A few firms — 15 percent of the advertisers — wanted to improve their product image. As in other developing countries, many natives lack confidence in products produced in their own country and, as a result, a firm making an outstanding product may have to work hard to convince the market of its quality. This problem can be overcome only with strong promotion, a general raising of quality standards, or a combination of the two.

The Advertising Audience and
Use of Media

The audiences that respondent advertisers sought to reach are indicated in Table 9-9. These were defined in broad terms. However, Peruvian businessmen generally lack complete data.

According to the interview results, 19 percent of the consumer goods producers who advertised did not attempt to reach the ultimate consumer with their advertising. The major purpose of their advertising must then have been to secure distribution with middleman outlets. Forty-one percent of the industrial goods producers did not attempt to reach industrial buyers with their advertising. Because their distribution channels tended to be short, they were

Table 9-8

Most Frequently Stated Advertising Objectives

| | | Percentage of Advertisers Stating | | | |
| | Total Firms | Peruvian–Owned Firms | Foreign–Owned Firms | Consumer Goods Producers | Industrial Goods Producers |
Objective					
To sell more	40	44	36	49	28
To announce products, offer information	27	20	33	21	34
To maintain brand awareness	17	17	17	23	9
To improve product image, show quality	15	13	17	14	16

Table 9-9

Intended Audience for Advertising

| | | Percentage of Respondents | | | |
| | Total Firms | Peruvian–Owned Firms | Foreign–Owned Firms | Consumer Goods Producers | Industrial Goods Producers |
Audience					
Ultimate consumers	72	79	64	81	59
Industrial buyers	32	36	28	12	59
Retailers	13	15	11	21	3
Others	20	20	19	30	6

[1]The columns in the table do not total 100 percent because of multiple answers.

not overly concerned with securing distribution. They were, however, interested in cultivating consumers. Almost six of every ten industrial goods manufacturers intended their advertising to reach ultimate consumers, though this percentage may be overstated. Although an attempt was made to explain the difference between industrial buyer and ultimate consumer, the two categories may not have been clear to respondents.

Advertising Media Used. One of the critical decisions to be made by an advertiser is the choice of a "media mix." The media chosen should fit the firm's objectives and reach the desired audience. Because objectives were not clearly stated and the measurement of the audience was somewhat confused, the choice of media is difficult to evaluate.

To ascertain the relative use of various media, we asked respondents what approximate percentage of their 1965 advertising budget (for the product being studied) went to each medium. Because the actual sizes of the advertising budgets involved were not known, averages were computed by averaging the percentages of each firm (see Table 9-10).

The use of different media has been discussed earlier in the section on marketing infrastructure. The breakdown of advertisers into ownership and industry classifications did, however, provide some interesting information. Peruvian-owned companies made greater use of some of the media traditional to Latin America, especially cinema and outdoor advertising.

Although it may be adversely affected by the increased use of television, cinema remains a useful advertising medium in Peru. Low admission prices result in large audiences; audiences tend to be local to the theater district, thereby offering selectivity of the audience (this is especially valuable to retailers who can reach an audience appropriate to their trading area); the varying admission prices by theaters add to audience selectivity, enabling advertisers to reach audiences whose income levels make them the best potential customers.

Industrial advertisers did most of their advertising in newspapers and magazines. It was surprising to find advertisements for industrial pumps and generators in newspapers such as *El Comercio,* but this was a reflection of the inadequate magazine media available. Obviously these advertisements, which were read by a general audience, result in much advertising waste. Some industrial advertisements were institutional, however, and intended for the general public.

Variances in media usage were most pronounced when the specific industries were used for cross-tabulation. Consumer products firms used a variety of media, but they seemed to have adapted their media selection to fit their needs: the textile group found newspapers best suited to its needs; food and beverage manufacturers preferred radio and television; the household products men emphasized both newspaper and television; producers of automotive products emphasized outdoor advertising, primarily in the form of signs and bumper stickers on the backs of trucks; the drug industry concentrated its advertising on samples and handout literature for doctors.

Industrial goods producers, as has been noted, spent a seemingly inordinate

Table 9-10

Average Allocations of the Advertising Budget (Percentage of Total Advertising Budget)

Type of Media	Total Firms	Peruvian-Owned Firms	Foreign-Owned Firms	Consumer Goods Producers	Industrial Goods Producers	Auto[2]	Food	Textiles
Newspaper	25	26	24	18	34	9	13	38
Magazine	17	16	17	7	31	10	5	2
Television	15	17	14	22	6	16	34	26
Radio	11	12	9	14	6	14	26	14
Outdoor	8	12	4	9	7	31	5	9
Direct mail, messenger	5	6	4	3	7	7		
Cinema	4	5	2	5	2	11	5	5
Other[1]	15	6	26	22	7	2	12	6
	100	100	100	100	100	100	100	100

Type of Media	Drug	Household	Office	Construction	Agriculture	Products for fishing and mining	Other Industrial
Newspaper		29	42	7	36	26	48
Magazine	6	14	31	1	15	53	30
Television		28	8	7			13
Radio		10	4	12	3	11	
Outdoor		1	2	42	9	1	2
Direct mail, messenger	2	5	3	4	19	6	7
Cinema		3		15	2		
Other[1]	92	10	10	12	16	3	
	100	100	100	100	100	100	100

[1]"Other" includes primarily sales promotion and sampling.

[2]The number of firms in each specific industry category is relatively small, for this reason, the resulting averages should be accepted with caution.

proportion of their budgets in newspaper advertising. Many of them also used magazines, a more selective medium in view of their potential customers. The construction industry was atypical, spending the greatest proportion of its funds on outdoor advertising. Although following the typical pattern of spending a large proportion in newspapers, the agriculture-related products group also made considerable use of direct mail.

Major Problems of Advertisers. The major problems of advertising in Peru, as seen by advertisers, are presented in Table 9-11. Their most common complaint was that costs are too high. The largest single advertising cost component was the charge for media space (usually considered on the basis of cost per thousand viewers/readers). Unfortunately, many advertisers did not have confidence in media audience data, so they were not able to accurately compute cost per thousand. Using the "official" circulation and audience estimates, some media rates in Peru are compared with some of those in the United States in Table 9-12.

Cost comparisons between media in the United States and Peru suggest that the Peruvian rates, in terms of audience, are lower. If it is true that advertising in Peru costs too much, the reason must be its low productivity relative to that in the United States. This could be explained by the low purchasing power of audiences or low quality advertising. However, it is interesting that relatively few foreign-owned firms made this complaint. Perhaps foreign-owned firms view advertising in relation to benefits, while Peruvian-owned firms only think in terms of dollar outflow. A different explanation could be that foreign-owned firms, more accustomed to advertising in other countries, automatically allocate funds to advertising, while Peruvian-owned firms view advertising expenses more critically.

One of every five advertisers complained that Peru lacks enough qualified advertising agencies. (In a 1964 study, this same complaint was made in Canada, Ceylon, Curacao, Ecuador, Lebanon, New Zealand, and Sweden, indicating that the problem of quality is not limited to developing countries.)[6] This problem was expecially prevalent in the provinces. A Lima advertiser stated that over a period of several years he had used many different agencies, but had not found one that showed originality or creative thinking. The problem of poorly qualified agencies may have been overstated. Many advertisers did not understand what advertising can and cannot accomplish; they had no definite objectives to give to the agency. As a result they were disappointed when sales and profits did not increase significantly. The blame fell on the agency, but it rightfully may have belonged elsewhere (for example, in pricing or product policy). Nevertheless, Peru needs more qualified marketing techncians, including specialists in advertising.

The problem of inadequate media is a real one. Because Peru is such a small market, it cannot support many special magazines tailored to segments of the market. Industrial goods producers are particularly concerned with this problem, although consumer goods manufacturers also find large segments of the

Table 9-11

Major Problems of Advertisers in Peru

		Percentage of Advertisers			
Problem	Total Firms	Peruvian– Owned Firms	Foreign– Owned Firms	Consumer Goods Producers	Industrial Goods Producers
No problems	17	19	15	12	24
Advertising costs	31	44	18	40	18
Lack of qualified agencies	20	19	20	24	15
Lack of good media	13	8	18	12	15
Inadequate statistics, poor measurements	13	11	13	14	9
Other problems	27	14	38	24	30

population difficult to reach. Communicating with the Indian in the sierra who may not read, who has no radio or television set, and who doesn't speak or understand Spanish is a difficult matter.

The needed written media will not arise in Peru until the population is educated enough to read it and the purchasing power of market segments rises enough to offer more significant market potential. The latter problem may be overcome by the publishing of magazines with general Latin American distribution. Such magazines currently exist, but the marketer who limits his market to a single country requires split runs to avoid waste. This raises costs.

The poor statistics available and the inability to measure advertising results were, in the authors' opinion, understated by the respondents. Only 13 percent of the advertisers sampled mentioned this as a major problem. In the United States, advertising effectiveness measurement would probably be the most important problem in advertising. Peruvian advertisers apparently are not concerned so much with the problems of controlling variables as they are with the more basic difficulties of obtaining sales information and knowing more about their audience.

Table 9-12

Media Rate Comparisons, United States and Peru, 1966

	Peru *Cost/1,000*	*United States* *Cost/1,000*
Television—range of costs per commerical minute	$.53–1.07 (estimate of large agency in Peru)	$1.50–1.90 (BBDO Audience Coverage and Cost Guide, 1966)
Newspapers—range of costs per black and white page in newspaper of approximately 100,000 circulation	$3.03 (one agency's estimate) $11.34 (another agency's estimate)	$5.97 (quoted price of *Wisconsin State Journal*)
Magazines—cost per black and white page	$3.87 (average for eight unidentified magazines; agency estimate)	$4.20 (average of *Life, Look, Saturday Evening Post,* and *Reader's Digest*) $5.84 (average of *Golf, True, Mademoiselle, Good Housekeeping*)

Personal Selling

The major advantage of personal selling lies in the salesman's ability to adjust the presentation as he gets customer reaction. A salesman can also command more attention than an advertisement or display. The major limitation of personal selling is its relatively high cost for each contact. While television may reach a thousand people at a cost of a relatively few dollars, paying a salesman to make the same contacts would cost several thousand dollars.

Personal selling by manufacturers' salesmen performs an important part of the demand activation process. The industrial salesman is frequently the first to present industrial buyers with more advanced technology, thus introducing innovation to the economy.

Effective promotion usually blends personal selling, sales promotion, and advertising, balancing the strengths and weaknesses of each.

The Importance of
Personal Selling to Businessmen

Respondents' attitudes about the importance of personal selling to product success were measured using a five-point scale, ranging from "of great importance" to "of little importance." Responses are averaged in Table 9-13.

The average point score for personal selling is 4.4, considerably above the average of 3.7 given to advertising. Businessmen in Peru apparently feel that personal selling is their most important form of marketing communication. A striking difference between attitudes toward personal selling and those toward advertising is that the former are considerably more uniform among the comparison groups. The small differences among categories suggests that the attitudes toward personal selling may not have been significantly influenced by the comparison variables.

Industrial goods producers were expected to rate personal selling as more important than were consumer goods producers. They did not. The averages of the two groups were virtually identical. Personal selling for the industrial goods producer generally means direct contact between salesmen and ultimate users; in the consumer goods field, salesman contact is more often limited to middlemen. The unexpectedly strong belief of consumer goods producers that personal selling was important may have been an indication of middleman problems. Salesmen apparently were needed to call on middlemen and get them to carry the product, display it properly, and sell it aggressively. Another possibility is that respondents interpreted the question broadly, and included the importance of the middleman's personal selling effort in their evaluation. If this is true the manufacturer's point score would have been inflated.

Competition seemed somewhat related to the importance attributed to personal selling, although intercorrelations with other variables may have accounted for the differences within the category. Firms with heavy competition felt personal selling was more important than did other firms. Personal selling is an extremely valuable approach to combating competition, especially in an

Table 9-13

Respondents' Evaluations and Use of Personal Selling

Classification	Importance of Personal Selling	Use of Personal Selling	
	Average Point Score[1]	Percentage of Respondents with Salesmen	Average Number of Salesmen[2]
Total firms	4.4	79	9.6
Peruvian–owned	4.3	75	6.9
Foreign–owned	4.4	84	11.5
Consumer goods	4.4	82	12.4
Industrial goods	4.3	75	4.7
Small	4.2	82	7.0
Medium	4.5	76	10.6
Large	4.2	78	10.0
Owner–managed	4.3	81	7.6
Professionally–managed	4.5	76	10.4
Heavy competition	4.6	88	13.2
Moderate competition	4.5	84	7.0
Light competition	4.2	63	7.1
Very high purchase value	4.1	50	3.1
High purchase value	4.4	77	5.8
Moderate purchase value	4.4	87	7.7
Low purchase value	4.4	83	14.2
Industry category			
Automotive products	4.1	90	7.8
Food and beverages	4.4	76	4.6
Textiles, clothing, footwear	4.4	83	7.4
Pharmaceutical	4.4	89	17.2
Household durables	4.6	78	10.3
Office products	4.6	89	6.3
Construction–related products	3.9	80	3.4
Agriculture–related products	4.1	50	7.5
Products for fishing and mining	4.3	83	5.0
Other industrial products	4.6	71	2.7

[1] 5 = of great importance; 1 = of little importance

[2] Among all firms in the group

industrial environment that places a high value on friendships and personal contacts.

Among the industry categories, the range in evaluations was from 3.9 points (for the industry manufacturing construction products) to 4.6 (for two industrial products groups and one consumer products industry). Firms producing food and beverages still consider personal selling important to them, although advertising would seem better fitted to their broad consumer and middleman markets.

Personal selling appears to be considered a more important promotional approach than advertising. Another important conclusion is that attitudes toward personal selling are quite uniform and cannot be attributed to the influence of any comparison variable. The importance of personal selling is apparently accepted by almost everyone.

Each respondent was asked if his firm had salesmen and, if so, how many. One would expect some correlation between attitudes and whether salesmen are employed. However correlation between attitudes and the *number* of salesmen employed would not be so definite because a firm could rate personal selling as being very important and still logically have only one salesman. The number of salesmen should fit the requirements of the product and market, and if these factors are equal, should be directly related to the size of the company.

Although some exceptions to the rule were found, 75 to 85 percent of all firms employ salesmen. Heavy competition apparently encourages more frequent use of salesmen. Purchase value is inversely related to the use of salesmen — the higher the value of the product the less likely the use of salesmen. The explanation of this unexpected finding is that many of these companies are settled comfortably in a product area where demand, even at high prices, exceeds supply. The Peruvian customer often comes to the seller, eliminating the need for salesmen. While it is understandable that firms of this type may not want to spend money unnecessarily, it can be noted that they are thereby left extremely vulnerable to competition. Their actual utilization of sales personnel may have been understated because many executives of these firms did extensive selling themselves; most likely they did not count themselves as salesmen.

Companies selling products whose average purchase value is low had more salesmen than any other category. These companies usually required wide distribution, and therefore needed many salesmen to make contact with a great many middlemen. A good example was found among companies producing candy and ice cream. These products were sold directly to the retailer by company salesmen. Company policy was that distribution should be as wide as possible — to movie theaters, *ambulantes* (street peddlers), grocery stores, restaurants, supermarkets, and others. The number of company salesmen needed to reach all these outlets each week was very high because wholesalers were not used.

At the other extreme were producers selling a product of very high purchase value such as production machinery. Potential customers often numbered no more than two or three firms of major importance and another ten to twenty of minor importance. One or two salesmen probably were able to cover the market adequately. The consumer-industrial goods breakdowns, closely correlated with the value of purchase, substantiated the latter.

Competition was directly related to the number of salesmen used. Heavy competition apparently forced some companies to use more salesmen.

Size did not greatly influence the number of salesmen used. Small firms had fewer salesmen than larger firms, but the difference was not very great; medium-sized firms actually had more salesmen than the large firms. The breadth of the market rather than sales volume was the more important determinant of sales force size.

Predictably, foreign-owned and professionally-managed firms used a somewhat greater number of salesmen than their counterparts did. Observations lead to the conclusion that this was due partly to a greater awareness in these firms of the need for aggressive marketing and partly to intercorrelations with other variables.

The use of salesmen and the number of salesmen employed varied considerably among industries. Salesmen were used least often (50 percent of the time) in the products for agriculture industry. They were used most in the automotive products, pharmaceuticals, and office products industries.

The average number of salesmen per firm, counting firms who use no salesmen, varied from 2.7 for the "other industrial products industry" to 17.2 for pharmaceuticals. The latter figure, however, was approximately 70 percent higher than the next highest one.

Very few firms used salesmen who worked parttime for other firms. Almost 90 percent of the respondents using salesmen hired full time salesmen exclusively.

Responsibility for Sales Management

In three of every four cases the sales manager was given responsibility for management of the sales force. Some firms not having a sales department left this responsibility to the general manager, who in effect acted as a part-time sales manager.

Although hiring of salesmen was generally the responsibility of the sales manager (59 percent of the firms) or the general manager (25 percent of the firms), some firms placed this function under someone else in the firm, usually a personnel or administrative manager.

Sales Training

Although the number of salesmen employed by a firm is important to adequate market coverage, the *quality* of each salesman is often the most important determinant of success. The statement the "salesmen are born, not made" is no longer accepted by modern business. Some personality types are more likely than others to be effective salesmen, but the quality of the sales force is most dependent upon the training provided by the company and the level of compensation paid the salesmen.

Each respondent was asked to describe any training his firm gives its salesmen. Answers were general and varied greatly among firms. Results, classified into several descriptive training categories, are presented in Table 9-14.

Two basic kinds of sales training were used: training new salesmen (categories 2-5) and continued training of the present sales force (category 6). Multiple answers were thus expected. The categories of sales training were arranged in an order reflecting increasing interest in sales training.

Thirty-one percent of the respondents indicated they did no sales training. Another 40 percent offered informal or on-the-job-training; only 31 percent offered some kind of organized training, either inside or outside the firm.

Peruvian-owned firms did relatively little sales training. Almost half of the Peruvian-owned firms offered no training at all. What training they did attempt was rather casual (only 8 percent offered an organized class to their salesmen). The 60 percent of the foreign-owned firms with an organized training class contrasts vividly. The Peruvian-owned firms apparently had not yet realized the potential benefits of sales training. Such training can be costly, but its potential value to the firm as well as to the economy is great. Poorly trained men tend to produce less volume for the firm, and they often resign because their personal earnings are low. High salesman turnover results in high marketing costs.

Industrial goods producers offered less sales training than their consumer goods counterparts. Respondents' comments indicated that this was because many of their industrial salesmen were highly qualified engineers who were sufficiently knowledgable when they were hired. Although such men may need to learn less because of prior training, the technical nature of their product may require greater product knowledge. Especially important, however, is the fact that these men are likely to be narrowly trained in the technical aspects of the job, and not trained at all in personal selling. The industrial salesman's responsibility is to sell his company's products. Understanding the product is a necessary part of this responsibility, but understanding the customer's purchase motivations and developing the ability to interact effectively with customers is also essential. The industrial salesman who understands human behavior and business practices is more likely than a poorly trained salesman to earn his employer a high return on investment. For example, a well-trained man may offer suggestions for new products because he has perceived a customer need that is presently not satisfied.

Owner-managed firms, relative to professionally managed firms, did less formal training and more informal training. The greatest contrast between these two groups of firms was that 53 percent of the professionally managed firms offered organized training sessions, whereas only 11 percent of the owner-managed firms did so.

Size did not play a particularly important role in stimulating sales training.

Table 9-14

Descriptive Categories of Sales Training Used by Sample Firms

Type of Training	Total Firms	Peruvian-Owned Firms	Foreign-Owned Firms	Consumer Goods Producers	Industrial Goods Producers	Owner-Managed	Professionally-Managed
				Percentage of Respondents [1]			
1. No training	31	46	13	19	43	44	21
2. A few days of informal training	18	22	13	17	18	20	12
3. On-the-job training in field or office	22	15	30	28	13	18	18
4. Organized class within firm	19	4	38	26	10	4	38
5. Organized class outside firm	12	4	22	9	15	7	15
6. Periodic sales meetings	23	20	27	26	18	13	26

Type of Training	Small	Medium	Large	Heavy	Moderate	Light	One	Two	Three	Four
					Percentage of Respondents [1]					
1. No training	36	30	35	30	33	45	17	61	42	86
2. A few days of informal training	22	15	10	17	14	23	17	15	17	--
3. On-the-job training in field or office	19	22	10	30	17	14	28	23	12	14
4. Organized class within firm	5	18	25	30	14	4	31	15	8	14
5. Organized class outside firm	11	7	20	17	11	4	17	--	8	--
6. Periodic sales meetings	17	22	15	13	25	14	31	15	8	--

[1] Columns do not add to 100 percent because of multiple answers.

Larger firms conducted more organized training within the firm, probably because they could spread the cost over more salesmen. The small firms settled for more casual training.

Competition was directly related to the use of sales training. Firms in a heavily competitive environment did more training and were likely to structure it more tightly.

Responses indicated that in general, the higher value of purchas roducts were sold by men with less company sales training. Although it is likely that these men are previously trained elsewhere — perhaps in engineering school — their high quality should have added incentive for further training. Such men are generally capable of learning the techniques of personal selling rapidly and well. Firms that sell products of low purchase value are probably hiring poorly trained men who actually are order-takers rather than salesmen. Training for these men is needed because they start at such a low level, but the total knowledge required is less because of the nature of their job.

Periodic sales meetings as a method of providing salesmen with continuous training were not well accepted in Peru. Only 23 percent of the respondents held these meetings.

Salesmen Compensation

Sales productivity is often closely related to both the level and the form of compensation. Although no question was asked concerning the level of salesman's pay, comments by respondents indicated that the average salesman was paid between $100 and $300 per month. One industrial firm had a salesman earning "about $10,000" a year. Although these pay scales may appear generally low to someone from a developed nation, they are reasonably high compared with other wages and salaries in Peru. Selling certainly offers greater income potential than most occupations in the country.

The most popular form of salesmen's compensation was a combination of salary and commission. Almost two of every three firms used some plan of this nature. The salary portion varied widely, but on the average it was fairly low — commissions were expected to contribute the bulk of the salesman's income.

Many firms paid their salesmen an allowance for *movilidad* (travel expense). Because this was usually a nominal amount, a firm offering *movilidad* plus commission was considered as offering "commission only." A few respondents told of salesmen who took jobs with several companies, collecting *movilidad* from each and working for none. As they lost their jobs because they were unproductive, they would look for work with other companies.

Peruvian-owned firms were more frequent users of the "commission only" plans (26 percent) than were the foreign-owned firms (11 percent). The opposite was true for "salary only" plans, where 24 percent of the foreign-owned firms and only 9 percent of the Peruvian-owned firms used them.

Consumer goods producers emphasized commission-salary combination plans only slightly more frequently than their industrial goods opposites. However, 24 percent of the industrial goods producers used "salary only" plans; only 8 percent of the consumer goods firms used these.

Compensation plans varied greatly among firms. In some situations, demand exceeded supply and the salesman was under little pressure. But in many other instances, the salesman had to sell a new idea to a tradition-oriented customer while facing strong competition. The personal incentive for the salesman in such circumstances must be significant if he is to succeed.

Major Problems in Personal Selling

Each respondent was asked to identify and discuss his major problems in personal selling and sales management. Multiple answers were permitted and expected. Responses of greatest frequency are presented in Table 9-15. Several important variations appeared among firm categories. Foreign-owned firms indicated they were more likely to have problems in personal selling than were Peruvian-owned firms. The major difference lay in the problem area of unqualified salesmen, where only 19 percent of the Peruvian-owned firms as opposed to 67 percent of the foreign-owned firms had problems. The difference was probably one of evaluation. The foreign-owned firm had often had experience with well-educated salesmen in a developed country; *by comparison,* the salesmen available in Peru performed poorly. The firm with no experience outside Peru did not judge its salesmen so harshly because it had no basis for comparison. It appears that the traditional standards for salesmen in Peru are low; unless these are raised it is doubtful that the quality of salesmen will improve.

Because the foreign-owned firms, which were most dissatisfied with salesman quality, had *less* difficulty with the moral character (laziness, dishonesty) of their salesmen than did Peruvian firms, it seems that the quality condemnation was not aimed at the Peruvian salesman as a "personality." It was instead a complaint about the poor education of the salesmen.

Industrial goods producers were less likely to have problems in personal selling than were consumer goods producers. Their market requires fewer but more highly qualified salesmen. Fewer problems arise as a result. Of the sixteen industrial goods manufacturers who used salesmen and had problems, however, fourteen had difficulty finding qualified salesmen.

Conclusions

Promotional activity in Peru is less vigorous than it would be in most developed countries. In many industries demand exceeds supply, and there is little pressure

Table 9-15

Major Problems in Personal Selling

		Percentage of Respondents With Salesmen			
Problem Area	Total Firms	Peruvian–Owned Firms	Foreign–Owned Firms	Consumer Goods Producers	Industrial Goods Producers
Have no problems	38	53	19	23	56
Lack of qualified salesmen	40	19	67	42	39
Lazy, dishonest salesmen	10	12	8	12	9
Collections are difficult	13	16	8	12	14
Other problems	47	44	50	51	42

by manufacturers for marketing communications; in other industries customers are few and sales traditionally are made on the basis of personal friendships. Marketing communication in many ways seems to be a relatively new activity for businessmen in Peru. The Peruvian-owned firms consistently displayed less interest in promotion than did the foreign-owned firms. The demonstration effects of the communications efforts of the foreign-owned firms, however, many of which have only recently located in Peru, seem to have stimulated the Peruvian-owned firms to pay more attention to promotion. At the time of this study it appeared that many Peruvian businessmen were concerned about the need for better marketing communication, although they did not yet fully understand the technology involved and had not yet implemented aggressive promotional programs.

Personal selling was the most important form of promotion used within the communications mix. Advertising, appearing less directly related to sales than personal selling, was less popular. Another reason for the less frequent use of advertising was the lack of supporting institutions. Managers may have felt that personal selling was easier to implement and more flexible than advertising, given the existing media and agency structure in the country. Manufacturers' concern with fragmented markets — the urban or the middle and upper class markets — also acted as a constraint on their use of mass media.

Businessmen felt that their major problem in the area of personal selling was the low quality of their salesmen. A major portion of the blame must be placed upon the manufacturer who fails to provide the needed training. Because many manufacturers do not employ enough salesmen to warrant a formal training program, one useful device might be a training center for salesmen (paid for by a group of manufacturers). General sales training would be given in this center, and specific product and company training would be offered within each member firm.

The visitor to Lima might well receive the impression that modern advertising has reached Peru. Magazines and newspapers are sold on almost every corner; television sets are displayed in store windows showing the frequent use of commercials; pedestrians often walk by carrying transistor radios blaring forth loud commercials; and billboards and signs seem to occupy every available space. Advertisements seem similar to those familiar to the United States citizen.

The investigation of manufacturers' marketing practices revealed that advertising is not very sophisticated in Peru. Objectives are seldom set; media audience data are generally poor; few advertising specialists are to be found. The situation is definitely worse in the provinces since specialized talent is not available and advertisements often show it. On the other hand, the interest in advertising is obvious and many managers recognize the need for improvement.

Improvements in the media structure, increased competition, and improvements in marketing technology can all be expected to increase the use of marketing communication in Peru as economic development takes place. It is particularly desirable that the efficiencies of mass communication be more fully utilized by the business community in the future and that the "subsistence" sector of the economy be more fully integrated into the total economy. Unfortunately, the negative attitude of the government toward advertising counters the fulfillment of these tasks.

If the *criollismo* spirit prevails, the importation of potentially useful foreign communications technology will come slowly. While many managers are more cosmopolitan than provincial, unless they show greater concern about reducing barriers between social classes, a marketing communications system that meets the needs of all major consumer groups in Peru will likely remain only a potentiality.

10 Distribution Management in Peru

Channels of Distribution

To be efficient and to best meet the needs of society, marketing must change in response to alterations in market conditions and in consumer needs. Distribution practices are changing in Peru, but there is reason to believe that modifications take place slowly and only when there seems to be no alternative. The apparent and relatively fast success of Sears Roebuck and Company, S. A., together with the rapid development of Lima's supermarkets, indicates that the consumer has been ready for modern retailing for some time, but that business has been unwilling to provide the necessary facilities. Similarly, wholesaling establishments have not provided retailers with the breadth and depth of goods which they desire. Many manufacturers and some retailers are attempting to devise means to bypass wholesalers as a result.

Discussions of the retail and wholesale sectors of distribution in Chapter 4 have indicated that Peru has a sprinkling of modern retailing and wholesaling establishments, but that the bulk of manufactured products moves through the old, traditional establishments. These establishments have limited stocks and an abundance of labor as compared with capital. This, it should be repeated, does not necessarily mean that wholesaling and retailing are economically inefficient. With a surplus of labor available, it may be that labor-intensive distribution facilities are as efficient (or more efficient) as capital-intensive ones. But traditional retailing must eventually give way to modern distribution facilities and to some extent this is now happening in Peru.

Channels of Distribution Used

An analysis of the distribution channels used by 110 manufacturers of diverse types of products located in both urban and rural areas is difficult. In many respects, 110 different distribution methods could be found. It is possible, however, to discuss the similarities and dissimilarities among the systems and to provide some reasons for the distribution practices followed by manufacturers.

Respondents were asked to give the proportion of total sales of the product under study which goes to each of several types of customers. Table 10-1 shows their replies. It was not possible to weight the proportions because respondents did not supply exact sales data.

Peruvian consumer goods firms showed a definite tendency to bypass the middleman and deal directly with the consumer, perhaps because this strategy has been economically feasible in a small market. Foreign-owned firms dealt more with middlemen, their usual practice when operating in other countries. (Foreign-owned industrial goods producers, however, tended to sell directly to their customers because of the small, centrally located market.) It is significant to note that producers in Peru generally planned to *continue* to bypass wholesalers and, where possible, retailers.

Respondents also were asked to trace which of the possible channels was used for the product in question. Frequency of use of the various channels is shown in Table 10-2. Some respondents were confused by the term "final consumer." In general marketing terms, "final" or "ultimate" consumer refers to the household consumer. But 24 percent of the industrial goods producing firms claimed their most important distribution channel was the "final consumer," rather than the industrial consumer. The industrial firm, as far as the respondent was concerned, *was* the final consumer. (Some industrial goods producers which sold over 50 percent of their output to industrial users did have their most important *single* channel in the consumer market.) In retrospect, a better choice of terms, perhaps, would have been "industrial" and "nonindustrial" users.

The majority of manufacturers interviewed (79 percent) did not consider the wholesaler their most important channel of distribution. Industrial firms' use of wholesalers as the most important channel was especially low.

There are three probable explanations for the apparent nonuse of wholesale establishments in Peru:

1. The 5 percent sales tax imposed by the government at every point of exchange in the distribution process discourages the use of wholesalers. Although there are ways of avoiding the tax, such as consignment selling, many manufacturers choose to eliminate the middleman.
2. The relatively small and concentrated market, especially for industrial goods, makes direct distribution to retailers or industrial and non-industrial buyers fairly easy.
3. Good wholesalers often are not available. Peru has five to ten outstanding wholesalers, but their principal role is in importing and distributing foreign-produced goods.

Even those manufacturers using wholesalers admitted they would like to exclude the wholesaler from the channel of distribution. This attitude is all the

Table 10-1

Manufacturer Sales by Type of Customer

Customer	Percentage of Total Sales
Retailer	27
Industrial user	25
Wholesaler	23
Ultimate consumer	15
Government	7
Foreign buyer	1
Others	2
	100

more disturbing when it is observed that at least some of the larger importer-distributor firms (such as Wiese, Ferreyros, Cosmana, International Machinery Company) have developed manufacturing enterprises to supplement their wares. In this respect they are like wholesalers in Turkey, India, Egypt and Brazil.[1]

The larger consumer goods firms, despite their greater resources, were less likely to sell directly to buyers than were the smaller consumer goods producers. Perhaps their market power enabled them to get better service from middlemen, or perhaps they were in a better position to analyze the economic efficiency inherent in calling on specialists for their distribution.

Industrial goods producers with light competition sold directly to their buyers more often. The reason may have been that the firms selling directly had more confidence in their competitive position and thus rated competition more lightly.

As might be expected, those products with a low value of purchase were sold principally through wholesalers or retailers; products with a higher value of purchase were more frequently sold directly to their final users.

To obtain an indication of aggressiveness, firms were asked, "How are negotiations usually begun with your customers?" Many respondents were unable to decide which was most important — salesman contact, distributor or wholesaler contact, or contact initiated by the potential customer. Responses did allow a general picture of the aggressiveness of the firms, however. More foreign-owned firms mentioned negotiations beginning with the visit of a company or distributor salesman while Peruvian-owned firms most often mentioned the importance of customer-initiated sales contacts. Perhaps foreign-owned firms had to do more contacting to capture some of the market originally held by Peruvian-owned firms. Peruvian-owned firms may not have been willing to pay the price for acquiring new business — the price being a willingness to make new customer contacts and to maintain continuity with present customers.

Customer-initiated sales contacts were more important to industrial goods producers than to consumer goods manufacturers. Although there is an incentive for industrial goods purchasers to seek out sources of supply, it was clear that industrial goods manufacturers were not aggressively seeking the new business necessary to maintain and build a growing economy.

Channel Selection and the
Choice of Middlemen

The selection of one or more channels of distribution is an important marketing decision. Each respondent was asked how his firm decided which channel to use for the product being studied. The factors considered are presented in Table 10-3.

Twenty-five firms did not answer the question. None of those responding were specific enough to suggest that firms had made a careful analysis of the situation. Some made the choice on grounds that "that's the way it has always been done." Such thinking fails to appreciate the competitive advantage that can be won with a better choice of channels. It was especially surprising that foreign-owned firms, which often had little market experience in Peru, proved more likely to take this approach. Past experience as the basis for channel choice has obvious merit, but this response does not mean that the firm has carefully studied the alternatives.

The consideration of least cost/most profit was mentioned by more firms than any other factor. Although this criterion should be a primary basis for selecting a channel of distribution, determination of costs or expected profits requires thorough study. For instance, a firm might look at two channels and decide that because one requires a 20 percent trade discount and another only 10 percent, the latter would be more profitable, neglecting to consider that the former channel might double the firm's sales volume and take over the credit function, thereby cutting total cost. We believe that the overall distribution network in the Peruvian economy could be improved significantly if manufacturers would audit their present channels and carefully consider alternatives.

The most important single factor considered in the selection of particular middlemen was financial strength, as indicated in Table 10-4. Many respondents sought information from banks, credit organizations, as well as other sources. Some required middlemen to submit financial statements. Because the cost of

Table 10-2

Most Important Distribution Channels of Manufacturers

Type of Respondent	M↓R↓FC	M↓W↓R↓FC	M↓FC	M↓IC	M↓W↓IC	M↓A↓IC	OTHER	Totals
Total Firms	28	17	12	29	4	3	7	100
Peruvian–Owned Firms	26	16	14	31	3	2	8	100
Foreign–Owned Firms	31	18	8	28	5	5	5	100
Consumer Goods Producers	42	27	15	6	2	--	8	100
Industrial Goods Producers	11	4	9	57	6	6	7	100
Small Firms	28	18	14	26	2	5	7	100
Medium Firms	32	17	7	24	7	3	10	100
Large Firms	33	19	5	38	5	--	--	100
Heavy Competition	36	20	4	28	4	--	8	100
Moderate Competition	19	21	19	24	5	5	7	100
Light Competition	30	11	6	41	4	4	4	100
Owner–Manager	27	15	18	29	2	3	6	100
Professional–Manager	29	19	5	31	7	2	7	100
Low Purchase Value	51	37	3	3	--	--	6	100
Moderate Purchase Value	22	21	22	21	--	--	14	100
High Purchase Value	8	4	31	41	--	8	8	100
Very High Purchase Value	--	--	--	80	20	--	--	100

Key: M — Manufacturer   R — Retailer
      A — Agent   FC — Final Consumer
      W — Wholesaler   IC — Industrial Consumer

Table 10-3

Factors Considered by Manufacturers
in Selecting a Channel of Distribution

| Factor Considered | Total Firms | Percentage of Respondents | | | |
		Peruvian–Owned	Foreign–Owned	Consumer Goods Producers	Industrial Goods Producers
Obvious choice	12	9	15	6	19
Least cost–most profit	22	33	13	21	27
Customary for industry	19	17	20	25	11
Trial and error, past experience	16	24	8	23	8
Company policy	9	4	15	10	8
Others	33	26	41	29	38

money was so high in Peru — at least 16 to 18 percent in effective money interest rates — manufacturers wanted their middlemen to pay bills promptly and assume the expense of carrying an inventory. At times, because of a lack of middlemen with adequate financial resources, manufacturers were forced to accept financial responsibility for inventories.

Several respondents claimed they selected the best overall merchant. This involved an evaluation of the middleman's total operation, including his sales force. We received the impression that this consideration was definitely secondary to a middleman's financial strength. Ten percent of the respondents expressed concern with the business morality of the middleman (could he be trusted to do his best and do it honestly). Sixteen percent of the foreign-owned firms mentioned this factor.

Manufacturer-Middlemen Relationship

The two most common formal relationships between producers and their middlemen are ownership ties and legal or contractual arrangements. The majority of business between manufacturers in Peru and their middlemen was done on an informal basis. No contract was prepared to protect each party. Common ownership links were not frequent, although they were more often found between industrial producers and their middlemen than in the consumer

Table 10-4

Manufacturers' Criteria for Selection of Middleman

Criterion	Percentage of Middleman Users Mentioning
Financial strength	36
Best overall merchant	31
Good business morality	10
No criteria—sell to all with credit standing	16
Others	24
No answer	53

Table 10-5

Formal Ties Between Manufacturers and Their Middlemen

Classification	Percentage Having Formal Ties
Total Firms	39
Peruvian–Owned Firms	30
Foreign–Owned Firms	49
Consumer Goods Producers	29
Industrial Goods Producers	55

goods field. Foreign-owned firms, possibly less sure of themselves in an unfamiliar market, indicated a greater tendency for ownership or legal ties with middlemen, as shown in Table 10-5.

Services to Middlemen

Because the marketing intermediary plays such an important role in sales and product success, many firms attempted to spur his cooperation by offering services. Middlemen usually sold and distributed the products of several companies. To ensure that his products were not neglected, the manufacturer often provided incentives for middlemen such as cooperative advertising, salesmen contests, consumer contests, salesmen training, and promotional aids, as well as other services such as credit and guarantees against price declines.

Each respondent was asked if he offered any special services to his middlemen. He was given a list of the services mentioned above and invited to add any others. (The list likely inflated the answers. If a firm *at any time* offered a particular service to a middleman, it was probably mentioned to the interviewer.)

Credit was commonly offered to or demanded by middlemen. A cash discount was almost always offered, but most middlemen were unable to pay within the normal ten-day discount period. Thus, a cash discount in Peru was usually allowed up to thirty and even sixty days before payment. The high cost of money in Peru led most middlemen to insist upon fairly lengthy credit terms from manufacturers. Industrial goods producers tended to give longer term credit, but even some consumer goods manufacturers extended up to one hundred eighty days credit. Several manufacturers made the comment that credit arrangements were often the key to making a sale. Credit was frequently more important than even product or price.

One manufacturer in the construction materials industry summarized the situation in this manner:

The three most important factors in selling in Peru are credit, credit, and credit. Those equipment dealers and material suppliers who come to Peru convinced that they can sell their product because it will reduce the cost of construction, or because they have a more competitive price, will be disappointed. Those offering their product at an average competitive price, but with substantially better financing terms, should find a land of opportunity. This is not because price and quality are not important, but because credit is more important.

In thinking of credit, the U. S. seller must keep one factor in mind: companies comprising the construction industry generally want credit not because they are shoestring operations or because they are fly-by-night operators who do not intend to meet payment responsibilities, but because they are subject to the pressure created by the unusual rate of return that capital in short supply demands.

As long as capital is in short supply and commands a disproportionate rate of return, even the best-financed construction companies will look upon credit as a major criterion in the purchase of equipment and supplies.[2]

The high cost of money also meant that manufacturers did not like to extend credit. Some of the stronger firms whose products were in great demand were able to insist upon cash payments. Manufacturers also disliked extending credit because of the difficulty of collections. Estimates of middlemen nonpayment ranged from less than one percent to 10 percent. Many firms turned their collections over to a bank. It appears the "typical" arrangement by a consumer goods producer with his middleman called for thirty to sixty days credit, and collection was apt to lag the due date by a month.

Foreign-owned firms generally extended more services to middlemen than did Peruvian-owned firms, especially where salesmen contests, consumer contests, salesmen training, and cooperative advertising were concerned. These incentive programs for increasing and improving the middleman's promotional effort suggest a greater marketing aggressiveness among foreign-owned firms.

Consumer goods producers, having a greater need to depend upon middlemen to promote to their widely scattered markets, typically extended more services than industrial goods producers did. Exceptions were salesmen training (industrial goods are more technical and salesmen require greater product knowledge) and guarantees against price declines.

Size was highly correlated with the number of services offered to middlemen. Large firms offered more of every service than did small firms. Competition also had a direct correlation with the number of services offered. A manufacturer faced with heavy competition usually offered more services and incentives to his marketing intermediaries.

Owner-managed firms gave a below average number of services. Professional managers more aware of the techniques of stimulating middlemen, tended to offer more services. Manufacturers of products of low average purchase value were more prone to offer incentives than other manufacturers. This is explained by the firms' need for help in promoting to widely scattered markets and by the need for promotional incentives when the average commission per sale was low. A product of 250,000 *soles* value could bring a middleman's salesman a commission of 10,000-25,000 *soles.* The salesman's incentive is obvious. However, the same salesman may need extra stimulation to promote a product for which the average order may be 500 to 1000 *soles,* and the commission only a few *soles.*

Manufacturers' Problems in
Dealing with Middlemen

Forty percent of the respondents indicated that they had major problems with their middlemen — foreign-owned firms (60 percent) more so than Peruvian-owned firms (24 percent). Foreign-owned firms do not have as many of the personal contacts necessary to maintain good working relationships; and they are more demanding in what they expect — wholesalers in the advanced economies probably offer better service than Peruvian wholesalers do.

The problems mentioned as being of major importance showed no pattern. The most common problem occurred in the area of collections. (Only eight respondents mentioned this.) Other problems, each mentioned by only a few firms, were that: middlemen want to buy in small quantities; no specialized dealers are available; the middleman does not want to push the manufacturer's brand; there is no information feedback from middlemen; the middleman tries to cut prices; the middleman is not very aggressive or is dishonest; and the middleman is apathetic to the manufacturer's promotions.

The complaints expressed about middlemen in Peru were similar to complaints United States manufacturers express about their middlemen. Although there is reason to believe that the middlemen in Peru are perhaps less effective than in some other parts of the world, there is also reason to believe that manufacturers themselves do not do their part to make middlemen more effective through better selection and training.

On a scale from *five* (very satisfied) to *one* (dissatisfied), manufacturers were asked to evaluate their relationships with middlemen. Average responses are shown in Table 10-6. Responses clustered around the median, indicating that the firms were somewhat less than fully satisfied with their middlemen.

The indication that manufacturers are dissatisfied with the performance of their middlemen, combined with the previously mentioned desire to bypass middlemen, perhaps foretells problems for wholesalers. "Economic development and its accompanying general increase in the standard of living often bring with them a host of problems for wholesalers. . . ."[3]

The Peruvian government, its agencies, and area development corporations could be the main driving force in improving distribution channels, but they are frequently ineffective because of their lack of marketing expertise. A few years ago a development corporation in Cuzco established a fertilizer plant at nearby Cachimayo. To justify the plant it was necessary to include in its "market area" the *departamentos* of Cuzco, Apurimac, Arequipa, Ayacucho, Puno, Madre de Dios, Moquegua, and Tacna, having a total cultivatable surface of approximately 48,800,000 acres.[4] In view of the lack of railroads and other transportation facilities in these areas there was little hope of marketing effectively to most of the area.

In addition, after investing some $19 million in the fertilizer plant,[5] the corporation made no provision for sale and distribution of their product. No studies were conducted to determine the ability of the sierra or altiplano farmer to buy fertilizer, or equally important, his willingness to do so. An effective distribution system would have called for a means of educating farmers about the importance of fertilizer.

Shortly after the Cachimayo plant began operation, it had accumulated what was described as a "year's inventory" because sales were negligible. At the same time, the Camana Valley in Southern Peru, which had unrealistically been included in the market area, reported drastic shortages of fertilizer.[6] Even had physical distribution been feasible for Camana farmers, the product was not designed for use in lowland rice and sugar producing areas such as Camana, and

Table 10-6

**Manufacturer Estimates of Middleman
Inventories**

		Percentage of Respondents			
Inventories in Days of Sales	Total Firms	Peruvian-Owned Firms	Foreign-Owned Firms	Consumer Goods Producers	Industrial Goods Producers
to 0	14	22	3	6	30
1 to 14	21	20	23	28	7
15 to 30	36	34	40	34	41
31 to 60	16	13	20	23	3
61 to 180	13	11	14	9	19
	100	100	100	100	100

the price was prohibitive — Camana farmers could buy fertilizer imported from Denmark at a lower price.

Evaluation of Distribution Channels

Manufacturers in Peru underrate the potential value of optimizing their distribution networks. Producers seem to accept the present state of affairs. The channels used by manufacturers vary widely, according to the needs of the individual producer. Channel choice appears to be made carelessly. Credit arrangements are often the single most important factor in the middleman-manufacturer relationship.

Because middlemen are generally looked upon as a principal reason for increased costs, some middlemen groups might do well to form associations designed to educate the public and government as to the vital role they play in the economy. The government should take a more active role in determining the functions and dysfunctions of the various middlemen and in encouraging those middlemen who help build the economy, while discouraging those who are detrimental to its growth.

After studying channel of distribution reports from Japan, Brazil, Venezuela, Puerto Rico, Turkey, Egypt, India, and tropical Africa, Wadinambiaratchi concluded that "the channels of distribution in a country reflect the stage of economic development in that country."[7] If we accept this hypothesis, the development of distribution channels in Peru would indicate a moderately well developed economy — one which would rank with neither the least developed countries nor the most developed ones. On the other hand, we cannot accept fully Wadinambiaratchi's conclusion that the businessman's role in developing channels of distribution is merely a passive one – that he must make major changes in the sociopsychological, cultural, or anthropological aspects of a country to change the distribution channels. The application of sound marketing principles in dealing with middlemen will go a long way toward changing and improving distribution channels.

Physical Distribution

Physical distribution was once considered one of the most important marketing functions. Then emphasis was placed on advertising and marketing research. In recent years, marketing specialists in the developed nations have begun to restudy the problems of physical distribution. The development of electronic data processing equipment has been followed by the development of models for improving the performance of physical distribution. Many marketing experts now feel that the major opportunities for increasing marketing efficiency lie in this area.

Physical distribution in Peru is a problem because the terrain is difficult and transportation facilities are inadequate. Much of the consumer population is scattered widely throughout some of the most mountainous country in the world.

Limitations on the Sales Area

The research team asked each respondent if his firm's sales were limited to a single geographic area. Responses are shown in Table 10-7. Almost half of the respondents indicated their sales were limited to a geographic area. Foreign-owned and industrial goods firms operated under this limitation most often. In the former case one could surmise that the explanation lies in the lack of contacts with distributors in the hinterlands. In the latter the market for industrial goods is heavily concentrated in the Lima-Callao area.

Transportation problems were the most frequent reasons for a limited sales area. These are discussed in some detail later in the chapter.

One-fourth of the firms with a limited sales area felt that the market outside the main metropolitan center was not worth cultivating. This was especially true of industrial goods marketers, but 19 percent of the consumer goods marketers also felt that this was so. The vast majority of the population lives outside the Lima-Callao area, but it is widely scattered and difficult to reach, with below average purchasing power. While the market potential in the provinces is considerable, development of this potential on a profitable basis would be difficult. It is not surprising that some firms chose to settle for the more accessible metropolitan market.

Twenty-two percent of the foreign-owned firms with a limited sales area and 11 percent of the Peruvian-owned firms with the same limitation had a market

Table 10-7

Geographic Limitations on Sales

Classification	Percentage of Firms with Sales Limited to an Area
Total firms	46
Peruvian–owned firms	42
Foreign–owned firms	51
Consumer goods producers	34
Industrial goods producers	58

divided by industry or government.[a] A possible explanation is that the government, under pressure from local firms, seeks to limit the market of the foreign competition. A few firms mentioned credit and collection problems as the main factor limiting their sales area. They were willing to undergo the expense of sending a salesman into the provinces, but unwilling to send him back to each customer two or three times to collect what was owed.

Four industry groups had a preponderance of their sales limited to the coast, particularly Lima-Callao. One obvious group consisted of manufacturers producing for the fishing industry. Firms producing for mining companies saw the sierra as their most important area.

Transportation

Transportation activity was usually (in 65 percent of the firms) centered under someone in the production or administration department. Warehousing was even more often centered outside the sales or marketing department — 79 percent of the respondents placed this under production or administration.

Although the potential difficulties of transportation are evident to anyone who has traveled in Peru, only 27 percent of the respondents indicated that they had major problems with transporting the specified product to its markets. The main problems in order of frequency of occurrence are listed below.

1. *Poor roads* — Even the best roads in Peru are poor by United States standards. Most mountain roads are dirt or gravel and are difficult to traverse during rainy weather. They are bumpy, so breakage of fragile cargo is common. In addition, maintenance of a vehicle using such roads is expensive. One respondent estimated that because of transportation problems his firm reached only 35 percent of its potential customers.

[a]The significance of the factors limiting market areas may not be great, because the bases used to calculate percentages are small: 27 Peruvian-owned firms had a limited sales area; 23 foreign-owned firms had one.

2. *High cost* — Several manufacturers complained that the costs of transporting goods are excessive. The seasonality of crops means that during certain months the demand for transportation between Lima-Callao and the provinces is particularly high. Rates soar during this period and transportation is simply uneconomical for marketers at this time, even if the available vehicle can be located. Little backhauling is available.

3. *Poor service* — Some producers felt that trucking service was not adequate. Deliveries are not made on schedule, breakage and theft occur more often than they should, and equipment breaks down frequently. Manufacturers felt truckers did not have enough initiative or accept enough responsibility. Problems also existed in shipping. It was reported that if a Peruvian manufacturer wanted to sell in Colombia he could expect his goods to sit in a Peruvian warehouse for up to a month before being cleared for shipment. Upon delivery in Colombia, a similar wait could be expected. The reason for the delay is primarily "paperwork." A shipment sent up the coast by steamer that should have taken perhaps a week actually took two or three months.

Not all firms are able to do anything about trucking service, but those controlled by Eduardo Dibos Chappuis, currently president of the Sociedad Nacional de Industrias, have some of their products carried to customers by trucks of their own commercial trucking company.[8]

Warehousing

The size of inventory in terms of days of sales varied widely, depending upon the many factors peculiar to the particular firms. In addition, estimates of the average inventory were difficult for many firms to make, because their inventory levels varied from period to period. Most errors in reporting, however, were of a random nature and tended to cancel out. The responses to the question of inventory size are found in Table 10-8.

Because the reasons for high or low levels of inventories are so different, it is difficult to evaluate responses to this question. In some cases a low inventory was a result of efficiency and good sales forecasting. In others it was due to poor forecasting or production inefficiency. A few generalizations, however, may be made.

Foreign-owned firms carried above-average inventories; industrial goods firms often produced to order. Medium-sized firms carried the largest inventories and large firms carried the smallest (in days of sales). Competition was directly related to inventory size — more competition forced the carrying of greater inventories which, of course, allowed the firm to give better order-filling service. Professionally managed firms carried larger inventories.

Seventy-one percent of the respondents indicated they did *not* have major inventory problems. Of the thirty-two firms having such problems, the difficulty of forecasting needs and lack of space were most often mentioned. Forecasting difficulties were to a great extent the result of poor quality marketing research.

Table 10-8

**Manufacturer Estimates of Average
Inventories in Days of Sales**

	Percentage of Respondents in Days of Sales Categories				
Classification	0	1–30	31–60	61 and Over	Average Number of Days
Total firms	14	34	26	26	48
Peruvian–owned firms	19	36	24	21	42
Foreign–owned firms	7	33	28	32	57
Consumer goods producers	4	41	26	29	54
Industrial goods producers	26	27	26	21	42
Small firms	15	36	21	28	49
Medium firms	6	28	33	33	59
Large firms	14	52	20	14	31
Heavy competition	8	28	24	40	62
Moderate competition	20	32	27	21	44
Light competition	14	48	21	17	39
Owner–manager	16	42	30	12	34
Professional–manager	10	25	19	46	69
Very high purchase value	30	10	40	20	56
High purchase value	17	35	21	27	30
Moderate purchase value	21	42	16	21	48
Low purchase value	- -	46	23	31	43

However, the difficulties of forecasting in Peru are certainly as great as they are in the United States. The smaller size of the market means that there is less likelihood of one mistake being counterbalanced by another mistake elsewhere. In addition, the lack of secondary information makes forecasting difficult and there are problems in predicting overall economic growth in a country whose industrial base is changing so rapidly.

Lack of space was a real problem in the Lima-Callao area. Rapid population growth was one reason. Indians have come down from the mountains in great numbers and taken up "squatters rights" on much available land, particularly in the industrial areas. Further, the rapid industrial growth has taxed the construction industry's ability to supply needed buildings. Added to this, of course, has been the necessity for building earthquake-proof buildings and the problem of largely antiquated building methods. In short, land and building prices along with the price of borrowed money have been high, and have caused problems for manufacturers and middlemen alike.

It was somewhat surprising not to find more problems with warehousing and handling stocks. Inventory control techniques were generally very elementary, although there were some outstanding exceptions. Perhaps the relative lack of concern in this area is explained by the fact that manufacturers do not know how much more smoothly their operations *could* run — what they do see is that things are continually getting better as minor improvements are made in inventory systems.

Evaluation of Physical Distribution

Within the Lima-Callao area, which holds a major portion of most producers' markets, physical transport of goods is not difficult. Transportation problems in this area are similar to those found in any large city, although traffic conditions may be worse than usual because of the great amount of road construction activity. Outside the main metropolitan area, however, transportation is extremely difficult. The terrain is rough and roads are poor.

Peru is in the unfortunate position of requiring very expensive transportation facilities but lacking the financial resources to provide such a system. Despite present efforts to improve transport facilities to the provinces, it was evident there will always be transportation difficulties in most of the country.

11 Pricing Management

Prices are of vital interest to buyers and sellers alike. The prices charged for goods or services are a major factor in determining the purchasing power of consumers, the volume of economic activity, and the profitability of sellers. Pricing management can be especially difficult in a developing nation. As Sherbini points out, "domestic manufacturers in developing countries often face a dual problem in setting their basic prices. First, imports frequently impose an upper ceiling on prices . . . and secondly, prices become rigid once they are set,"[1] due to government price controls and needed approval.

Although the breadth of this study precluded a detailed investigation of pricing practices in Peru, information was gathered on the major factors considered in setting prices, the margins used, price variations (for example, discounts and negotiations), and major pricing problems.

Responsibility for Pricing

In most of the firms interviewed the general manager accepts pricing as his responsibility. Pricing was the responsibility of the sales manager in one of every four firms, and of someone else (usually the administrative manager or accountant) in the few remaining firms.

Responsibility for pricing policy and responsibility for pricing are not necessarily the same. A general manager may set the company's general policy, while a lower level executive may determine the actual price for a given transaction. The interviewees were asked, "Who in your firm has the authority to set the price of the product being studied?" The general manager alone had this authority in 49 percent of the firms interviewed. He shared his authority with the sales manager and others in another 25 percent of the firms interviewed. The "sharing" situation was one where the general manager met with others to discuss alternative prices. General managers most likely retain their supreme authority in these cases, but probably consider the suggestions of others. The general manager, then, was the major pricing decision maker in 74 percent of the firms interviewed.

The sales manager alone was given pricing authority in only 7 percent of the firms interviewed. Accountants, administrative managers and others had the authority in 14 percent of the firms. Although it is understandable that the chief executives would want to give their approval for decisions as basic as the setting of prices, it is not so clear that accountants and administrative managers, who are often far removed from customers, should have this authority. The reasons they frequently do have the authority to set prices are undoubtedly their knowledge of costs and the fact that much pricing in Peru is done on a "cost-plus" or other formula basis.

The home office retains authority for pricing in only 11 percent of the foreign-owned firms. It appears that decentralization of pricing authority is dominant among the international firms operating in Peru.

One pricing situation that did not come forth in the question, but which does exist, is the case where an important customer is affiliated with the manufacturer by common ownership or common directorate. This situation was prevalent among 24 percent of the foreign-owned firms, 11 percent of the Peruvian-owned firms, 26 percent of the industrial goods producers, and 7 percent of the consumer goods producers.

One industrial goods firm was established by a group of manufacturers who were not satisfied with existing suppliers. The newly created firm's basic role was to service the founding group of manufacturers. Sales to firms outside this group were not considered particularly important. When the manager of the supplying firm felt that rising costs indicated the need for increasing his prices, he had to receive the approval of a directorate composed of his principal customers. The directors, not wanting to increase their costs, were reluctant to grant permission for increased prices. Pricing decisions, therefore, were made on a very artificial basis, and the supplying firm's prices tended to be unrealistically low in view of production costs and competitive prices.

Major Factors Considered in Pricing

In the United States, surveys of pricing practices indicate "that price policies are much more cost-oriented than demand-oriented. This tendency is reflected in the industry practices of cost-plus, rate-of-return, administered pricing, and so on, in which some 'normal' margin of profit (conditioned by competition) is added to full production costs of the product in question."[2] This tendency may be due to the fact that businessmen normally know more about product costs than consumer demand.

The interviewers asked each respondent what major factors were considered in determining the price of the product being studied. Five factors were suggested and the respondent was asked to include any others that were important. Responses appear in Table 11-1.

Production costs, mentioned by 86 percent of the respondents, were by far the single most important factor considered in establishing prices. This held true

Table 11-1

Major Factors Considered in Pricing
(Percentage of Respondents)

Factors	Total	Peruvian	Foreign	Consumer	Industrial	Small	Medium	Large
Production costs	86	86	86	89	82	84	81	83
Prices of competition	54	46	65	54	53	53	60	39
What the customer is willing to pay	24	28	19	32	16	20	24	22
Tariff protection	8	6	12	7	10	4	6	17
Agreements with other firms	7	3	14	11	4	7	6	9
Other	14	5	28	21	6	13	12	26

Factors	Heavy	Medium	Light	Owner	Manager	Purchase Value			
						1	2	3	4
Production costs	80	80	90	85	72	78	87	90	90
Prices of competition	96	40	41	55	42	57	47	60	50
What the customer is willing to pay	33	22	17	31	9	25	20	27	--
Tariff protection	4	11	7	5	12	6	7	7	20
Agreements with other firms	--	9	10	6	7	9	13	3	--
Other	21	9	10	6	30	22	13	17	10

for all categories of firms. Competitors' prices, mentioned by 54 percent, ranked second in importance as a factor in price setting. Almost all firms with heavy competition considered the prices of their competitors, foreign-owned firms more than Peruvian-owned firms. Large firms, apparently more confident of their strength, were less disposed to consider competitive prices. Suprisingly, the owner-managed firms appeared more concerned with competitors' prices than did the professionally managed firms, even though the owner-managed firms faced considerably less competition. Perhaps professionally managed firms differentiated their products or were more efficient and found it easier to meet competition.

The factor "what the consumer is willing to pay" met with mixed responses. Some respondents laughed at the idea that this factor should influence price setting. Assuming that respondents interpreted the statement to mean a consideration of consumer or customer demand, it is apparent that pricing in Peru is definitely oriented toward cost rather than demand. While almost nine of ten firms considered costs in their pricing, only one in four considered demand. Most respondents took the attitude that "customers will pay what we want to charge." We believe this attitude is primarily due to (1) the generally high level of prices and the tendency of prices to rise continually; (2) relatively frequent excess demand; (3) a failure to consider the potential importance of lower income mass markets; (4) high protective tariffs; (5) the lack of effective competition in some industries; and (6) a lack of information about demand. Indeed, many firms are able to earn a satisfactory return on investment without considering demand, although this does not mean they are maximizing or optimizing their profits.

The tendency to avoid lower prices apparently is shared by businessmen in other countries. Galbraith and Holten reported a similar situation in Puerto Rico:

Price competition is virtually nonexistent. The sellers believe that they are confronted by demand curves which are inelastic — that a lower price would not increase total sales sufficiently to enhance or even maintain their margin of profit. The signs of nonprice competition exist in the varying services offered by different stores. However, because of the live and let live approach to business typical of most entrepreneurs, analysis in terms of monopolistic competition, or any other type of competition, may be inappropriate. It is doubtful whether owners seek to maximize profits, either by price or nonprice competition, in the usual sense. They may be thought of as maximizing profits if one includes in marginal costs the subjective costs of becoming unpopular with competitors.[3]

The implications for economic development are far-reaching. First, industry's lack of interest and information concerning the nature of demand suggests that resources may not be allocated to their most productive ends, i.e., demand and the marketplace are not acting as an allocator of resources. Second, by not considering the nature of demand (and therefore price elasticity) adequate consideration is not given to the potential market that might be reached through lower prices. It is conceivable, especially if there are economies of large scale, that a much higher proportion of the market could be served at a lower price without decreasing (and perhaps increasing) the profits of the company. Third, the low volume, high price policy that industry is using implies that only affluent customers are being served. The less affluent members of the economic system are probably being priced out of the market and must go without.

Tariff protection was an important factor in pricing in 8 percent of the firms interviewed. When important competition from imported goods existed, the prices of these imports determined, to a great extent, the prices of locally produced goods. Domestic firms, seeking and obtaining protective tariffs, tended to set their prices just below the tariff-laden import prices. Unlike some of the larger firms, smaller firms apparently have not been able to receive tariff protection. It also appears that producers of high value equipment, mostly capital-industrial goods, have been more aggressive and successful than the average firm in obtaining tariff protection. Tariffs were an important consideration in the pricing of 20 percent of these firms.

Tariff protection was decreased somewhat in May 1969 when the government eliminated the 10 percent surcharge on the importation of capital goods financed by foreign credits and not domestically produced.[4] Except for food staples, fuel, and several other basic items, all imported articles had been subject to the surcharge since June 1968. A number of other stipulations must be met to qualify for the exoneration, but the clear result is that costs of equipment will be lowered somewhat. This should tend to hold down prices.

Agreements with other firms appeared much more common among the foreign-owned firms than among Peruvian-owned firms. This could suggest a foreign business group that controls competition by maintaining close contacts. Foreign firms were shown earlier to be more likely to divide the market. However, the impression was also given that foreign firms were often more candid than domestically owned firms.

The most important pricing consideration in the "other" category was government control of prices. Because 16 percent of the foreign firms felt government controls were important to their prices and only 3 percent of the Peruvian-owned firms took this view, it might appear that government discriminates against the foreign-owned firms. Actually, the difference in percentages is explained by the preponderance of foreign capital in the price-controlled drug industry.

Manufacturers' Gross Margins

Gross margin is the difference between selling price and cost of goods sold. A firm's average percentage of gross margin is determined by subtracting the cost of goods sold from net sales, and taking the difference as a percentage of sales. The resulting percentage margin is an average of all sales and may not represent the margin for any one sale. Discounts often differ from sale to sale. Some sales are made to retailers while others are made through wholesalers who receive a lower price to compensate them for their services, and margins may vary during the year depending upon product category, type of distribution system used, manufacturers' services and the like.

Making a meaningful analysis of the gross margins of one hundred ten different manufacturers is difficult. Only sixty-six of one hundred ten respondents were willing to provide information on their gross margins. In addition, some who did may have given an inaccurate figure because of a lack of information or a fear of disclosing the actual margin. If it is assumed that since any such inaccuracies are random, comparisons may be made among groups of the respondents. It should be recognized, however, that the data may be highly inaccurate.

The average percentage gross margin for all firms was 30 percent. Based upon gross margins in developed nations this percentage does not seem unusually high. Two industries — those producing drugs and household durables — reported high gross margins and raised the average above what it would have been for the remaining firms. Three industries — products for automobiles, for agriculture and for fishing and mining — reported rather low gross margins.

Industrial goods reportedly received a lower markup over manufacturing cost, probably because less margin is needed to cover marketing costs than is the case with consumer goods. Large firms also reported a smaller than average gross margin as did firms having a product with very high purchase value, the latter because these firms were industrial goods producers.

Completely surprising was the inverse relationship between the degree of competition and percentage gross margin. One would expect that greater competition would result in lower gross margins. One explanation is that many manufacturers are averse to price competition. They prefer to compete on the basis of quality and promotion. Greater competition may force them to raise their prices to provide a sufficient margin to cover the added service and marketing costs. On the other hand, the variation in margins among the groups with varying degrees of perceived competition may have been attributable either to inaccuracies in the data or to other factors not related to the degree of competition.

When the firms were classified into ranges of average gross profit margin, approximately half of the respondents utilized a margin of 21 to 40 percent. Only 14 percent had a margin of 41 to 50 percent, and only 9 percent had margins over 50 percent. A frequency distribution of the percentage gross margins peaked at about the average of 30 percent.

Negotiation of Prices

The traveler or tourist in a Latin American country gets the impression that bargaining or negotiating at the retail level is a normal Latin practice. This impression is somewhat misleading, because he shops for art and craft items, which are particularly subject to bargaining. Especially with foreigners, vendors

Table 11-2

Gross Margin Percentages

Classification	Percentage Gross Margin
Total firms	30
Peruvian–owned	31
Foreign–owned	29
Consumer goods	35
Industrial goods	25
Small	34
Medium	28
Large	23
Heavy competition	32
Moderate competition	28
Light competition	27
Owner–managed	29
Professionally–managed	30
Very high purchase value	17
High purchase value	30
Moderate purchase value	28
Low purchase value	33

try to start as high as possible and then work down through bargaining to the "right price." It is accurate to say that bargaining on price at the retail level is more prevalent in Latin America than it is in the United States.

Indications are, however, that the amount of bargaining at the retail level is being reduced over much of Latin America. Fewer stores are "coding" prices and allowing sales clerks to reduce a price when a potential buyer asks for a discount or makes an offer for the merchandise. At least some of this tendency is due to the fixed price policy followed by Sears Roebuck. Sears competes with the department stores and higher priced speciality shops, which in turn compete with, or at least influence, the prices of smaller stores. With only two stores in Peru, one in downtown Lima and the other in a Lima suburb, Sears still has a definite influence on retail prices.

Discussions of price uniformity and discounts in the international marketing literature almost always dwell on discounts at retail. Little or nothing has been reported on price discounts by manufacturers.[5] How much negotiating do manufacturers do with their customers in establishing prices? When asked if negotiation was involved in their pricing, 40 percent of the respondents replied "yes." Negotiations were more common among industrial goods producers (55 percent) than among consumer goods (23 percent), undoubtedly due to the relatively high value of the industrial sale, the leverage of the industrial purchaser, and the made-to-order nature of many industrial products.

The larger, more powerful sellers did less negotiating of prices. Competition and nationality of ownership did not appear to influence whether a firm negotiated its prices. However, the fact that owner-managed firms negotiated more often (45 percent) than professionally managed firms (29 percent) suggests that price negotiating may be a dying tradition. This conclusion assumes that industry will tend to become more professionally managed as time passes.

The general manager did the negotiating more often than any other executive in the firm, alone in 45 percent of the negotiating firms and with others in another 26 percent. The sales manager negotiated alone in only 17 percent of the respondent firms and with the general manager in another 12 percent. Thus, the sales manager was left out of negotiations on price in 71 percent of the respondent firms. This is clearly a potential cause of difficulty between the general manager and the sales manager. Sales volume was one of the major bases for evaluating the sales manager's performance.

Another question was asked to determine the uniformity and variability of the price discount schedule. Responses are shown in Table 11-3. A uniform price discount schedule, of course, may mean that different customers pay different prices. For example, a large buyer is able to take advantage of discounts for buying in large quantities. What we wanted to determine, however, was whether negotiations or "special arrangements" between firms enabled two similar buyers to receive different prices. Essentially, this question provided another means of determining the amount of negotiation used with the basic price discount schedule.

Table 11-3

**Uniformity–Variability of Prices and
Discounts**

	Percentage of Respondents				
Response	Total	Peruvian	Foreign	Consumer	Industrial
Prices and discounts are uniform to *all* customers	62	55	72	69	55
Some customers receive special prices and discounts	31	37	21	31	30
Most customers receive special prices and discounts	7	8	7	- -	15
	100	100	100	100	100

Approximately six of every ten firms maintained a uniform price discount schedule. In some instances, the response to this question conflicted with the response to the earlier question about price negotiations. For example, in the direct question about price negotiations, Peruvian and foreign firms showed a similar tendency to negotiate, but in the price discount schedule question, Peruvian-owned firms showed a greater tendency to negotiate.

The authors have no explanation for the variation in answers. However, because the price discount question clearly "spelled out" the alternative situations, the authors accept answers to that question as being the more accurate. In any event, it appears that negotiation of prices, while a fairly common practice, is not by any means the primary way of conducting business in Peru. In response to both questions, slightly less than 40 percent of the firms claimed to negotiate over prices.

The Use of Discounts

In the drug industry it is illegal to discount from established prices, but firms do discount by giving a "baker's" or "long" dozen to customers. It is said that this "long" dozen sometimes stretches to eighteen or more. The government has attempted to restrict this practice without any particular success. This willingness to discount apparently carries through to the retail level because many drug retailers automatically discount from the prices marked on the items in their stores.

Discounts offer the manufacturer flexibility in his pricing. By using various types of discounts he can provide incentives for customers to purchase as he prefers them to purchase — in cash, during off-season months, and in large quantities. The researchers asked each respondent what types of discounts his firm utilized.

It was found that discounts were an important part of manufacturers' pricing strategies in Peru. Almost nine of every ten firms offered at least one type of discount, and the "average" firm offered one and one-half discount types.

The most popular discount was based on size of order. Almost half of the respondents used quantity discounts. Other discounts in order of importance were functional discounts (those varying by type of customer), those based on the cumulative volume of purchases, those varying according to the results of negotiation, and those varying by season. In addition, although not specifically mentioned in Table 11-4, most firms offered a cash discount. The results of cross-tabulations are listed below.

1. Foreign-owned firms made greater use of customer type and cumulative purchase discounts, and used other discounts about as frequently as did the Peruvian-owned firms.

2. Industrial goods producers used all discount forms more often than did consumer goods firms, except for cumulative purchase discounts. The latter is undoubtedly due to the fact that many industrial sales are made only infrequently, as when a new machine is purchased. Another machine may not be purchased for several years.

3. Large firms tended to use fewer discounts than did small and medium-sized firms, perhaps because their strength puts them in a position to avoid discounts. However, large firms *were* the most frequent users of the cumulative purchase discount.

4. Owner-managed firms used cumulative purchase discounts and negotiated discounts most frequently, while professionally-managed firms made the most frequent use of functional and quantity discounts.

5. Heavy competition seemed to encourage the use of quantity and functional discounting, but had little influence on the use of other types of discounts.

Price Competition

A firm may have several competitors, but if they do not compete vigorously the firm will have little actual *competition*. As one measure of competition, respondents were asked to rate the degree of price competition they faced, using a five-point scale ranging from "very strong" (5 points) to "not very strong" (1 point). We expected that businessmen would tend to overrate the amount of price competition.

Using this approach, the results are actually measures of management's perception of price competition. Because management action is based upon management's perception of its environment, those perceiving stronger competition probably would tend to compete more aggressively than those perceiving weak competition.

Table 11-4

Types of Discounts Used (Percentage of Respondents Using)

Type of Discount	Total	Peruvian	Foreign	Consumer	Industrial	Small	Medium	Large
Size of order	46	47	45	42	51	51	36	26
Type of customer	35	30	42	32	38	31	33	22
Cumulative purchase	26	20	35	26	26	18	33	30
By negotiation	20	20	20	13	28	13	27	9
By season	8	8	7	8	9	7	12	– –

Type of Discount	Owner	Manager	Heavy	Medium	Light
Size of order	38	42	52	40	33
Type of customer	26	33	48	31	27
Cumulative purchase	31	13	16	36	17
By negotiation	25	9	20	18	20
By season	8	7	8	11	3

Table 11-5

Respondents' Evaluations of Price Competition (3 = moderate price competition)

Classification	Average Point Score
Total firms	3.1
Peruvian–owned	2.8
Foreign–owned	3.4
Consumer goods	3.1
Industrial goods	3.1
Small	3.1
Medium	3.6
Large	2.7
Owner-managed	3.0
Professionally–managed	3.2
Very high purchase value	2.8
High purchase value	3.0
Moderate purchase value	3.4
Low purchase value	3.2
Automotive products	2.6
Food and beverages	2.4
Textiles, clothing, footwear	4.1
Pharmaceutical	3.8
Household durables	2.9
Office products	3.4
Construction–related products	2.3
Agriculture–related products	3.0
Products for fishing and mining	3.5
Other industrial products	3.2

Price competition was perceived as being stronger by the foreign-owned firms than by Peruvian-owned firms. As mentioned earlier, we believe that this may be because the foreign-owned firms expected to find little competition and were surprised, or because they have shown a willingness to enter into industries with strong price competition. Managers of medium-sized firms, in all classifications, perceived the strongest price competition. This may be due in part to the above average number of foreign-owned firms in this category. However, it can be hypothesized that many of the medium-sized firms were competing on a price basis with larger firms in their industries.

Of all the specific industries studied, textiles, clothing and footwear producers perceived price competition as being highest, while those manufacturing products for the construction industry rated it lowest. Other evidence indicates that these perceptions were probably accurate. However, the pharmaceutical industry rated price competition second highest of all the industries. This was difficult to understand in view of the rather overt price discussions which were reported to occur among the industry leaders. The high rating may have been a reflection of industry's distaste for government price approval or the price competition which takes the form of extra quantities at existing prices.

Although price competition within the products for the automobile industry didn't appear to be very high, indications were that the more important factor was government control (as in gasoline) or the threat of government control over prices. The firms knew that if their prices got too far out of line the government would require price approval or would actually set the prices of their products or their return on investment. This is especially true since the government, in the fall of 1968, nationalized International Petroleum Company, Ltd. (I.P.C.), a subsidiary of the Canadian affiliate of Standard Oil of New Jersey. All foreign-owned firms, not just those in the automotive products field, are concerned that the government may decide to expropriate their factories and distribution facilities. The government's denial of further intentions to appropriate has not been successful in alleviating these fears, especially in view of the expropriation of W.R. Grace and Company's sugar holdings at Paramonga and Cartavio in the early summer of 1969, and current pressures to nationalize the automobile assemblers.

Major Pricing Problems

The researchers expected almost every respondent firm to report some major pricing problems. However, 40 percent of the respondents did not feel that they had any major pricing difficulties. Of those who did mention specific problems, few appeared to be overly concerned about them.

The most frequently expressed problem, mentioned by 24 percent of the respondents, was that of meeting competition. Foreign-owned firms and industrial goods producers mentioned this difficulty more often than other types of firms. For some reason industrial goods manufacturers emphasized competition somewhat more in this question than they had earlier when asked to rate their price competition.

Ten percent of the respondents mentioned government price controls or the threat of controls as being a major problem. This was mentioned by 18 percent of the consumer goods producers and 2 percent of the industrial goods producers. The responses reflect government control of pharmaceutical prices and of prices for "essential" foods.

Ten respondents felt that high and rising costs were a major pricing problem, because these costs set a floor below which prices could not be set. Several of these respondents specifically mentioned their high labor costs. Better training programs could do much to raise productivity and thus lower the cost of labor going into any one article. However, some firms did have cost problems of great seriousness. A textile manufacturer who had recently purchased some modern machinery pointed out that mills' in the United States could use one man to operate thirty or more looms, while work rules in Peru prevented him from using more than ten looms per man. He also pointed out the difference between his situation and that of the United States mill, which could run its loom for days without changing the setup because demand was so great. Because its demand for any one cloth was so small, the Peruvian mill had to stop its looms every hour or so to adjust them for production of another product.

Fringe benefit costs are very high in Peru. They were generally equal to 50 to 60 percent of the basic wage costs at the time of the study. Like most laws, those laws dealing with social benefits sometimes have loopholes. Some of the newer firms in Peru, having greater flexibility in their organizational structure, appear to be capable of taking advantage of these loopholes and gaining some cost advantages over the older firms.[6]

Ten respondents also mentioned the difficulty of raising prices. Except for cases where government pressure exists, this did not, in our judgment, seem to be too great a problem because the public was accustomed to inflation, and price increases were met with less resistance than they would have been in a more stable financial environment.

A few firms had difficulty justifying their price differentials. They felt their quality was more than worth the difference between their prices and those of their competitors, but they had difficulty convincing customers of this. This problem frequently arises in developed as well as underdeveloped nations, and the best solution seems to be a better planned and more aggressive marketing program.

Summary and Evaluation

Prices are high in Peru. The reasons for this are many, but one of the most important is the manufacturers' emphasis on production and a neglect of demand. Because demand analyses and cost accounting are seldom used, the setting of prices is usually highly arbitrary.

Pricing strategy is nonetheless an important element in the marketing strategy of manufacturers in Peru. Management is generally aware of the many possible variations in pricing, and many types of discounts are used. Negotiation of prices was an important factor for almost 40 percent of the firms studied.

Foreign-owned firms seemed to make significantly greater use of uniform price schedules and felt that they faced stronger price competition than did Peruvian-owned firms. Consumer goods producers tended to make above average use of uniform prices; their margins were also greater than those of the industrial goods producers.

Price, being a very visible element of marketing strategy, is subject to close observation by the government. Needs of consumers for low priced essential goods are met somewhat by government price controls on certain basic food products and by the relatively recent introduction of low priced − low quality goods by some manufacturers.

However, we do not believe that aggressive price competition will predominate in Peru until (1) production becomes more efficient, enabling the most efficient producers to lower their prices substantially; (2) production increases to the point where supply exceeds demand at current levels of price; (3) accounting improves to give manufacturers the information needed for intelligent costing and pricing; and (4) there is a greater recognition of demand elasticity and the concept of increasing profits through a larger volume of sales at a lower price and profit margin.

12 Overall Marketing Strategy

In the preceding chapters, discussion has been limited to the investigation of specific marketing practices. At this point it is appropriate to examine how these practices combine to form the overall marketing strategies of Peruvian manufacturers.

The Question

Respondents were asked to allocate 100 points among the facets of competitive strategy (product efforts, sales efforts, distribution, and pricing) according to the perceived relative importance of each. The question did not distinguish whether relative importance was to be evaluated on the basis of inputs or outputs. For example, an input measure of personal selling might be the percentage of the marketing budget devoted to personal selling; an output measure might be an estimate of the actual contribution of personal selling in achieving the firm's marketing objectives. Hindsight suggests that the point allocations probably were based on a combination of inputs and outputs. This may not constitute a problem because there should be a correlation between the input and output of any given factor. In other words, the inputs should be determined according to their estimated outputs. If a manager feels that product quality is the major determinant of the product's success, one would expect that product efforts would constitute the most important input to the firm's marketing program.

It should be recognized that the allocations are based on perceptions – the subjective evaluations of marketing executives. As a practical matter, marketing strategies are primarily determined on the basis of management perceptions and subjective evaluations. This is especially true in Peru where so little emphasis is placed on research.

The actual question read:

Please allocate 100 points among the following major policy areas according to their relative importance in your *marketing strategy* for [*product being studied*]:

_____Product efforts   Includes product planning, product
                                           research and development, and the
                                           services accompanying the product.

_____Sales efforts   Includes sales management and
                                           personal selling, advertising,
                                           promotion programs, and all other
                                           marketing communications.

_____Distribution	Includes the selection, coordination, and evaluation of channels, transportation, and inventory control.
_____Pricing strategy	Includes price determination, pricing policies, and specific strategies over which you exercise some degree of control.
_____Other	

The question was taken from a fairly extensive study of the marketing strategies of United States manufacturers.[1] Therefore, the following analyses will present some comparisons of the allocations of Peruvian and United States manufacturers.

Differing Marketing Strategies

The point allocations of Peruvian executives differ significantly from those of executives in the United States who placed more emphasis on the product facet of marketing strategy. In view of the research and development orientation of United States industry, this is not surprising. However, Peruvian managers, like their counterparts in the United States, perceived product efforts as being more important than sales efforts, distribution, or pricing. They allocated 35 percent of their points to product efforts, whereas United States manufacturers allocated 41 percent.

In both the United States and Peru, sales efforts were perceived as the second most important facet of marketing strategy. Peruvian manufacturers allocated 25 points to this facet, and U. S. manufacturers 28 points. Distribution was perceived as being about equally important in both nations, with 17 and 18 points being allocated to it.

Pricing was perceived as being substantially more important to Peruvian manufacturers than to U.S. manufacturers. The Peruvian respondents allocated 22 of their 100 points to pricing; among U.S. executives, only 12 points were allocated to pricing. As indicated earlier there is far less competition in Peru than in the United States. The less competitive environment gives manufacturers more pricing freedom. As a consequence price is a more controllable and a more important facet of competitive strategy in Peru than in the United States. In the

United States the prices of many products are established by the forces of demand and supply with little freedom left for the manufacturer to vary his price from those of his competitors. Consequently, the manufacturer strives to differentiate his product. Nonprice competitive strategy is extremely important for industry in the United States.

Nationality of Ownership

As shown in Table 12-2, the perceived importance of the various facets of marketing and competitive strategy in Peru varied considerably by nationality of ownership. The outstanding difference between Peruvian and foreign firms is that Peruvian firms attached greater importance to price and product, while foreign firms attached more emphasis to sales efforts. The following hypotheses are possible explanations for the differences:

1. Foreign-owned firms often sell the products that have been developed in another country. They have little to do with the actual development of products and consequently, allocated fewer points to product efforts than the managers of Peruvian-owned firms.
2. Foreign management, accustomed to business practices in a more developed economy, place heavy reliance on sales efforts. A well-developed industry, led by a few strong firms, will often try to avoid price-cutting because price cuts can be matched by the competition and result in lower margins for all firms. Thus, many of the foreign managers in Peru are accustomed to using nonprice competition and they have the experience and creative talent to incorporate it into their strategy. In some cases, they can use the promotional campaigns developed by other divisions of their company in other nations.

Type of Industry

The United States study showed that marketing strategies vary significantly from industry to industry, depending upon characteristics such as the motivation of the purchasers, the value of the product, the technicality of the product, the knowledge of the buyer, and purchasing efforts of the buyer. As shown in Table 12-3, a similar pattern is prevalent in Peru.

Consumer goods producers weighted sales efforts and distribution most heavily, while industrial goods producers gave greater relative weight to product efforts and pricing. This agreed with the pattern of the United States study and our expectations. Industrial buyers tended to buy more on the basis of price and product quality, while nonindustrial buyers were less qualified to evaluate product quality and, therefore, price. In addition, consumers' purchase motivations were often psychologically based; consequently, sales efforts were highly influential and in many instances created psychological utility. Industrial

Table 12-1

Relative Importance of Major Facets of Marketing Strategy

Policy Area	Average of Points Allocated	
	Peruvian Manufacturers[1]	U. S. Manufacturers[2]
Product efforts	35	41
Sales efforts	25	28
Distribution	17	18
Pricing	22	12
Other	1	1
	100	100

[1] Results of Peruvian study

[2] Results from the previously–mentioned Udell study in the United States

Table 12-2

Relative Importance of Major Policy Facets, Peruvian–Owned and Foreign–Owned Firms

Policy Area	Average of Points Allociated	
	Peruvian	Foreign
Product efforts	37	32
Sales efforts	20	32
Distribution	17	17
Pricing	26	18
Other	- -	1
	100	100

buyers in Peru are heavily concentrated in the Lima-Callao area. Distribution to them is fairly simple. Consumer goods producers, on the other hand, were more apt to sell in the provinces where distribution is difficult. Also, consumer goods have a longer channel of distribution while industrial goods are often sold directly to their users.

Professional and Owner-Managers

Allocations among owner-managed and professionally managed firms do not show large differences. Owner-managed firms placed slightly more emphasis on product efforts and pricing, while professionally managed firms rated sales efforts and distribution above average. Because this classification closely parallels that of ownership it is difficult to distinguish whether the differences are due to type of management or nationality of the firm. However, the point allocations in Table 12-4 do not differ as markedly as those in Table 12-2 where nationality of ownership was considered. It appears that type of management did not greatly affect the perceived importance of the various facets of marketing strategy.

Competition

Manufacturers in Peru apparently react to heavy competition by emphasizing advertising, sales promotion, and personal selling. This may be due, however, to the fact that foreign-owned firms were predominantly in the highly competitive classification. As shown earlier the foreign firms placed the most emphasis on product efforts. We suspect that pricing and sales efforts are visualized as the more aggressive aspects of marketing and are therefore perceived as the appropriate areas for emphasis when the competition gets heavy. In truth, of course, the less dramatic policy areas of product and distribution often provide the best means of competing effectively.

Summary and Evaluation

The major facets of marketing strategy of manufacturers in Peru were, in order of their perceived importance: product efforts, sales efforts, pricing and distribution. Product efforts received above-average emphasis in the marketing plans of Peruvian-owned firms, industrial goods producers, owner-managed firms, and companies with light competition. Sales efforts were especially emphasized by foreign-owned firms and consumer goods producers. Distribution was emphasized by consumer goods producers; pricing was given above-average importance in the marketing plans of Peruvian-owned firms, industrial goods producers, and companies that faced heavy competition. Business firms in the

Table 12-3

**Relative Importance of Marketing
Facets to Consumer and Industrial
Goods Producers**

	Average Points Allocated	
Policy Area	*Consumer Goods*	*Industrial Goods*
Product efforts	32	38
Sales efforts	30	20
Distribution	20	14
Pricing	17	28
Other	1	- -
	100	100

Table 12-4

**Relative Importance of Major Facets,
Owner-Managed and Professionally-
Managed Firms**

	Average Points Allocated	
Policy Area	*Owner*	*Manager*
Product efforts	36	33
Sales efforts	23	27
Distribution	16	18
Pricing	25	20
Other	- -	2
	100	100

United States apparently attribute more importance to product efforts and less to pricing than do firms in Peru.

Marketing Success and Aggressiveness

The multiplicity of management goals — profits, growth, survival, public service, and recognition — makes the evaluation of marketing success difficult. Even the evaluation of the attainment of a single objective may involve several problems. For instance, profit can be measured in absolute or relative terms. It can be measured as a percentage of sales or as a percentage of investment. In the latter case the investment base can be measured on the basis of historical cost or replacement cost. Obviously, "profitability" will vary substantially depending upon the basis used. When multiple goals are present, many of them difficult to quantify, success becomes even more difficult to measure and each factor must be weighted to arrive at an overall indicator of success.

Somewhat arbitrarily we have chosen to examine two of the possible indicators of marketing success — profits and sales. Despite current concern with multiple management goals we believe that profitability is the single most important goal of management. Without profits, a firm cannot remain in business and has no opportunity to achieve its other objectives.

Profitability

Each respondent was asked to indicate his firm's rate of return on investment after taxes. Because some reticence was expected on the part of respondents in giving this information, the question was presented so that they could select from classifications of percentage return (for example, 6 to 10 percent), rather than given a specific answer.

Unfortunately, one-fourth of the respondents refused to answer the question. Nonresponse tended to be more common among Peruvian-owned and owner-managed firms and among firms facing light competition. In addition, the definite impression was given that many firms reported an inaccurate figure, and two well-known accounting firms in Peru warned that even with a truthful response answers were not likely to be accurate because accounting standards have not been clearly established in many Peruvian businesses. Thus, in many cases the general manager of the reporting company may not have known what his actual profits were. Noting these limitations, the reader may evaluate the profitability of businesses in Peru in Table 12-6.

The average return on invested capital after taxes for all firms responding was 13.5 percent. This is above the 11.8 percent return on invested capital recorded by the 500 largest manufacturing firms in 1964 in the United States.[2] However, if the greater risk and inflation are taken into consideration, the profits of

Table 12-5

**Relative Importance of Major Facets,
Firms with Heavy, Moderate, and
Light Competition**

| | Average Points Allocated | | |
Policy Area	Highly Competitive	Moderately Competitive	Lightly Competitive
Product efforts	24	37	41
Sales efforts	30	26	20
Distribution	18	14	19
Pricing	27	22	19
Other	1	1	1
	100	100	100

Table 12-6

Average After–Tax Profit as a Percentage of Invested Capital

Classification	Number of Firms Responding	Average Percent Return on Investment
Total firms	75	13.5
Peruvian–owned	44	14.0
Foreign–owned	31	12.9
Consumer goods	40	12.2
Industrial goods	35	15.0
Small firms	35	13.3
Medium firms	23	14.5
Large firms	16	12.7
Owner–managed	42	15.7
Professionally–managed	33	10.8
Heavy competition	16	10.4
Moderate competition	30	12.7
Light competition	20	17.7

manufacturers in Peru are not substantially disproportionate to those in the United States.

The frequency distribution for levels of profitability shows that 47 percent of the respondents claimed they earned 0 to 10 percent on invested capital after taxes; another 25 percent stated earnings as being between 11 to 20 percent. A few firms reported rates of return above 30 percent, and two firms enjoyed more than a 70 percent return.

Nationality of ownership and firm size did not appear to have a major effect on profitability. Industrial goods producers earned a somewhat higher return than consumer goods producers, but the difference was only 2.8 percent.

One surprising result is that owner-managed companies earned a 45 percent higher rate of return than did the professionally managed firms (15.7 percent versus 10.8 percent). Several hypotheses can be offered to explain this: 1) the greater competition faced by the professional managers holds their profits down; 2) professional managers may not have felt as free to tell the truth about rate of return as did the owner-managers; 3) professional managers by taking advantage of accelerated depreciation and similar opportunities were able to keep their "book" profits lower for tax reasons; and 4) the owners may have taken small salaries for their management services, preferring to be compensated through capital gains.

Although it was expected, one of the most interesting results is the inverse correlation between profitability and the degree of competition. The most profitable firms (17.7 percent return) faced the least competition, while the least profitable firms (10.4 percent return) faced the most competition.

Sales Success

Because of the doubtful reliability of the profitability data, we wanted to use an additional measure of marketing success. Since the traditional objective of marketing management has been sales, and because profits cannot be achieved without sales, sales were utilized as a success indicator. This had an advantage over profitability because respondents were more willing to give sales information, probably were more honest about it, and because sales volume is relatively easy to measure accurately.

The absolute level of sales is to a great extent the measure of customers won in the past and held in the present. The rapidity with which the firm has been able to expand its clientele, as well as develop existing clientele, can be measured by the percentage growth in sales over a specific period of time. The authors chose to combine sales strength (volume) with sales growth (percentage growth in past five years) into a single index of sales success.

The sales success index was arrived at by awarding each respondent points for sales volume and percentage growth over the past five years as follows:

Sales Volume

Less than 26.8 million soles = 1 point
26.8 − 150 million soles = 2 points
Above 150 million soles = 3 points

Sales Growth (past five years)

Less than 50 percent = 1 point
50–100 percent = 2 points
Over 100 percent = 3 points

The range of point scores was 2 through 6 points. Firms scoring 6 points were rated as the most successful. Because we have used the 5-point scale often during the discussion, the sales success index was adjusted downward to 1 through 5 points by subtracting one from each company's index.

The sales success indexes of the various categories of firms are shown in Table 12-7. Probably the most striking aspect of the table is the closeness of the average sales indexes among the various categories of firms. Given the size of the sample, most of the differences that do exist are not statistically significant.

In terms of sales success, foreign-owned firms were somewhat more successful than their Peruvian counterparts. This would be expected because an international corporation would not be likely to consider an investment in Peru unless the potential sales volume was fairly large.

Industrial goods manufacturers had a greater degree of sales success than consumer goods manufacturers, in spite of the rather small market for industrial goods in Peru. The explanation may lie in the fact that industrial goods producers in Peru are "younger" than consumer goods producers. Percentage growth of sales is likely to be greater in the early years of a company, because the base used to compute the percentage gain is very small. In fact, 41 percent of the industrial goods firms responding had grown over 100 percent in the past five years. Only 14 percent of the consumer goods manufacturers enjoyed similar rates of growth.

The type of management did not result in very large differences in sales success. Firms with light competition had greater success, as measured by the sales index, than firms with more competition. Because size was a component of the sales index, a cross-tabulation was not made between the success index and firm size.

Marketing Aggressiveness

Each firm's marketing aggressiveness was also rated. At first an attempt was made to compute an index based on quantifiable factors such as percentage of sales spent on advertising, number of salesmen, training offered salesmen, and number of employees employed in service activities. This proved to be more misleading than informative, because each firm's activities were organized differently. For instance, manufacturer A might have no salesmen and manufacturer B might have many. However, the reason for A's not having salesmen could be that he preferred to sell through an aggressive distributor who provided the personal selling.

Abandoning the idea of a quantitative index of many factors, we decided to make a subjective evaluation of the marketing aggressiveness of each firm. Three classes of marketing aggressiveness were defined:

Classification	Marketing Aggressiveness Index Points
Very marketing-oriented, highly aggressive	3
Somewhat marketing-oriented, moderately aggressive	2
Not very marketing-oriented, not very aggressive	1

Admittedly, the index is based on the interviewers' subjective evaluation of each firm. However, it proved to be relatively easy to classify firms into one of the three categories. Table 12-8 shows some fairly wide variations in aggressiveness and marketing orientation among the different firm classifications. Foreign-owned, consumer goods, and professionally managed firms showed an above-average marketing aggressiveness. Larger firms, however, were more aggressive than small firms. Competition appears to have some effect on marketing aggressiveness — greater competition forces a greater marketing orientation and more aggressiveness. However, the competition variable is subject to the greatest potential distortion because of intercorrelations, a fact that may reduce the significance of differences within this category.

*Profitability and
Marketing Aggressiveness*

Return on investment was cross-classified with marketing aggressiveness to determine if any relationship existed between the two variables. Those firms with the lowest marketing aggressiveness rating (1) had an average reported return on investment (ROI) of 12.7 percent. The firms with a median marketing aggressiveness rating (2) enjoyed a 13.1 percent ROI. The companies with the highest marketing aggressiveness rating (3) had a 14.8 percent return. Therefore, profitability and marketing aggressiveness were positively related.

Table 12-7

Sales Success Index

Classification	Number of Firms Reporting	Average Index
All firms	86	2.7
Peruvian–owned	52	2.5
Foreign–owned	34	2.9
Consumer goods	46	2.5
Industrial goods	40	2.8
Owner–managed	50	2.7
Professionally–managed	36	2.6
Heavy competition	19	2.6
Moderate competition	33	2.4
Light competition	25	2.9

Table 12-8

Marketing Aggressiveness Index

Classification	Average Index Score
Total firms	1.8
Peruvian–owned	1.6
Foreign–owned	2.1
Consumer goods	1.9
Industrial goods	1.6
Small	1.5
Medium	2.0
Large	2.0
Owner–managed	1.6
Professionally–managed	2.0
Heavy competition	1.9
Moderate competition	1.8
Light competition	1.6

Because of widely differing returns among the ten industries studied, the positive relationship could be due to industry differences rather than differences in marketing aggressiveness. To adjust for industry differences, percentage deviations in profits among the marketing aggressiveness groups of each industry were calculated. These deviations were then added and averaged, the result being a calculation of average deviations in ROI by marketing aggressiveness groups with the impact of industry differences removed.

Those firms with a marketing aggressiveness rating of 1 had average profits which were 10.6 percent less than those of their industry. More aggressive firms with a rating of 2 had an average ROI which was .6 percent above the industry average. The most aggressive firms (a rating of 3) had an ROI average 16.8 percent above the industry average.

Similar calculations were made for competitive groups. It was found that the ROI of marketing aggressiveness 1 firms averaged 4.6 percent less than the group average for firms facing the same degree of competition. Marketing aggressiveness 2 firms were 5 percent below the industry average, while marketing aggressiveness 3 firms enjoyed profits 17.4 percent above the average for their competitive group.

In summary, profits were positively related to marketing aggressiveness, especially when differences in profitability among industries were considered.

13 Synopsis: Marketing Strategies and Practices in Peru

Because the foregoing chapters have contained a great amount of data about a diverse number of subjects, it is appropriate at this point to highlight the major findings of the study. One major study objective was to describe, with an empirical base, the conduct of marketing in Peru. Thus the first part of this chapter focuses on marketing practices in Peru, relating these to the influence of general social, economic, and political variables. Where appropriate these practices are evaluated as to their implications for the economic development of Peru as well as their meaning to the marketers themselves. The latter part of the chapter deals with several specific variables (nationality of ownership, types of management, and the like) that were hypothesized to influence marketing practices in Peru.

The Practice of Marketing in Peruvian Manufacturing

In keeping with the earlier format, this synopsis of marketing practices is presented by functional classification.

Marketing Organization

On almost any terms, the marketing organizations of many firms were primitive. Specific marketing responsibility had not been delegated in more than half. Among these, the general manager performed the most necessary marketing functions, such as specifying price and credit policies, while other functions, such as marketing research and forecasting, were ignored. Foreign-owned firms and those firms producing consumer goods were more likely to have marketing responsibilities assigned to a specific department than were Peruvian-owned firms and industrial goods producers.

The amount of marketing technology present in a firm can be measured, to an extent, by the development of its marketing organization. Each firm was therefore placed in a marketing development stage essentially based upon the amount of marketing specialization in the firm. Five stages of marketing organization development were used. These generally parallel the historical evolution of marketing organizations in the United States. Foreign-owned firms and consumer goods producers were found to have more advanced organizations than Peruvian-owned firms and industrial goods producers. Likewise, professionally managed firms and larger firms were more advanced than owner-managed and smaller firms. Some degree of intercorrelation certainly exists here because professionally managed firms and larger firms were more likely than their counterparts to be foreign-owned. On the other hand, foreign ownership was more common among industrial goods producers than among consumer goods producers, which had relatively advanced marketing organizations.

Two considerations appear relevant in the explanation of this anomaly. In the first place, the consumer goods manufacturers included in our sample were generally among the larger and more well-established firms; in hundreds of the smaller firms which operate in the consumer goods sector (which would include a good many artisan-type workshops) the situation would be quite different and the level of marketing organization much more rudimentary. Second, when contrasted with the situation of the consumer goods producers, the market for domestically manufactured producer goods is of relatively more recent origin, and for the most part far smaller (in terms of the total potential number of customers and the number of units of goods produced and sold). It tends to be even more geographically concentrated and less complex in the sense that cultural heterogeneity and cultural factors in general probably play a much smaller role in the buying decisions of industrial goods purchasers than they do in the market for consumer goods. Accordingly, producers of industrial goods can make do with a less differentiated marketing organization than can the larger consumer goods producers, at least at the present stage of development.

Another aspect of the findings regarding the level of development of marketing organization and marketing technology bears explicit comment. In observing that marketing organizations were generally primitive in Peru, we do not mean to suggest that matters would necessarily be greatly different for firms *of comparable size* in the United States — or elsewhere, for that matter. It must be remembered that even the larger Peruvian manufacturing enterprises would be small or, at best, medium-sized producers in the United States, and we should not want to imply that among these latter the level of marketing organization is generally quite advanced. We suspect this is not the case.[1] Nevertheless, the firms included in our study may be taken as fairly representative of the *leading* manufacturing concerns in Peru; and if the leading firms of the country operate as our study seems to indicate, an important social judgment is raised concerning the adequacy of their performance for national development requirements. In other words, can a country like Peru afford to have its leading industrial producers behave as casually as many of them do regarding efficiency levels in the marketing process? A number of factors may be advanced to explain the current level of performance: managerial inexperience, a critical shortage of trained and specialized marketing cadres, the rudimentary state of market information (and information-gathering channels), protection from external competition through national trade policies and protection from aggressive internal competition (in several of the industries studied — eg. food, drug, household goods, construction — there is a strong suspicion that market-sharing and price-rigging arrangements are operative).

Marketing Research

The objective need for marketing research in a market such as that of Peru which has been relatively unexplored would appear to be great, yet Peruvian manufacturing firms do not consider it very important. Only 62 percent of the firms interviewed reported conducting marketing research, and the great majority of this "research" consisted of informal observation by top management. Most of the specific marketing research projects undertaken were of a very elementary nature.

Consumer goods producers and foreign-owned firms were more likely than industrial goods producers and Peruvian-owned firms to conduct marketing research. In the case of the industrial goods producers, the characteristics of the market would probably explain the relative lack of research, just as they explain the less sophisticated marketing organization which prevailed among these firms.

A number of circumstances seemed to account for the pervasive neglect of (or even disinterest in) marketing research, one of which was the paucity of market information from secondary sources, a feature which implied that a great deal of marketing research would have required an expensive confrontation with the complexities of primary data collection. Also, as continuous increases in the price level suggest, there was a general condition of excess demand in the market which forgave marketing errors and permitted firms to grow even when marketing management was desultory. Finally, the process of import displacement — a policy increasingly favored by governmental authorities — permitted data on the composition of imports to substitute, at least partially, for other elements of marketing research. Thus, to some extent firms were dealing with a captive market protected from external competition and, as noted previously, sometimes protected as well by collusive agreements from sharp domestic competition.

We also derived a very distinct impression that the prevailing perception among the firms is that they are dealing with a known and quite circumscribed market demand, one which is comparatively static over the short run and subject to expansion over the longer run, chiefly as a function of population growth, increasing urbanization, and a general rise in income levels. Much less frequently was any awareness detected that the size of the market for particular products could be partially a function of the marketing behavior of the firms themselves, including their widespread disregard of marketing research.

Product Activities

Very little original product development is conducted in Peru. Although almost all firms had introduced new products at some time in their history, more than half had done so during the year preceding the study and new products tended to be copies of those made in more developed countries. Because this approach allows Peru to increase its product technology rapidly at relatively little expense, it might seem appropriate that Peruvian manufacturers should concentrate on product imitation at this stage of the country's development. In general, product planning was viewed as a function of production management — a practice which tended to reinforce the essentially imitative character of product introduction and which stemmed in part from the fact that trained engineers were more readily available in Peru than were trained marketing specialists. Indeed, it was not uncommon to find engineer training being employed as a substitute for specialized training in a number of other fields such as economics and management, just as accounting training has occasionally functioned in this surrogate capacity.

Even though producers introducing new products complained that major problems of new product introduction were "strong competition" and that "traditional consumers are slow to adopt new ideas," little evidence was found to support them in these assertions. Competition, whether external or domestic, often did not appear to be so strong as was claimed (for reasons noted previously), although for a number of products, such as textiles, the situation may be changing. Moreover, many firms apparently did little to induce their customers to adopt new ideas, much less engage in research to ascertain what alternative product preferences might exist. On the contrary, the excess demand for many goods resulted in situations in which producers were able to dispose of their output — on a "take it or leave it" basis so far as concerned their captive-market clientele — with little marketing effort and scant regard for product inferiority and inappropriateness for consumer needs. The sacrifice of consumer welfare (in the form of unmet or poorly met needs and preferences) resulting from this practice is especially great considering the low income levels and resource scarcities which prevail in Peru. In this connection, some limited Peruvian experience would even seem to belie the supposed resistance of consumers to new products; witness the popularity of cheap (less than $1 a pair) plastic shoes or the prevalence in rural areas of sandals made from old tire casings. While plastic shoes may be expensive in the long run because they wear out more quickly than leather shoes, they have found considerable acceptance among lower-income consumers who seldom have, at any one time, the money for purchasing the higher priced leather footwear. Such examples of product adaptation, however, are less frequent than one might expect to find were manufacturers more concerned with seeking a mass market for their products.

It may also be noted that the rather widespread failure to develop products more adapted to the particular conditions of the Peruvian market involves the sacrifice of a potential competitive advantage *vis à vis* imported products. In recent years, for example, there has been a growing concern in the United States that export goods designed for the affluent home market may not be particularly well adapted to overseas market preferences and requirements. From the perspective of manufacturers in less developed countries, the predicament of United States exporters implies the possible existence of an area of competitive advantage which local manufacturers could exploit by developing products better adapted to local needs than are goods imported from — and designed primarily for — the more industrially advanced and wealthy nations. The point is germane to the production and marketing of both consumer goods and producer goods. Lacking this genuine element of competitive advantage, which also works to enhance consumer welfare, Peruvian industry would necessarily have to continue to rely on artificial restraints of trade as a major support for its operations. Moreover, if Peruvian manufacturers hope to find future success in exporting manufactures to other Latin American countries or elsewhere, product adaptation based on original market research would seem essential as a replacement for the present, somewhat *dolce far niente,* approach to these matters.

Service

Service was categorized by the authors as either presale (directly related to making the sale) or postsale (designed to keep customers content so that they will make repeat purchases). Slightly less than two-thirds of the firms interviewed stated that they provided presale product service to their customers, although, as with marketing research, what the firms regarded as service was often minimal. Foreign-owned firms and firms producing industrial goods were more likely to provide presale service than Peruvian-owned firms and consumer goods producers were. Presale service usually consisted of consultations concerning buyer's needs, and on the average, firms reported employing about six people for this work out of more than 250 employees.

Postsale service, on the other hand, was offered by only 54 percent of the firms. Again, foreign-owned firms and industrial goods producers were more likely to offer postsale service than were Peruvian-owned and consumer goods producing firms. These firms also employed about six people for the service. In a number of cases the same people supplied both presale and postsale service.

This inadequate service was likely due to a lack of concern with customer satisfaction and to the difficulty of obtaining qualified personnel to perform the service, given the low educational level of the country. Very few firms, however, appeared willing to provide the training and education necessary to develop qualified service personnel. In the case of the consumer goods industries, this may be a comparatively minor shortcoming, although even here a more concerted effort to provide postsale servicing might well be a vital component of any serious campaign to develop wider provincial markets for consumer durables. In the marketing of industrial goods, the matter is of much greater social importance, particularly as presale and postsale servicing are related to sales promotion and selling — for reasons which will be set forth below.

Advertising and Sales Promotion

Over two-thirds of the firms reported advertising in the year prior to the interview. Foreign-owned, professionally-managed firms and consumer goods producers were more active here than Peruvian-owned, owner-managed firms and industrial goods producers. Neither size of firm nor amount of competition, however, appeared to have a great influence on whether a firm advertised.

Attitudes toward advertising did not correlate with advertising behavior as closely as might be expected. Several firms that did not advertise nevertheless believed that advertising was important to the sale of their products. This can be traced to such factors as government taxation based on advertising volume (beer industry), the inability of marketing managers to convince general managers of the need for advertising, and the lack of suitable media for some products. Where excess demand gives rise to a strong seller's market, the felt need to advertise is undoubtedly weakened.

Firms interviewed spent an average of 1.8 percent of sales on advertising. Considering only the firms that advertised during the previous year, the percentage was 2.7. Of this group, Peruvian-owned and foreign-owned firms estimated exactly the same advertising percentages, and consumer goods producers and small firms reported spending a larger percent of sales on advertising than did their counterparts. As might be expected, the lower the purchase value of the product advertised, the larger the percentage of sales spent on such promotion.

The pharmaceutical industry, much as in the United States, had the largest percentage of sales used for advertising. The other industrial products group, encompassing heavy industry and those firms which did not seem to fit in the other industrial product categories, had the lowest percentage of sales for advertising. Less than half of all firms in all industries reported using an advertising agency.

On the average, Peruvian-owned firms made greater use of traditional Latin American advertising media, such as cinema and outdoor media, than did foreign-owned firms. Newspapers were used more than any other media, but television was the fastest growing in terms of advertising volume. Some advertisers complained about the lack of high quality media. Indications were that this complaint, particularly outside the Lima-Callao metropolitan area, was justified. Media were being improved in the *departamentos,* but not fast enough to satisfy advertisers. On the other hand, there was little evidence that much of a creative or imaginative character was being done to take full advantage of such promotional and communications possibilities as are afforded in the extensive network of provincial markets.

In connection with the pervasive lack of market research and the general tendency to concentrate marketing efforts on the more accessible markets of the coastal zone, especially the Lima-Callao metropolitan area, this inadequacy of provincial advertising media may partially explain another feature observed in the Peruvian marketing scene. Thus far only very slight attention has been devoted to using promotion to develop markets for manufactured consumer goods and producer goods in the highlands where the bulk of the population lives. While political parties have, in recent years, made considerable efforts to peddle their wares among the provincial population, private businesses have been much less active in this respect, and only a modest amount of attention has been given to the matter of communicating effectively with the non-Spanish-speaking population. As a result, there has been a failure on the part of the modern sector to supply the traditional sector with either an adequate range of incentive (i.e., consumer) goods or suitable types of producer goods, the introduction and utilization of which would contribute to higher levels of productivity and income among the farm population.

Another element which probably contributed to the shortcomings of marketing communications strategies derives from the joint operation of cultural dualism and the sharply drawn system of class stratification. Generally, major marketing decisions (and most other managerial decisions) are made by persons whose sociocultural background and frame of reference is distinctly urban and upper-middle or upper class. Among this group, firsthand knowledge of the life situation — the attitudes, preferences, job activities, and life style — of the provincial and rural populace seemed rather limited, or even distorted,[a] and convincing evidence could not be found indicating that the growing body of anthropological literature which deals with subordinated groups in Peruvian society had been studied (at least systematically and with any frequency) in an effort to bridge this gap in understanding.

For some products, especially luxury goods, the problems of marketing communication are not particularly severe. Since the upper-class consumers of these goods are cosmopolitan in orientation, such items may be advertised in the fashion of the more developed countries. And some adaptation of advertising has occurred in the marketing of goods among urban middle-class consumers as well as among lower-class consumers who often seek to be identified with the middle class and who share the so-called *criollo* outlook. A soft drink manufacturer, for example, advertised his product as having a "Peruvian flavor" (*de sabor nacional*). In general, however, the cultural milieu does present complexities for designing effective promotional programs, even for urban markets, and it may have been this, at least in part, which discouraged firms from a greater use of advertising. Because of the lack of education, for example, it is often necessary to design advertising messages at a fairly low level; yet even then the advertiser is not certain his message is registering. In other instances, the locus of the buying decision is not clear; upper-class and upper-middle class households sometimes send their servants to shop for certain items so that point-of-sale advertising may be less appropriate than other media. The tendency of many Peruvians to view shopping as a social event involving discussion and bargaining with a variety of small shopkeepers and *ambulantes* adds further complications since particularistic, affective, and personalistic considerations may color purchasing decisions and reduce their instrumental or neutral character. The general lack of verified audits of readership (for printed media) and of reliable estimates of listeners and viewers (for radio and television) also inhibited the development of marketing communications strategies.

---

[a]One of the lasting benefits of the Cooperacion Popular Program, a national community development effort not unlike the Peace Corps, may be its role in familiarizing the educated youth of the coast with the highland ways of life. Never before has Peruvian industry been able to draw upon such a reservior of personnel so well acquainted with the highland markets.

Personal Selling

Seventy-nine percent of the firms employed salesmen. Foreign-owned firms, consumer goods producers and professionally managed firms employed a greater number than their counterparts. Firms with heavy competition used more salesmen than those with lighter competition, and the lower the typical value of purchase the more salesmen the firms had. The average firm employed ten salesmen.

With few exceptions, the firms did not provide their salesmen with good sales training, yet they complained of a lack of qualified salesmen. Thirty-one percent stated they gave their salesmen *no* training. Some firms desired to hire accomplished salesmen but were only willing to pay them beginning wages. In spite of this limited investment in sales training, however, personal selling was considered by the respondents to be more important to the success of their product than advertising.

Peru has established what appears to be an excellent, if still small-scale, training system (the *Servicio Nacional de Aprendizaje y Trabajo Industrial,* or SENATI) for blue-collar workers; we believe that such a center for sales training may well be in order, financed, perhaps, on the basis of a tax similar to that used in Great Britain's manpower training programs. Of the various professional associations found in Peru, ADV and IPAE had some good sales training facilities, but more were needed in view of manufacturers' stated needs for salesmen. Two considerations in particular suggested the desirability of greatly supplementing the limited in-company training programs with programs external to individual firms. In the first place, a good many firms were so small in terms of their total resources and had such a small sales force that they probably could not have justified setting up really adequate training facilities on an individual basis. Second, and this may be a factor of reckoning for large and small firms alike, the value of any substantial investment in company training programs must, from the firm's point of view, be weighed against the risks inherent in interfirm labor mobility in a market in which competent salesmen tend to be scarce — if not necessarily rewarded according to their scarcity value because of job-market imperfections.[b]

However understandable the low priority accorded in practice to investment in effective sales training procedures, the behavior of the firms in this regard seems questionable from a social perspective — and dubious from the perspective of long-range prospects for firm growth. For many types of goods, given the problems which exist in the marketing communications system, the tradeoff between advertising and personal selling may well be favorable to the latter, especially in the underdeveloped provincial markets. Consequently, as Peruvian industry begins to approach the domestic market saturation limit, marketing strategies, like personal selling, which might serve to relax the constraints of domestic market size by taking greater advantage of the latent provincial market potential should receive a higher priority than they apparently have. Considering, too, the difficulties which impede marketing research based on analysis of secondary data, the feedback effects of information transmitted to companies

[b]Among other things, the nature of Peruvian social legislation tends to reduce labor mobility, and though one would expect this to reduce the risks of a company's losing its investment in sales training, firms seems not to have reacted according to expectations. This suggests that sellers' market conditions may be the chief explanatory variable in the situation we are describing.

from their sales personnel in the field could conceivably function in an important way to improve the design of marketing programs.

National development requirements imply another value of efficacious sales training programs, particularly when these are taken in conjunction with educational advertising and the provision of service on a presale and postsale basis. Since economic development consists, in part, of effecting innovations in the production techniques of a wide range of industries and in thousands of firms, the promotion and sale of producer goods becomes, in economies which are not centrally planned, a function of vital importance: that of a change agent. As a means of disseminating innovations and providing technical assistance to client firms whose owners may be largely unaware of the potentially available production-technology alternatives, personal selling, sales promotion, and service take on many of the functional characteristics of a system of extension education. "Extension agents" of the private sector, the salesmen of industrial goods, are thus directly (through sales of their employer's output) and indirectly (through enhancing the income-earning capacity of their customers) contributing to the necessary amplification of the domestic market on which the momentum of industrial growth largely rests.

Channels of Distribution

Approximately one-fourth of the average manufacturer's sales were made to each of three types of customers: retailers, industrial buyers, and wholesalers. An additional 15 percent of sales went directly to the ultimate consumer and the balance was sold to other types of buyers, including the government.

Although wholesalers were important to some manufacturers, 77 percent of the manufacturers interviewed believed that their most important channel of distribution did not include a wholesaler. This belief can be attributed to three factors:

1. The 5 percent sales tax imposed by the government each time goods change hands (a factor which encourages vertical integration).
2. The relatively small and concentrated urban market, especially for industrial goods but for a number of consumer lines as well, which makes short channels of distribution more feasible than would otherwise be the case.
3. The lack of good, efficient full-line wholesalers willing to promote domestically produced goods. Many existing wholesalers, especially the larger ones, spend most of thier effort promoting imported lines. Some of these, again particularly the larger ones, also have ties through common ownership and/or interlocking directorates with local manufacturers (including some firms in which foreign capital participates), the distribution of whose output receives their major attention.

Peruvian-owned firms were more likely to exclude a wholesaler from their distribution system than foreign-owned firms were, but this may have been partly a function of their somewhat smaller average size. It was found, for instance, that larger consumer goods firms were generally less likely to bypass marketing intermediaries than were smaller consumer goods firms, and while this may have been to some extent attributable to their use of market power to obtain better service from middlemen, the larger Peruvian-owned consumer goods firms were also, in some instances, affiliated through common ownership or other business ties with important middleman enterprises. These connections may often have been a significant part of the explanation for the size of the larger Peruvian-owned firms. The former firms are most likely passing up the benefits of the wholesaler's specialization, and often would be well advised to establish a somewhat less direct channel of distribution. This would be especially true as domestic manufacturers attempt to reach out beyond the Lima-Callao metropolitan market to provincial areas and as sellers' market conditions diminish. On the other hand, since this relationship is a matter in which wholesalers might reasonably be expected to take some of the initiative, a fuller explanation of this situation awaits more detailed research on the structure and functioning of Peruvian wholesaling. Possibly wholesalers will seek out domestic suppliers more aggressively as import substitution industries accelerate their growth.

Thirty-nine percent of the firms interviewed had a legal (contractual) or economic (involving common ownership or interlocking directorates) relationship with a wholesaler, with a retailer, or with both types of middlemen. These relationships were also, for some firms, probably tied in with the reasons for selecting a particular middleman. While vertical integration carries certain benefits for the firms which are linked together, especially when the marketing intermediary is among the stronger or larger members of the group, it is at least possible that manufacturers not so directly affiliated with a large marketing intermediary firm might experience less satisfactory service in the distribution of their output. Thirty-six percent of the firms using middlemen replied that they sought middlemen with the best financial strength, which would depend on both the marketing intermediaries' internal resources and access to bank credit.

A somewhat surprising finding in this connection was the extent to which manufacturing firms provide credit to marketing intermediaries, a factor which would explain the importance assigned to the middleman's financial strength — through affecting the credit-worthiness of the middlemen-borrowers and the likelihood of the middleman's making demands upon the manufacturer for credit. Backward financing (i.e., the extension of credit by wholesalers or retailers to manufacturers) was not as important as had been expected considering experience reported for other less developed countries. But it is possible that backward financing would have been more in evidence had we covered firms smaller than those included in the sample.[c] Thirty-one percent also said they look for the best merchants, but exactly what they meant by this was not always clear. While it could have referred to such aspects as the

[c] A number of writers have suggested that this indirect channeling of commercial credit into production may constitute an important source of funds for small manufacturers.

geographical coverage of the middleman's operations, middleman services, the prestige or reputation for probity of the intermediary, his aggressiveness in sales promotion, and so on, the impression given was that such factors were generally not evaluated in any consistent fashion.

On the average, firms were only moderately satisfied with their middlemen. They appeared not to have systematically studied alternatives in the channels of distribution, and therefore may not have been either minimizing opportunity costs in distributing their products or putting themselves in touch with the largest number of potential consumers. That the situation seems to be so generally satisfactory to the manufacturers involved is probably attributable, as are so many other aspects of marketing behavior, to the prevalence of a sellers' market and to preoccupation with exploiting the possibilities of the most accessible and affluent markets of the country. At the same time, however, it must be observed that such an undynamic approach to the question of selecting channels of distribution does not do much for incorporating provincial regions into a well-integrated national market system. This interpretation would seem to be confirmed by our findings on the subject of physical distribution.

Physical Distribution

Nearly half the firms reported that their sales were limited to a single geographical area, usually the Lima-Callao metropolitan area. This area is the only market of any size because it is the easiest to reach (in making sales and deliveries), and because many transportation problems are inherent in selling to the rest of the country. Organizational problems such as the maintenance of satisfactory communication and the management of accounts receivable also deter firms from extending their operations geographically, but a more aggressive development of markets in outlying regions is generally not thought to be worth the effort.

Firms were asked to estimate the number of days of inventory they had. The average firm reported 48 days of inventory; if this is accurate, it means a stock turnover of more than seven times per year — rather high by the standards of developed countries. This may be a reflection of the capital shortage and concentrated market in Peru, but it could also suggest that much of the inventory-carrying function is shifted to other units in the chain of distribution to marketing firms which perhaps enjoy superior access to bank credit, or which can extract credit for such a purpose from manufacturers. Indirectly, in other words, manufacturers may be financing larger inventories through the financing they provide to market intermediaries.

Pricing

Imports, of course, generally set an upper limit on prices. Sherbini's observation that once prices are set they tend to become rigid is to some extent borne out by this study, although obvious allowance must be made for general upward movement of the price (and cost) level. Most pricing was done on a cost-plus basis, with prices of competitors and tariff protection also being considered by some of the firms.

It was interesting that some respondents actually laughed when asked if they considered what the consumer is willing to pay in determining prices. Other firms stated that they do this as a matter of course. Nonetheless it was apparent that cost was by far the most important factor in price determination. In spite of the casual traveler's impression that there is no such thing as a fixed price in Latin America, the study indicated that prices were relatively fixed at the manufacturer's level. Many firms did negotiate prices, but the practice was not as prevalent as one might have expected.

As one measure of competition, respondents were asked to estimate the level of price competition. On the five-point scale from "of great importance" (5) to "of little importance" (1), the average firms chose near to the 3-point level, "moderate." Indications were that price competition in the past was very low. Responses to this question, then, suggest that price competition was increasing over what it once was, but was still only moderate. At the same time, however, in a number of instances imports (and hence the prices of imports) were included in the reference group of competitors; in these cases, tariff readjustment or import restrictions probably can be relied upon to reduce the pressure of price competition.

The interviews also provided little evidence of an awareness of the price elasticity of demand concept. Very few firms considered that their sales and profits might have increased if they had lowered prices; it was rare to find firms which employed developmental or penetration pricing as a means of cultivating wider markets through tapping the purchasing power of lower-income regions and classes. In this, of course, pricing behavior was consistent with the general pattern of performance in other aspects of the marketing process and shared the implications of those other practices with respect to both assumptions and consequences.

The foregoing, for instance, can probably be traced largely to insufficient supply relative to demand, to oligopoloid market structures and collusive practices, to the psychological and other effects of perennial inflation, and to management perception of the limited size and potential of the Peruvian market. Firms have continually had to do something to cover rising costs, and it has been easier to raise prices than to lower or maintain prices and increase sales.

Overall, firms reported their gross margins to be 30 percent. This is not very high compared to that obtained in the United States. There is reason to believe, however, that some firms understated their margins because of the fear of government control over prices, or to deter the drawing of inferences regarding profitability. Only 14 percent of the firms reported a gross margin of 41 to 50 percent, and only 9 percent reported a gross margin of over 50 percent.

Ten percent of the respondents mentioned government price controls as a pricing problem. The belief that if prices had become too high in the opinion of the government, controls would have been applied, was more a factor in the drug industry than elsewhere.

Overall Marketing Strategy

A measure of the relative importance of the major marketing strategy variables was obtained by asking respondents to allocate 100 points among the areas of product efforts, sales efforts, distribution, and pricing strategy, according to their relative importance for the product being studied.

Ostensibly, manufacturers in Peru feel that pricing is of greater importance and product efforts of less importance than do manufacturers in the United States. The product research and development orientation of United States industry is well known, and it was not surprising that firms in Peru were less oriented in this direction.

Some of the outstanding differences in respondents' allocations of points representing the importance of the four strategy variables are:

1. Peruvian-owned firms attached greater importance to price (in the sense indicated above) and product, while foreign-owned firms attached greater importance to sales efforts. The importance accorded product variables, however, probably refers less to product development and adaptation (product differentiation) than to efforts to convince skeptical consumers that Peruvian-made goods are not inferior in quality to imported goods.
2. Consumer goods producers weighted sales efforts and distribution most heavily, while industrial goods producers gave greater relative weight to product efforts and pricing.
3. Allocations among owner-managed and professionally-managed firms did not show large differences, although the former were slightly above average in their allocations for pricing and product efforts.
4. Firms facing heavy competition tended to emphasize promotion and pricing in their overall strategy; firms facing light competition emphasized product efforts far above all other strategy variables.

Marketing Success and Aggressiveness

The reported after-tax net profit for all firms was equal to 13.5 percent of invested capital, a rate of return not substantially different from the effective interest rate on bank loans to prime private sector borrowers in the Peruvian money market. This return on investment, as expected, showed a strong inverse relationship to the degree of competition, but in general it was not nearly so high as is often asserted to be the case for profit rates in underdeveloped countries. One reason probably lies in biased responses: i.e., the understandable reluctance of firms to report their true rate of earnings. On the other hand, the prevailing high prices on goods sold in Peru may not be very closely correlated with high returns on invested capital, even considering the substantial imperfections in the market, because of inefficiency and a high level of costs.

Summary and Evaluation

At this point it seems reasonable to evaluate the study results from the viewpoint of the businessman operating in the environment of a developing country. What do the results mean to him? We have tried to avoid the implication that marketing strategies and practices not conforming to those in the United States are undesirable in the Peruvian environment.[d] Certainly many marketing practices followed in Peru represent reasonable attempts to adapt to market needs.

There are, however, some indications that businessmen in Peru have reason to alter their current approach to marketing. One of the more interesting results of the study came from a cross-tabulation of marketing aggressiveness and profitability. Aggressive marketing firms enjoyed an average return on investment that was 17 percent *above* their industry average; those firms that were not very marketing oriented and not very aggressive had an average return on investment that was 11 percent *below* their industry average. This spread would suggest that there are substantial rewards for the businessman who shows an above-average interest in his marketing program.

Specific examples of how better marketing could affect a firm's profitability are not difficult to find. The investment in the fertilizer plant that was mentioned in an earlier chapter represents an expensive mistake made because of inadequate market study and distribution planning. The high selling costs mentioned by many firms, resulting from a high turnover of salesmen, could be lowered with adequate salesmen training. Firms producing equipment for the fishing industry saw their markets fall sharply without new customers to replace them. Market evaluation and related product development could have predicted and prepared them for the sales decline.

The marketing strategies and practices used in Peru must, of course, be adapted to the environment. Without dealing in specific strategies, however, one would judge that a basic change in attitude toward marketing by managers in Peru would be in their own self-interest. The businessman who can design and implement efficient marketing programs can:

1. Expand his market size by capturing customers from his less marketing-oriented competition,
2. Expand the total market for his product through previously untapped market segments,

[d]In fact, many of the practices discussed in this study closely parallel those of similar manufacturers in the United States.

3. Strengthen his political position by displaying his capacity to effectively satisfy the demands of consumers,

4. Build up marketing skills to compete more effectively in foreign markets as trade barriers are lowered, and

5. Increase the profitability of his present markets by developing more efficient techniques for satisfying consumer demands.

Marketing changes will occur in Peru. Undoubtedly, many Peruvians will soon be bringing newly acquired specialized competence in business matters to bear in the business community, for the dearth of trained personnel in the managerial field suggests opportunities for fairly rapid upward mobility in management for those young men and women who possess the skills necessary for sustaining business expansion. While management skills will surely be, as they have been, a continuing factor in the assignment of managerial roles, no one supposes that particularistic considerations of class and family will rapidly lose their significance. The point to be kept in mind, however, is that the present thrust of Peruvian educational development provides greater possibilities than have existed heretofore for effecting at least a measure of reconciliation between the traditional basis of role assignment and a more instrumentally oriented basis of recruitment on criteria of achievement or technical competence. Consequently, as newer managers arise, bringing with them a more professional type of preparation and orientation, it seems safe to assume that there will gradually be a progressive modification of the kind of marketing behavior depicted herein. To the extent that this occurs the present study may serve as a baseline from which the evolution of Peruvian marketing behavior may later be traded.

The Influence of Product, Firm, and Market Variables on Marketing Strategy

This section will relate the study results to the hypotheses stated in Chapter 1. In the few industries within which firms had very similar products, such as the pharmaceutical industry, there was some slight but not very clearcut evidence that marketing strategies fell into similar patterns. Even in the narrowly defined industries, however, dissimilarities were found. Other variables, such as firm size and marketing technology, seem to offset the superficial similarity of firm strategies within the same industry in Peru. This study does not indicate that firms within a given economic, political, and social environment have similar marketing strategies.

Nationality of Ownership Variable

Considering a number of the findings, it is clear that foreign-owned firms were generally more aggressive in their marketing efforts than were Peruvian-owned firms. Moreover, for questions asked during the interviews regarding marketing technology and aggressiveness, the nationality of ownership variable showed, in cross-tabulations, some of the widest variations in answers. The differences revealed by these variations tended, on the whole, to support the conclusion that foreign-owned firms employed a more advanced marketing technology than did Peruvian-owned firms. Some of the pertinent findings are:

1. Foreign-owned firms tended to delegate marketing responsibility more often than did Peruvian-owned firms.
2. Foreign-owned firms were much more likely to conduct marketing research.
3. Foreign-owned firms were more likely to engage in both presale and postsale service and to employ more personnel in this work.
4. Foreign-owned firms were more likely to use advertising, advertising agencies, and cooperative advertising.
5. Foreign-owned firms were more likely to have sales training programs and to recognize problems in personal selling; they were less likely to rely on commission-only compensation plans.
6. Foreign-owned firms were more likely to utilize a greater number of channels of distribution, to have formal ties with their middlemen, and to offer dealer services.
7. Foreign-owned firms were somewhat more likely to consider factors other than costs in establishing their prices.

The question on overall marketing strategy suggests that foreign-owned firms are also more cognizant of the benefits of adequate sales efforts than are Peruvian-owned firms — or at least that the former give greater relative weight to sales efforts.

Type of Management Variable

Marketing aggressiveness also appeared to be greater among the professionally managed firms (nonowner-managed) than among the owner-managed firms. Because the type of management variable was subject to an above-average amount of intercorrelation with other comparison variables, there is the possibility that its influence may have been somewhat exaggerated. Yet a review of the many questions connected with marketing aggressiveness and technology indicates that the type of management variable may have had an influence somewhat above the average for all comparison variables. These apparent influences support the view that professionally managed firms tended to employ a more advanced marketing technology and to display more marketing aggressiveness than owner-managed firms. Some of the more interesting results are:

1. Professionally managed firms were more likely to have an advanced marketing organization than were owner-managed firms.
2. Professionally managed firms were likely to employ more presale and postsale servicemen.
3. Professionally managed firms had a more positive attitude toward advertising's importance and made greater use of advertising.
4. Professionally managed firms were somewhat more likely to conduct sales training programs.

Size of Firm Variable

The difference in marketing aggressiveness between the small and large firms was greater than that for any other comparison variable. This difference supports the view that firms with high sales volumes tended to employ more advanced marketing technologies and to be more aggressive in their marketing than firms with low sales volumes, especially because size was subject to less inter-correlation than all other comparison variables.

Some of the more interesting revelations of the cross tabulations are:

1. Small firms definitely tended to have the most primitive marketing organizations; medium-sized firms showed the greatest tendency to have rather highly advanced marketing organizations.
2. Large firms were more likely to conduct almost all types of marketing research; medium-sized firms were generally closer to the large than the small firms in this tendency; small firms were least likely to conduct marketing research.
3. Large firms employed, on the average, a greater number of personnel in both presale and postsale service.
4. Large firms tended to rate advertising as being more important than did other firms, but they did *not* make greater use of advertising.
6. Small firms spent the greatest percentage of sales on advertising, and large firms spent the least.
6. Large firms tended to have somewhat more organized sales training programs than did the small firms.
7. Large firms were more likely to offer dealer services.
8. Large firms tended to operate on lower gross margins than did small and medium-sized firms.
9. Size did not seem to have a great influence on the number of salesmen employed by the respondents.
10. Large firms tended to use fewer discounts than other firms, although they made greater use of the volume discount.

The findings reveal the selective influence of size on marketing aggressiveness and technology. Because the data represent a greater portion of the study findings than the single evaluation of marketing aggressiveness does, we weighted them more heavily in our judgments. Thus, while overall the evidence supports the hypothesis that large firms are more aggressive and employ more advanced marketing technologies than smaller firms, the qualification must be made that size is apparently fairly selective in its influence on marketing strategy.

Type of Industry Variable

Consumer goods producers were, in general, more aggressive in their marketing efforts than were industrial goods producers. The type of industry variable was less subject to the influence of intercorrelations than were many other variables. Thus an assessment of firms' marketing aggressiveness supports the hypothesis that consumer goods producers tend to employ a more advanced marketing technology and to be more aggressive in their marketing than do industrial goods producers.

Cross-tabulations of responses to several pertinent questions, in fact, suggested that the type of industry was perhaps the most influential variable in determining marketing strategy, and the variable's influence was generally in a direction that would tend to support the hypothesis. Again, the relatively low intercorrelation of other variables with this one suggests that study findings related to type of industry were especially significant. Some of the pertinent findings are:

1. The marketing organizations of consumer goods producers were significantly more advanced than those of industrial goods producers.
2. Consumer goods producers were slightly more likely to conduct sales and market analyses; consumer goods firms were almost twice as likely to conduct product tests, consumer surveys, advertising research, packaging tests, and psychological tests.
3. Consumer goods producers seemed to have the greatest recognition of the full implications of product planning.
4. Consumer goods producers showed an above-average tendency to have introduced new products within the year preceding the study.
5. Consumer goods producers were well above average in their rating of advertising's importance, in their usage of advertising, and in the percentage of sales spent on advertising.
6. Consumer goods producers employed, on the average, almost three times as many salesmen as did industrial goods producers; they also were much more likely to provide training programs for their salesmen.
7. Consumer goods producers generally showed an above-average tendency to offer dealer services.

8. Price elasticity of demand was considered more frequently by consumer goods firms.

9. Consumer goods producers were less likely to provide presale and postsale service.

10. Consumer goods producers employed higher margins.

11. Consumer goods producers were less likely to negotiate prices.

At the same time, however, it must be observed that the varying marketing strategies of consumer and industrial goods producers most often appear to be a reflection of the varying characteristics of the consumer and industrial markets as these are now constituted in Peru.

Market Competition Variable

Competition was the comparison variable subject to the greatest intercorrelation with other variables; this would tend to exaggerate or perhaps confuse differences. Even so, we rated firms facing heavy competition as being only 10 percent more aggressive than firms facing light competition. This was one of the lowest differentials registered within a comparison variable category. This higher aggressiveness rating for firms facing heavy competition tends to support the hypothesis that such firms employ a more advanced marketing technology and are more aggressive in their marketing than firms facing light competition – but the support is rather weak.

A review of questionnaire responses also suggests that competition was not strongly related to marketing aggressiveness and technology. Some of the more important cross-tabulations showed the apparent varying influence of competition:

1. Firms facing the heaviest competition were more likely to conduct the various types of marketing research.

2. Heavy competition apparently encouraged substantially more frequent use of salesmen, as well as the use of a greater number of salesmen.

3. Heavy competition encouraged the use of sales training programs.

4. Heavy competition seemed to encourage the offering of dealer services.

5. Heavy competition encouraged the consideration of factors other than costs in setting prices. That is, competitors' prices and what the consumer is willing to pay were more often considered when competition was heavy.

6. Competition had little or no influence on the number of personnel employed in presale service; it was somewhat related to the number of postsale service personnel.

7. Attitudes toward and use of advertising were not related to the degree of competition; the percentage of sales spent on advertising showed no clear relation to the amount of competition.

8. Gross margins were inversely related to the degree of competition.

Respondents who faced heavy competition felt that sales efforts and pricing were of the greatest relative importance in their overall marketing strategy. We felt that these two strategy variables connote marketing aggressiveness somewhat more strongly than product efforts and distribution do. If this is so, responses to this question seem to support the hypothesis. In general, however, we believe that study findings offer less support for this hypothesis than for any of the others, in part because the intercorrelations of other variables with the degree of competition are so strong.

Value of Purchase Variable

A review of responses to questions pertaining to marketing aggressiveness and technology suggests that the value of the typical purchase was highly related to marketing strategy in some instances, but not clearly related in many. Because this variable was rather highly intercorrelated with the type of industry variable, it is very difficult to evaluate which of the two variables was more influential. Also, value of purchase was highly intercorrelated with other variables in a direction that would tend to offset its influence. An additional weakness of the cross-tabulations was that two of the four classifications for this variable included relatively few firms. Some of the study findings are listed below:

1. Firms selling products of very high value were least likely to have made recent product introductions.

2. There was some evidence that value of the typical purchase was directly related to the number of presale service personnel employed; the evidence is quite definite that a direct relationship existed between value of the typical purchase and the number of postsale service personnel.

3. Advertising played a greater role in the success of products of low and moderate purchase value than it did for those of high and very high purchase value, according to the respondents' evaluations of advertising's importance; use of advertising, however, did not vary with the value of the typical purchase.

4. The percentage of sales spent on advertising increased as the value of the typical purchase decreased.

5. Value of the typical purchase held no discernible relationship to attitudes toward the importance of personal selling, although it was inversely related to both the use of personal selling and the number of salesmen employed.

6. As a general rule, higher value of typical purchase was associated with less sales training by the firm.

7. Products with a low value of purchase were more often sold through middlemen; products with a higher value of purchase were more often sold directly to industrial and non-industrial buyers.

8. Gross margins were lowest for products of very high purchase value, but were similar for all other classifications.

9. Price competition was somewhat less strong for products of very high purchase value; it was highest for products of moderate purchase value.

All things considered, we conclude that the evidence generally supports the hypothesis that firms selling a product with a low value of typical purchase tend to employ a more advanced marketing technology and to be more aggressive in their marketing than firms selling a product with a high value of typical purchase.

It is important to note that the cross-tabulations suggested by the hypotheses were made primarily to enrich the description. Testing of the hypotheses can best be described as exploratory, because the study design did not permit detailed investigation of any single one of them. The hypotheses were stated in general terms regarding the influence of the comparison variables on the total marketing strategy and practices. Yet results invariably showed that the comparison variables were influential in some aspects of marketing, and not influential in others. Tentative conclusions, then, had to be based upon the balance of the influences of each variable. Further study is needed to give conclusive proof or refutation of the hypotheses.

In our judgment, a clear view of the full range of marketing behavior placed in its environmental context is prerequisite to meaningful investigation of more detailed aspects of marketing practice. Hopefully, the present research will serve as a point of departure for later studies,[2] many of which will undoubtedly be done by the young Peruvian scholars who are now beginning to emerge from the recently established centers for specialized business education in that country.

14 Conclusion: Development and the Marketing Concept

Although the importance of the market was recognized in such early writings as *The Wealth of Nations,* the mainstream of economics has traditionally concentrated on the production process, public and private finance, and the distribution of factor returns. Under the impact of Keynesian analysis, with its extension by Harrod and Domar into long-run growth theory, the emphasis was placed more than ever on the strategic role of the level of fixed capital investment. This variable was perceived as the primary determinant of the level of income and employment and, indeed, the growth rate of the economy. Such factors as the acquisitions and accumulations of managerial and industrial labor skills — and marketing skills — were scarcely considered, or altogether ignored. The spokesmen of economic dissent — the Marxians, the institutionalists, and others — were similarly preoccupied, while twentieth century socialists have been, until quite recently, chiefly concerned with such matters as production-oriented centralized economic planning, general income redistribution policies, and the nationalization of industry.

Thus it is not surprising that economists in the less developed nations have generally followed suit in their thinking about economic processes — and more often than not preoccupation with production has in practice come to mean a nearly exclusive preoccupation with industrial production. Considerable reliance has ordinarily been placed on the "simple" expedient of import substitution, helped along by subsidized investment in one form or another.

As W. W. Rostow has pointed out, marketing has usually been regarded as a subordinate kind of economic activity, and "down to the present day it is difficult to get development economists and policymakers to accord to problems of efficiency in distributing the same attention they give automatically to problems of production, investment, and finance."[1] Economists such as Rosenstein-Rodan, Nurske, and Mosk have acknowledged that the extent of the market may be a principal limiting factor in the development process, and Paul Strassmann has argued that a widening of the market has important repercussions on the efficiency of investment in less developed areas.[2]

But if there has been recognition of the importance of markets, there has been much less concern with marketing as such, at least outside the field of agricultural economics. For the most part, and particularly in respect to industrialization, it has apparently been assumed that marketing progress would automatically accompany progress in production and the provision of physical distribution elements such as roads. Thus changes in market structures and marketing policies have usually been treated as derivative or induced aspects of economic development, not as initiating or possibly autonomous sources of growth and higher productivity.

In this study, marketing has been defined as the planning, promotion, distribution, and servicing of the goods and services desired by consumers. "Planning, promotion, distribution, and servicing" delineate the most prominent functions of marketing, while "desired by consumers" suggests the basic business orientation which is known as the "marketing concept." From the perspective of this concept, a private or public enterprise must cater to the needs and desires of the people if it is to attain maximum success and contribute to the social welfare. Accordingly, the consumer (broadly defined to include households, industrial buyers, and institutional users) becomes the focal point of most business decisions. Production is geared to creating the goods and services the public needs and desires as these are ascertained through extensive and intensive market research. Finance is organized to provide the capital required to produce and facilitate the sale of desired products. And marketing, in turn, is employed to effectively communicate with as well as deliver the goods and services to the intended markets. In short, the marketing concept argues that a consumer orientation should be a foundation for the planning and execution of most business activites.

This assignment of social validity to needs expressed in the market is not, of course, absolute. To further long-run national development, not all possible demands registered freely in the marketplace should necessarily be ratified by corresponding shifts in the pattern of production. Indeed, a good many should not. For example, pandering to an antisocial degree of conspicuous consumption is hardly supportable on any grounds while more urgent claims on resources go unmet, although ideally, effective fiscal policy should capture the private spending power which seeks expression in conspicuous consumption in the first place. (Unfortunately, in some parts of the world the operations of the fiscal system have merely substituted public waste for private waste.) Similarly, there may be harmful products for which a demand might conceivably exist or be cultivated (e.g., narcotics). Conversely, where significant externalities are present, the market may not adequately register the real social need for a particular product or service. In still other cases, production of an item may justifiably be undertaken even when not immediately profitable if supply discontinuities require anticipating an eventual growth of demand.[3] Generally speaking, to handle cases such as the foregoing, the operations of the public sector are of paramount importance.

These cases aside, however, and with all due recognition of the social validity of certain contraventions of the market mechanism, it remains true that effective marketing, i.e., the set of business policies implied by the marketing concept, can play a valuable part in reducing the manifold market imperfections which tend to depress the efficiency of resource use in the economic system.

In the United States, the spreading acceptance of the marketing concept has a certain experiential basis; the force of interproduct and interindustry competition, in a setting of affluent consumers, has placed a premium on skill in detecting the subtleties of a sophisticated market demand. In the less developed countries such as Peru, where modern marketing techniques have only recently begun to penetrate into the practices of local industry, relatively passive forms of marketing efforts have frequently sufficed for a captive local market in which the range of buying alternatives has been limited by protective tariffs and a scarcity of domestic competitors. Many of the newly established local manufacturers have had an acceptable volume of sales virtually assured in markets previously developed by imports. In addition, demand has been subject to some expansion because of population growth, accelerated urbanization, and rising incomes generated by export growth and by public and private investment activity. Given this setting, it is not surprising that the chief focus of private business activity has been on the investment and production aspects of development.

At present, however, judging from the Peruvian experience, it is questionable that the prevailing approach to marketing represents the most promising basis for sustaining the industrial momentum already achieved. The degree of protection accorded new industrial ventures has permitted a fairly high level of costs to develop in national industry. Partly the result of simple managerial and labor inexperience, which is unavoidable in a newly industrializing society, the high cost level also reflects the choice of capital-intensive production technologies which are not always the most economical choices for capital-scarce and labor-abundant economies. Where import substitution policies have pushed investment into industries with inflexible, capital-intensive technological characteristics, the dilemma has often been that of selecting between high-cost suboptimal-scale plants and more nearly optimal-sized facilities used at less than capacity and therefore, at a high cost. The fact is that very often both the production technologies and the products these technologies are designed to produce have been borrowed from abroad with remarkably little regard for questions of whether they are the most appropriate for the less developed economic setting.

Beyond these factors, domestic competition is often weak owing to a variety of causes, including rather limited access to capital supplies, lack of effective legal safeguards on collusive and monopolistic practices, and the inability of the small domestic market to support more than a handful of firms in particular lines of production. This has permitted production to be carried on without a constant effort to reduce cost and to cater to the needs of the market. Undoubtedly the sellers' market conditions which frequently prevail have facilitated continuation of this pattern of business behavior.

Combined with the foregoing is a common predilection for pricing policies based on a high unit markup and low volume sales principle. In addition, there is a generally casual approach to the selection and development of efficient channels of distribution. The result is a final product price level so high that the potential market, small to begin with, is reduced even further. Still other marketing limitations on the size of the available domestic market derive from the widespread failure to train qualified sales personnel, inadequate provision of presale and postsale services, the difficulties of (or disinterest in) developing more effective marketing communications strategies, and the common disregard of product development and product adaptation based on systematic research of market needs and preferences. Because the market is still primarily a seller's market, the offering of goods is in too many instances, from the standpoint of those consumers who are not priced out of the market, on a "take it or leave it" basis, and choice is limited.

The result is a paradox. On one hand the impression is widespread in Peru that the total market size is relatively static or fixed, that there are no more than 3.5 million or so active consumers in a nation with some 12 million people. The large majority of the inhabitants are simply not participating (or believed not to be participating) in the national economic development process; this means that over 70 percent of the Peruvian population does not have the opportunity to contribute in any meaningful way to the economic growth and strength of the country.

Insofar as the market for national production is thought to be subject to expansion, it is largely a process that involves selling the same set of consumers a wider range of locally manufactured goods — except to the extent that income and employment multiplier effects may accompany trade expansion and domestic investment. However, these latter marketing-expanding influences are limited by the high cost and price levels of national production and aspects of marketing behavior, both of which tend to reduce effective demand by eliminating the lower-income groups from the market. Therefore, the perception of a comparatively fixed total market tends to be confirmed. Clearly, however, the market size described by this set of conditions is partly a function of prevailing business practice itself. To the degree that business behavior is predicated on the assumption of a relatively inelastic market, a situation arises which approximates a self-fulfilling prophecy.

To be sure, economists probably bear some share of the blame for this predicament; more often than not they have described economies such as Peru as dual economies consisting of a modern sector and a subsistence sector. The latter sector would include the population of the sierra, which is generally held to be outside the consumer market of the nation. The term "subsistence sector," however, can be misleading. In one sense the subsistence label indicates a standard of living which is little above the level necessary for survival. In everyday usage, however, subsistence defines a system of production and consumption in which households are almost entirely self-contained units, producing most of what they consume. In such a system there is little or no opportunity for commercial trade and monetized exchanges.

Of these two connotations of subsistence, there can be little doubt that the former is indeed an accurate characterization of *serrano* life in Peru and, for that matter, of the life of many in the coastal zone. But, as the colorful indigenous fairs and markets attest, there is a striking amount of exchange occurring within and among the villages and regions of the highlands, and in most such fairs (as well as in permanent shops) goods are sold which have been brought in from outside the sierra.[4] Some of this trade is conducted by barter, but in many or even most instances, money is used. Moreover, the experience of the credit cooperative movement in Peru suggests that the amount of hoarded money (latent spending power) in low-income sectors of the economy may be considerably larger than would be suspected from the conventional descriptions of subsistence sectors.[5] In short, it is a gross exaggeration to view the less developed portion of the Peruvian economy as a nonmarket region completely divorced from the centers of economic modernization, even though much of current business practice tends to reinforce the marginality of provincial regions and of low-income groups in general. The same may be said of many other less developed countries in which "dualism" is a feature.

All this affects the validity of the widespread assumption that there are only about 3.5 million active consumers in Peru. The assumption seems valid only to the extent that the definition of the market is based on prevailing pricing policies, the kinds of goods currently manufactured, the existing distribution system, and the degree of effort currently employed in detecting consumer demand patterns and in operating marketing communications systems. In other words, the prevailing assumption of a fairly static market size inherently assumes that income and the other codeterminants of the market must remain constant, that the distribution system must continue to be relatively unresponsive to the interests and needs of the populace, and that there will be no development of improved marketing practices.

To state the issue in this way is virtually tantamount to suggesting a remedy which would help to relax the growth constraints currently imposed by the apparently small size of the national market — namely, the adoption of a "marketing concept" approach to business management.[a] While the concept is

[a]While we are here dealing primarily with the improvement of marketing policies, no implication is intended that this is the sole requisite of advance, or that marketing progress constitutes a panacea. Continued development of infrastructure, improved industrial relations, fiscal and agrarian reform, education improvement, the more effective use of cost accounting as a basis for managerial decisions, and many other developmental activities are all of great importance. There is not, of course, any single necessary and sufficient condition for development.

complex in its ramifications, it may be summarized as a shift in approach from the policy of attempting to market what is produced to a policy of gearing investment, production, and distribution to an intimate knowledge of the requirements of the market, *in both its consumer goods and producer goods segments.*

A strong case for this change in orientation can be made by considering the costs of the prevailing approach which, in its preoccupation with production, leads to business policies that are poorly conceived and executed. Given the current scarcity of aggregate national resources and the tremendous development needs of the Peruvian economy, the prime social task for the economic system is to allocate effectively the available resources according to the particular needs of the market. In so doing, consumer welfare would be increased substantially and greater realized value would be generated by the use of the resources. With the current production orientation, however, available resources are not being stretched to meet the unfulfilled needs of the populace and, because so little thought is devoted to consumer requirements, consumers are forced to select from what is offered by producers in a quite imperfectly competitive situation. Therefore, it is evident that a misallocation is occurring which involves a substantial sacrifice of consumer welfare and economic growth. This sacrifice is especially costly since the marginal value of a given volume of misdirected resources tends to be great at low levels of national per capita income.

It has, of course, been argued that aggregate consumption must be restrained in the interests of greater capital accumulation. Yet, this is a painful process in view of the low-income levels which prevail in Peru and elsewhere in the less developed parts of the world. Thus, if the development process is to be socially tolerable, it is essential to organize the output of goods in a way that minimizes the sacrifice of short-term consumer welfare. For that matter, application of the marketing concept to the current output of consumption goods should also serve to enhance their value as incentive goods and in that manner contribute to eliciting a greater effort to raise future output levels. In light of the politically explosive situation throughout the underdeveloped world, it is not an exaggeration to assert that the ability of a mixed economic system to survive may in part depend on its capacity to give the consumer what most nearly corresponds or conforms to his needs within the limits set by current resources availabilities.

In addition, it must not be overlooked that the effective marketing of all sorts of producer goods – with its strong resemblance to the adult (or extension) education process and to technical assistance programs contributes directly to an increase in resource availabilities. While this is important in fostering technological change and higher productivity through the economic system, it is an especially pressing concern for the agricultural sector of Peru where, in the highlands in particular, technical assistance from outside that sector is prerequisite to upgrading its performance and to alleviating the lot and raising the purchasing power of the people in it. In fact, in an impressive recent theoretical analysis of rural development, it was concluded that the results of the model constructed "stresses the importance of the variety and quality of manufactured goods offered to the rural area" and that "an industrial program which fails to open up the national market and indeed provides shoddy goods to substitute for goods previously imported from abroad can bring about a retreat . . . away from specialization and exchange."[6] Now that a serious agrarian reform effort is at last under way, implementation of the marketing concept in the production and distribution of agricultural products is unusually opportune.[7]

In addition to improving consumer welfare, the widening of the domestic market which would follow from implementation of the marketing concept should enable more Peruvian industries to attain a larger and more economical scale of production, just as it would tend to foster capital accumulation by expanding the supply of investment opportunities. On both counts, employment and income levels would benefit accordingly. Moreover, the resulting efficiency and growth of national industries would provide a better foundation than now exists for the development of industries which could compete effectively in the international markets of the world — in Latin American as well as elsewhere — or even, as a defensive matter, withstand the competition from imports originating in other Latin American countries should the movement toward regional integration ever gain momentum. It may well be that the Peruvian domestic market, even with maximum expansion, would still be insufficient to support the range of industrial undertakings which seems to be required to produce a satisfactory standard of living for Peruvians. Yet unless the kind of marketing behavior which would enlarge the now protected domestic market is adopted, it would be vain to expect much from efforts to develop the more competitively structured foreign markets for a growing volume and variety of Peruvian manufactures. Doubtless the preferential reduction of the advanced countries' barriers (the external obstacles) to imports from less developed countries would create a potential for export expansion and diversification in the latter group. Such, for example, is the clear belief of many associated with the United Nations Conference on Trade and Development. Whether that potential can be realized, however, depends mainly on overcoming the assorted internal market obstacles which at present operate strongly to thwart such an outcome.

In Peru's case, at least, there seems to be a number of latent opportunities in the economy which, if properly exploited, could be translated into an actual competitive advantage in fabricated goods. The diversity of domestically available raw materials, the considerable reserves of hydroelectric power, the readily trainable labor force with its comparatively low usage level, the littoral location of most manufacturing plants (i.e., so that cheap maritime transport costs apply to both imported industrial inputs and exported manufactured outputs), and the extensive communications links of Peru with various areas in the world market all suggest that Peru may be more favored than many other newly industrializing nations in having real, if still unexplored, possibilities for promoting the export of its manufactures. Additionally, it is quite conceivable that careful attention to product design would result in a better adaptation of Peruvian manufactured goods to the peculiar characteristics of the low-income home market and thus give Peruvian exporters a competitive edge over manufacturers from the developed countries whose output is, by and large, geared to the attributes of relatively affluent markets.

Yet there are obstacles which could negate most of these potentialities as they often have elsewhere in the world. They derive from poorly conceived government policies and other conditions external to the firm, factors which are unfortunately fairly common among the less developed countries: complicated export controls and time-consuming export procedures, export taxes, unrealistic export exchange rates, inadequate transport and port facilities, limited credit, domestic inflation, and overly protected price structures.

Other obstacles, though, stem from factors internal to the firms themselves: the lack of expert manufacturing knowhow in such fields as market research, product promotion, selection of effective representation in overseas distributional channels, the inability as well as disinclination to satisfy foreign importers' demands by adhering to the competitive trade practices that advanced industrial nations take for granted (such as maintaining an acceptable level of quality control, assuring promptness in shipments, seeing to the adequacy of packing, packaging, and servicing, the use of promotional pricing), and a practical disregard of the need to give careful and creative attention to product design and styling.

Unless these dysfunctional aspects of business behavior are remedied, both the removal of trade barriers to foreign markets (or even the obtaining of preferential access to them) and the institution of suitable export promotion policies by the national government are largely useless. Moreover, since the behavioral disabilities of firms from the standpoint of export marketing are substantially the same as their shortcomings in domestic marketing performance (when measured against the marketing concept criterion), it seems logical to conclude that implementation of the marketing concept would be doubly beneficial to national development in Peru, and indeed in underdeveloped countries generally.

Appendix

Literature on Marketing and Development

Although marketing has suffered from comparative neglect, there has never-theless been some recognition of its role in economic development. What follows is an effort to indicate the general categories under which the literature on the subject may be classified. By no means should this be viewed as a comprehensive bibliography; rather it should exemplify the nature of the work which has been done thus far.

General

One of the earlier articles to ask what bearing marketing organization had on development was published in 1953 by Richard H. Holton.[1] Using data derived from research in Puerto Rico, Holton questioned the suitability of the existing distributional network on the island for rapid industrialization and economic growth, and came to the conclusion that the latter would necessitate a considerable modernization of the marketing system. (A number of questions were left unanswered by his analysis, however, notably the relation of the marketing system to efficient use of the existing factor endowment.) In approximately the same period, Peter Bauer and Basil Yamey discussed the economics of marketing reforms, particularly in the area of agricultural marketing in the British African Colonies.[2] Recognizing that a number of proposals for reform had been made (and in some instances actually imple-mented), Bauer and Yamey observed that a number of the suggested changes were in fact undesirable from an economic point of view. Sometimes arbitrary and ill-conceived, the reforms were demonstrated to be unwittingly prejudicial to the interests of producers and consumers alike.

Somewhat later the importance of market organization for the development process was underscored again by two noted agricultural economists, Willard Mueller and George Mehren,[3] while in the early 1960's Norman Collins and Richard Holton urged that appropriate market reforms should be considered an integral part of a development plan. The latter authors favored a goal of establishing for the distributive sector

> ... a set of organizations and practices which would maximize the rate of growth of the primary and secondary sectors. This goal views marketing as playing an active, rather than merely a passive, cost-reducing role in economic development, and admits the possibility that more, instead of fewer, resources might well be devoted to the distributive sector.[4]

While much of the earlier writing on the subject was concerned directly or indirectly with agricultural marketing, there has been in more recent times an awakening of interest in nonagricultural marketing and development. A. A. Sherbini, for example, has pointed out the strategic role that marketing plays in optimizing the use of capital in newly industrializing nations; he has also emphasized the pitfalls that await management in making the change from marketing imported goods to marketing locally made products.[5] Moyer's study, *Marketing in Economic Development*, represents an initial attempt to snythesize the findings of the literature on the subject, and in 1965 the American Marketing Association adopted the role of the distributive sector in development as a major item for discussion at its fall conference.[6] Unfortunately, in recent years emphasis has shifted to management of the *international* firm as opposed to in-depth study within developing nations.

Market Studies

The fact that many businesses have recently begun to operate on an international scale, producing and/or marketing in unfamiliar environments, has led to many investigations of particular markets. The United States Department of Commerce has sponsored several of these studies, and others have been produced by local governments, research agencies, and the companies themselves.

This type of market investigation is usually a collection of pertinent statistical data, which gives a useful but rather general impression of local market conditions. Such items as income distribution, per capita income, population concentrations, educational levels, import-export trends, exchange rates and the like are usually presented. An example of a rather complete study of this kind is *A Marketing Guide to Peru,* which is helpful in that it contains a great many useful statistics.[7] Its principal deficiency is that it fails to explain just how Peruvian marketing is carried on, a limitation that is generally characteristic of most market studies.

Textbooks

A third source of information related, at least indirectly, to marketing practices and development are the textbooks written for courses in international marketing. The focus of these books varies from Philip MacDonald's *Practical Exporting and Importing,* which centers on problems of trading internationally, to Roland Kramer's *International Marketing,* which also considers the problems of marketing within a foreign country.[8] Traditionally, however, such books have been written to give advice to domestic businessmen so that they can enter and profit from the international market. Rarely have the studies been analytical in the sense of contributing to a satisfactory understanding of how foreign marketing systems actually operate and how their operations relate to economic growth. The problems of marketing abroad are so many and varied that any text which attempts to deal with them must also necessarily be quite general. Textbooks may point out, for instance, that attitudes toward competition vary widely from country to country, and give a few examples. But they offer few insights into the problems of competing within particular markets.

Somewhat different from the foregoing class of books is John Fayerweather's *International Marketing,* which attempts to explain *why* marketing differs from country to country rather than to advise *how* marketing should be conducted.[9] In his third chapter, Fayerweather discusses the economic, cultural, and political roots of marketing systems. Later in the book, he considers consumer purchasing power, motivations, decision-processes, and similar factors, attempting to explain how these factors differ from country to country. He also discusses the adaptation of strategy in the areas of product, distribution, promotion, and market research (unfortunately leaving out the problem of pricing). Similar in approach, but more extensive in its treatment of the subject, is David Carson's *International Marketing.*[10]

Although these textbooks, and others like them, are not directly concerned with the developmental aspects of marketing, they do point out some of the important differences in marketing systems, often emphasizing the differences between developed and underdeveloped countries.

Studies of Marketing Systems

The combination of increased travel by educators supported by government and private grants and the willingness of professional journals to publish articles on marketing systems has resulted in a significant body of literature on the subject. These articles are usually entitled "Marketing in . . . ," "Retailing in . . . ," "Wholesaling in . . . ," or something of that sort. They are basically descriptive with little detailed analysis. The information has generally been gathered from observation and informal discussion with businessmen of the specified country. Frequently the material has been gathered casually while the researcher's main responsibility during his stay in the foreign country was to organize a business school or teach in a university. The *Journal of Marketing* has shown particularly strong interest in papers of this kind. While they often provide valuable insights into marketing patterns throughout the world, such articles just as frequently fail to offer empirical data to substantiate the conclusions presented. More systematic and empirically grounded is the Marketing Science Institute's *Marketing Development in the European Economic Community,* which is concerned primarily with the impact of the EEC upon the role of marketing in the firm, trends in the allocation of marketing funds, and other aspects of marketing.[11]

Also of considerable interest are a number of extensive studies which have been made of the marketing systems of peasant economies and, to a somewhat lesser degree, the many village or community studies which anthropologists have made in various parts of the world.[12] Studies of these types allow the researcher the opportunity to gain an understanding of the marketing arrangements which prevail over large portions of the globe and are particularly valuable in pointing up the relationships which link the marketing system to other aspects of the socioeconomic complex.

To date, the most ambitious and comprehensive work in the area of marketing systems is Robert Bartels' *Comparative Marketing,* in which fifteen different authors present descriptions and interpretations of wholesaling in fifteen countries. Bartels, in a short summary, concludes that:

1. Channels tend to be more similar among free market economies than among those which are planned.
2. Certain types of functionaries exist in both the planned and unplanned economies.
3. The wholesaler's prominence is dependent on the producer's willingness to assume marketing responsibility.
4. Wholesaling structures differ quantitatively, as well as qualitatively, among countries.
5. The wholesaling system is the design of a social power structure.
6. Wholesaling structure and practices are determined not only by internal management strategy, but also by external circumstance.[13]

Formal Studies of Business Practices

As serious interest in marketing in foreign countries grows, there is a demand for more tightly structured research studies based upon organized interviewing. Illustrative of this newer type of business study (although neither is specifically concerned with marketing) are books by David Granick and Albert Lauterbach. Granick's contribution is in the area of executive attitudes, the research for which included organized interviewing of executives of several of the European countries.[14] Dealing with another area of the world, Lauterbach's book is based upon the results of 403 interviews in various Latin America countries. As the nature of his questions was essentially qualitative, he does not attempt to quantify the answers. He used an " . . . approach based upon relating the nature and functioning of management in a given area to the prevailing social system and cultural values both before and during a major development effort."[15]

The Marketing Science Institute is presently engaged in a project involving the use of an extensive questionnaire with personal interviews in countries which are at various stages of development.[16] The object of the study is to learn more about marketing practices and strategies and to compare results in eight countries. To our knowledge, this is the first multination detailed survey of marketing practices that has been undertaken. One must hope that, as there is a need for information of this nature, more will follow.

At present there is a lack of specific data about management practices, strategies, attitudes and the like in marketing as it exists in underdeveloped areas. This is true of Latin America as well as other areas of the world.

Bibliography

Bibliography

Books

Abramovitz, A. "Economics of Growth," in B. F. Haley, ed., *A Survey of Contemporary Economics*. Homewood, Illinois: Richard D. Irwin, Inc., 1952.

Adams, Richard N. *A Community in the Andes*. Seattle: 1959.

Alderson, Wroe, and Green, Paul. *Planning and Problem Solving in Marketing*. Homewood, Illinois: Richard D. Irwin, Inc., 1964.

American Association of Advertising Agencies. *The Advertising Agency Business Around the World, Parts I and II*. 1964.

American Institute of Certified Public Accountants. *Professional Accounting in 25 Countries*. 1964.

Bartels, Robert. *Comparative Marketing: Wholesaling in Fifteen Countries*. Homewood, Illinois: Richard D. Irwin, Inc., 1963.

Basadre, Jorge. *Peru: problema y posibilidad*. Lima: 1931.

Belaunde, Victor Andres. *La realidad nacional*. 2nd ed. Lima: 1945.

Bennett, Peter D. (ed.). *Marketing and Economic Development*. Chicago: American Marketing Association, 1965.

Bohannan, Paul, and Dalton, George (eds.). *Markets in Africa*. Evanston, Illinois: Northwestern University Press, 1962.

Broehl, Wayne Jr. *The International Basic Economy Corporation*. Washington: 1968.

Cappa, Ricardo. *Estudios criticos acerca de la dominacion expanola en America*. Madrid: Libreria Catolica de Gregorio del Amo, 1890.

Carson, David. *International Marketing: A Comparative Systems Approach*. New York: 1967.

Chaplin, David. *The Peruvian Industrial Labor Force*. Princeton, New Jersey: Princeton University Press, 1967.

Cortes, Alberto Baltra. *Crecimiento Economico de America Latina*. 4th ed. Santiago: Editorial del Pacifico, S. A., 1964.

Del Prado, Oscar Nunez. "Aspects of Andean Native Life," in D. B. Heath and R. N. Adams, eds., *Cultures and Societies of Latin America*. New York: 1965.

Dewey, Alice. *Peasant Marketing in Java*. New York: 1962.

Dobyns, Henry F. *The Social Matrix of Peruvian Indigenous Communities*. Ithaca, New York: Cornell University Press, 1964.

Doughty, Paul L. *Huaylas: An Andean District in Search of Progress*. Ithaca, New York: Cornell University Press, 1968.

Duffield, A. J. *Peru in the Guano Age*. London: 1877.

Dunbaugh, Frank M. *Marketing in Latin America*. New York: Printers' Ink Book Company, 1960.

Enke, Stephen. *Economics for Development*. Englewood Cliffs, New Jersey: Prentice-Hall, Inc., 1963.

Fayerweather, John. *International Marketing*. Englewood Cliffs, New Jersey: Prentice-Hall, Inc., 1965.

Galbraith, John K., and Holton, Richard H. *Marketing Efficiency in Puerto Rico*. Cambridge, Massachusetts: Harvard University Press, 1955.

Garland, Alexander. *La industria Azucarera en el Peru.* Lima, n.d.

———. *Peru in 1906 and After With a Brief Historical Sketch.* Lima: 1908.

Glade, William P. *The Latin American Economies: A Study of Institutional Evolution.* New York: 1961.

Granick, David. *The European Executive.* Garden City, New York: Doubleday & Company, Inc., 1962.

———. *The Red Executive.* Garden City, New York: Doubleday & Company, Inc., 1960.

Hammel, Eugene A. *Wealth, Authority, and Prestige In the Ica Valley, Peru.* Albuquerque: 1962.

Hirsch, Leon V. *Marketing in an Underdeveloped Economy: The North Indian Sugar Industry.* Englewood Cliffs, New Jersey: Prentice-Hall, Inc., 1961.

Hirschman, A. O. *The Strategy of Economic Development.* New York: McGraw-Hill, Inc., 1958.

Kindleberger, Charles P. *Economic Development.* New York: McGraw-Hill, Inc., 1958.

———. *International Economics.* 3rd ed. Homewood, Illinois: Richard D. Irwin, Inc. 1963.

Korb, George M. *Ticaco: An Aymara Indian Community.* Ithaca, New York: Cornell University Press, 1966.

Kramer, Roland. *International Marketing.* Cincinnati: 1959.

Lauterbach, Albert. *Enterprise in Latin America: Business Attitudes in a Developing Economy.* Ithaca, New York: Cornell University Press, 1966.

Levin, Jonathan. *The Export Economies.* Cambridge, Massachusetts: Harvard University Press, 1960.

Lockley, Lawrence, Lockley, Noemi Hewes, and Winston, Temple S. *A Marketing Guide to Peru.* Lima: Instituto Peruano de Administracion de Empresas, 1965.

MacDonald, Philip. *Practical Exporting and Importing.* 2nd ed. New York: The Ronald Press Company, 1959.

McMillan, Claude Jr., *et al. International Enterprise in a Developing Economy.* East Lansing, Michigan: Michigan State University, 1964.

Mangin, William P. "The Role of Regional Associations in the Adaptation of Rural Migrants to Cities in Peru," in D. B. Heath and R. N. Adams, eds., *Contemporary Cultures and Societies of Latin America.* New York: 1965.

———. "Mental Health and Migration to Cities: A Peruvian Case." *Ibid.*

Marketing Science Institute. *Marketing Development in the European Economic Community.* New York: McGraw-Hill, Inc. 1964.

Martin, Percy F. *Peru of the Twentieth Century.* London: 1911.

Mosher, Arthur T. "Research on Rural Problems," in Robert F. Asher, ed., *Development of the Emerging Countries: An Agenda for Research.* Washington, D. C.: 1962.

Moyer, Reed. *Marketing in Economic Development.* East Lansing, Michigan: Michigan State University, 1965.

Myrdal, Gunnar. *An International Economy.* New York: Harper & Row, 1956.

Norris, Vincent. "Advertising and Value Added," in Charles H. Sandage and Vernon Fryburger, eds., *The Role of Advertising*. Homewood, Illinois: Richard D. Irwin, Inc., 1960.

Nurske, Ragnar. *Equilibrium and Growth in the World Economy*. Cambridge, Massachusetts: Harvard University Press, 1961.

Owens, R. J. *Peru*. London: Oxford University Press, 1963.

Pan American Union, Division of Economic Research. *The Peruvian Economy*. Washington: 1950.

Partners in Growth. Wausau, Wisconsin: Northern Wisconsin Development Center, University of Wisconsin Extension, July 1969.

Payne, James L. *Labor and Politics in Peru*. New Haven, Connecticut: Yale University Press, 1965.

Pike, Frederick. *The Modern History of Peru*. New York: 1967.

Prescott, William. *The Conquest of Peru*. New York: Mentor Books, 1961.

Reyes, Oscar. *Breve historia general de Ecuador*. Quito: 1955.

Robinson, David A. *Peru in Four Dimensions*. Lima: American Studies Press, S. A., 1964.

Romero, Emilio. *Historica economica del Peru*. Buenos Aires: 1949.

Rostow, W. W. "The Concept of a National Market and Its Economic Growth Implications," in Peter D. Bennett, ed., *Proceedings of the American Marketing Association 1965 Fall Conference*.

_____ . *The Stages of Economic Growth: A Non-Communist Manifesto*. New York: Cambridge University Press, 1960.

Ryans, John K., Jr., and Baker, James C. *World Marketing*. New York: 1967.

Stanton, William J. *Fundamentals of Marketing*. 2nd ed. New York: McGraw Hill, Inc., 1967.

Stein, William W. *Hualcan: Life in the Highlands of Peru*. Ithaca, New York: Cornell University Press, 1961.

Stewart, Watt. *Chinese Bondage in Peru*. Durham: 1951.

Theobald, Robert. *Profit Potential in the Developing Countries*. New York: American Management Association, 1962.

Udell, Jon G. *A Model of Non-Price Competitive Strategy*. Madison: University of Wisconsin, 1963.

Valcarel, Luis E. "Indian Markets and Fairs in Peru," in Julian H. Steward, ed., *Handbook of South American Indians*. Washington, D. C.: 1947.

Von Tschudi, J. J. *Travels in Peru During the Years 1838-1842*. London: 1847.

White, William F., and Williams, Lawrence K. *Toward an Integrated Theory of Development*. Ithaca, New York: Cornell University Press, 1968.

Withers, William. *The Economic Crisis in Latin America*. London: Collier McMillan Limited, 1964.

The 1963 World Almanac and Book of Facts. New York: New York World-Telegram, 1963.

Youngson, A. J. *Overhead Capital*. Edinburgh: William Blackwood and Sons, Ltd., 1967.

Periodicals

Barrett, John L. "Peruvian Economic Conditions Continue Favorable," *Peruvian Times*. Lima (March 11, 1966).

Bauer, P. T., and Yamey, B. S. "The Economics of Marketing Reform," *Journal of Political Economy*. LXII, 3 (June 1954).

Bourricaud, Francois. "Structure and Function of the Peruvian Oligarchy," *Studies in Comparative International Development*, II, 2, Original Series 016 (1966).

Boyd, Harper W. Jr., *et al.* "On the Use of Marketing Research in the Emerging Economies," *Journal of Marketing Research* (November 1964).

Clark, Ronald J. "Land Reform and Peasant Market Participation on the Northern Highlands of Bolivia," *Land Economics*, XLIV (May 1968).

Collins, N. R., and Holtan, R. H. "Programming Changes in Marketing in Planned Economic Development," *Kyklos*, XVI, Fasc. 1 (1963).

Drucker, Peter F. "Marketing and Economic Development," *Journal of Marketing*, XXIII, 3 (1958).

Ewing, John S., and Yoshino, M. Y. "Some Issues in International Marketing," *Business and Society* (Autumn 1966).

"The Five Hundred Largest U. S. Corporations," *Fortune*, LXXIV (July 1966).

"Good News From the Andes," *Fortune*, (August 15, 1969).

Halper, Donald G. "The Environment for Marketing in Peru," *Journal of Marketing*, XXX, 3 (July 1966).

Holtan, Richard H. "Marketing Structure and Economic Development," *Quarterly Journal of Economics*, LXVII, 3 (1953).

Hymer, Stephen, and Resnick, Stephen. "A Model of an Agrarian Economy With Nonagricultural Activities," *American Economic Review*, LIX, 4, Part I (September 1969).

International Commerce. LXXI (March 26, 1965).

La Fabril, Lima.

La Prensa, Lima, 1965 and 1966.

Levitt, Theodore. "Innovative Imitation," *Harvard Business Review*, XLIV, 5 (September-October 1966).

Mehren, George L. "Market Organization and Economic Development," *Journal of Farm Economics*. XLI, 5 (1959).

Mueller, Willard F. "Some Marketing Structure Considerations in Economic Development," *Journal of Farm Economics*, XLI, 2 (1959).

Peruvian Times, Lima, 1965.

Prebisch, P. "International Trade and Payments in an Era of Coexistence: Commercial Policy in the Underdeveloped Countries," *The American Economic Review*, XLIX, 2 (May 1959).

Samli, A. Coskun. "Wholesaling in an Economy of Scarcity: Turkey," *Journal of Marketing* (July 1964).

Sherbini, A. A. "Marketing in the Industrialization of Underdeveloped Countries," *Journal of Marketing*, XXIX, 1 (January 1965).

Smithies, Arthur. "Rising Expectations and Economic Development," *Economic Journal*, LXXI, 282 (1961).

Strassmann, W. Paul. "Economic Growth and Income Distribution," *Quarterly Journal of Economics* (August 1965).

"Texto del Proyecto que el Peru presento en Panama sobre integracio economica," *El Commercio,* Lima (1966).

Udell, Jon G. "The Perceived Importance of the Elements of Strategy," *Journal of Marketing,* XXXII, 1 (January 1968).

"What Is Happening in Peru, South America?" *Now,* XX, 3 (March 1966).

Wadinambiaratchi, George. "Channels of Distribution in Developing Economies," *The BusinessQuarterly* (Winter 1965).

Technical Bulletins and Government Reports

Arancel de Aduanas (importacion). Lima: Ministerio de Hacienda y Comercio, 1964.

Business in Peru. Lima: Price, Waterhouse, Peat and Co., 1966.

Censo nacional de 1940. Lima: Republica Peruana, 1941.

VI Censo nacional de Poblacion. Lima: Direccion Nacional de Estadistica y Censos, Tomo III, Cuadro 52 and 67, 1965.

Cuentas nacionales del Peru, 1950-1965. Lima: Banco Central de Reserva del Peru, 1966.

De las Casas M., Lizardo, *et al. Estudio de Factibilidad Economica para la Ubicacion del Mercado de Productores.* Lima: Ministerio de Agricultura, 1965.

Diagnostico del Sector Industrial. Lima: Instituto Nacional de Planificacion, 1966.

Estudio Sobre la Produccion Horticola y Tenencia de Tierra en las Provincias de Lima y Callao. Lima: Republica Peruana, Informe No. 1, 1965.

Gillin, John. *Moche, a Peruvian Coastal Community.* Washington, D. C.: Smithsonian Institution, 1945.

Industria Manufacturera Peruana. Lima: Sociedad Nacional de Industrias, December 1965.

Las Empresas estatales en el Peru. Lima: Centro de Documentacion Economico-Social, 1965.

Mainwaring, Thomas A., *et al. Estudio Factibilidad para una Planta de Envasado de Pasas en Ica.* Lima: Stanford Research Institute and Instituto Nacional de Promocion Industrial, 1966.

Mainwaring. *Mercado de Productos Alimenticios y Bebidas en 1962 y Algumos Productos Industrializables.* Lima: Instituto Nacional de Promocion Industrial y Banco Industrial del Peru, 1965.

Miller, John F. *Food Distribution Survey, Lima/Callao Area.* Lima: U. S. Agency for International Development, 1965.

Moderno Desarrollo en un Pais de Antiguas Culturas. Dortmund, Germany: Corporacion de Reconstruccion y Fomento del Cuzco, 1965.

Padron de Industrias Manufactureras. Lima: Ministerio de Fomento y Obras Publicas, 1960.

Primer Censo Nacional Agropecuario. Lima: 1965.

Primer Censo Nacional economico (1963), Directorio de comercio al por mayor. Lima: 1965.

Relacion de Socios. Lima: Instituto Peruano de Administracion de Empresas, 1965.

Resena industrial del Peru. Lima: Ministerio de Fomento, 1902.

Roberts, J. Reynaldo. *Comentarias Sobre la Publicidad en el Peru.* Lima: Escuela de Administracion de Negocios para Graduados, 1967.

Shepherad, Geoffrey. *Low Income People in Peru Need More Protein: Here Is How They Can Get It.* Lima: Iowa Universities Mission, Alliance for Progress, 1966.

_____ . *Market News for Farm Products in Peru.* Lima: Iowa-Peru Agency for International Development Team, 1967.

Summary of Franchises and Benefits of the Industrial Promotion Law. Lima: Instituto Nacional de Planificacion, 1964.

Tenencia de la Tierra y desarrollo socio-economico del sector agricola. Washington, D. C.: Comite Interamericano de Desarrollo Agricola, 1966.

Thompson, J. Walter. *Perfil del Merado Peruano.* 1966.

Toschopik, Henry. *Highland Communities of Central Peru, a Regional Study.* Washington, D. C.: Smithsonian Institution, 1947.

Tosi, Joseph A. Jr. *Zonas de Vida Natural en el Peru.* Instituto Interamericano de Ciencias Agricolas de la OEA, Zona Andina, 1960.

United Nations. *1964 Yearbook of National Account Statistics.* New York: 1965.

U. S. Council of Economic Advisors. *Annual Report,* 1964.

U. S. Department of Commerce. *Basic Data on the Economy of Peru.* OBR 65-46. Washington, D. C.: USGPO, July 1965.

_____ . *Foreign Trade Regulations of Peru.* OBR 64-99. September 1964.

Vidal, Pedro Pulgar. *Situacion de la Industria Peruana en 1964.* Lima: Instituto Nacional de Promocion Industrial y Banco Industrial del Peru, 1965.

Willy, Adolph G. *Retail-Wholesale Meat Distribution.* Lima: U. S. Agency for International Development, 1964.

Other Sources

Bowers, Martha-Belle. "The Dawn of Manufacturing in Peru." Unpublished M. A. thesis in International Relations, University of Chicago, 1946.

Comite de Fabricantes de Cerveza. Lima.

Fisher Rossi, Dr. Konrad. Unpublished student papers. San Isidro, Peru: Escuela de Administracion de Negocios para Graduados, 1966.

Harms, Pablo L. "Total Satisfaccion del Consumidor — o Fin de la Empresa Libra." A speech made at the monthly meeting of ADV, May 10, 1966.

Marrou, J. Estuardo. "Marketing Strategies and Practices in Small and Medium-sized Wisconsin Food and Beverage Manufacturers: Comparisons With Similar Manufacturers in a Developing Economy." Seminar paper in lieu of thesis, University of Wisconsin, January 1968.

Saulniers, Alfred H. "Communications and Economic Development: A Descriptive Analysis of Peru." Unpublished paper, University of Wisconsin, May 3, 1968.

Thorelli, Hans B. "The Political Economy of the Firm: Basis for a New Theory of Competition?" Address at the annual meeting of the Schweizerische Gesellschaft fur Statistick und Volkswirtschaft at St. Gallen, May 28, 1965.

Udell, Jon G., and Glade, William P. "The Implications of Marketing Behavior for Economic Development." Unpublished monograph, 1966.

Vergara, Mejia Mercedes. Unpublished thesis in Economic Science. La Universidad del Centro Huancayo, Peru, 1966.

Wood, Richard H. "The Agricultural Supply Industries in the Economic Development of the Peruvian Sierras." Unpublished doctoral thesis, University of Wisconsin, 1969.

Notes

Notes

Preface

1. William F. Whyte and Lawrence K. Williams, *Toward an Integrated Theory of Development* (Ithaca, New York: 1968), pp. 30-31.

2. Arthur T. Mosher, "Research on Rural Problems," in Robert E. Asher, ed., *Development of the Emerging Countries: An Agenda for Research* (Washington, D. C.: 1962), p. 104. Mosher's argument rested upon the assumption that "both cultural history and the small and highly local nature of merchandising firms (in low-income countries) make integrated advertising campaigns not feasible if left (entirely) to private support."

3. Stephen Enke, *Economics for Development* (Englewood Cliffs, New Jersey: 1963), pp. 364-365. It is interesting and relevant to note that Charles N. Myers, in his *Education and National Development in Mexico* (Princeton, New Jersey: 1965), p. 65, recognizes the role of agricultural marketing as a form of extension education.

Chapter 1
Introduction

1. In the useful survey by Hahn and Matthews, "The Theory of Economic Growth" (*Economic Journal,* LXXIV, 296, 1964, pp. 779-902), over half the space concerned with alternative theoretical approaches was devoted to the savings-investment causes of growth. Nearly two-thirds of M. Abramovitz's survey of the "Economics of Growth," which is in Vol. II of B. F. Haley, ed., *A Survey of Contemporary Economics* (Homewood, Illinois: 1952, pp. 132-78), is devoted to capital formation as the cause of growth.

2. Peter F. Drucker, "Marketing and Economic Development," *Journal of Marketing,* XXIII, 3 (1958), p. 255.

3. Charles P. Kindleberger, *Economic Development* (New York: 1958), p. 107.

4. Arthur Smithies, "Rising Expectations and Economic Development," *Economic Journal,* LXXI, 282 (1961), p. 269.

5. See, for example, W. W. Rostow, "The Concept of a National Market and Its Economic Growth Implications," in Peter D. Bennett, ed., *Proceedings of the American Marketing Association 1965 Fall Conference,* pp. 11-20. During the same period, of course, there came to be, in the centrally planned economics of Europe, a new recognition of the importance of the marketing process.

6. Reed Moyer, *Marketing in Economic Development* (East Lansing, Mich.: 1965), p. 1.

7. *Ibid.*

8. William J. Stanton, *Fundamentals of Marketing,* 2nd ed. (New York: 1967), pp. 12-18.

Chapter 2
The Evolution of the Peruvian
Enterprise System

1. Ricardo Cappa, *Estudios críticos acerca de la dominación española en América* (Madrid: 1890), V and VI.

2. Cappa, op. cit., VIII. Oscar Reyes, *Breve historia general de Ecuador* (Quito: 1955), I, pp. 209-215, 246-247.

3. Jorge Basadre, *Perú: problema y posibilidad* (Lima: 1931), p. 108, for example, notes that wealthy merchants in Lima sometimes purchased aristocratic titles from the Spanish crown.

4. J. J. von Tschudi, *Travels in Peru During the Years 1838-1842,* (London: 1847), p. 177. Alexander Garland, *La industria azucarera en el Perú* (Lima: n. d.), p. 6.

5. *Ibid.* pp. 174, 238.

6. Alexander Garland, *Peru in 1906 and After with a Brief Historical and Geographical Sketch* (Lima: 1908), p. 260.

7. An excellent account of the political problems of the day may be found in Frederick Pike, *The Modern History of Peru* (New York: 1967). For more detail on economic events and trends, see Jonathan Levin, *The Export Economies* (Cambridge: 1960).

8. Levin's book covers this period to some extent, but for an interesting contemporary account the reader may consult A. J. Duffield, *Peru in the Guano Age* (London: 1877).

9. Levin, pp. 87-88; Watt Stewart, *Chinese Bondage in Peru* (Durham: 1951), pp. 27, 75, 85-86; Percy F. Martin, *Peru of the Twentieth Century* (London: 1911), p. 125.

10. Pan American Union, Division of Economic Research, *The Peruvian Economy* (Washington: 1950), p. 35, and Emilio Romero, *Historia económica del Perú* (Buenos Aires: 1949), p. 284.

11. Useful for its findings on this early period is Martha-Belle Bowers, "The Dawn of Manufacturing in Peru," unpublished M. A. thesis in international relations, University of Chicago, 1946. Also helpful is David Chaplin, *The Peruvian Industrial Labor Force* (Princeton: 1967).

12. Peru, Ministerio de Fomento, *Reseña industrial del Perú* (Lima: 1902).

13. See William Glade, *The Latin American Economies: A Study of Their Institutional Evolution* (New York: 1969), for a fuller discussion of these circumstances as they affected the structure of the economy in other countries.

14. República Peruana, Banco Central de Reserva del Perú, *Cuentas nacionales del Perú, 1950-1965* (Lima: 1966), p. 7. The average annual rate of price increase for 1950-1965 was 8 percent, the increase in 1964 and 1965 being 12 percent and 15 percent, respectively. *Ibid.,* p. 8.

15. *Ibid.,* p. 7.

16. *Ibid.,* p. 10. Fishing products, iron, and coffee constituted 39 percent of exports in 1965 as against 4 percent in 1950. Copper production and exports were also rising quite rapidly, from 5 percent of exports in 1950 to 18 percent in 1965.

17. Estimated from Table I of *Cuentas Nacionales,* using the 1963 *soles* equivalent of GNP and per capita gross product in 1965 and an exchange rate of 27 *soles* per dollar.

18. *Ibid.,* Table 8.

19. Comité Interamericano de Desarrollo Agrícola, *Tenencia de la tierra y desarrollo socio-económico del sector agrícola* (Washington: 1966).

20. Labor force distribution figures are computed from *Tenencia de la tierra,* Table 11.

21. República Peruana, Instituto Nacional de Planificación, *Diagnóstico del sector industrial* (Lima: 1966), p. 25.

22. *Diagnóstico,* pp. 1-11.

23. *Cuentas nacionales,* Table 19.

24. *Ibid.,* Table 18.

25. U. S. Department of Commerce, OBR 65-46, p. 18.

26. *Ibid.,* p. 19. (All statistics in the section about customers and suppliers are derived from this source.)

27. Pedro Pulgar Vidal, *Situación de la industria peruana en 1964* (Lima: 1965), p. 98.

28. *Ibid.,* p. 99.

29. U. S. Department of Commerce, OBR 65-46, p. 14.

30. *Ibid.,* p. 14.

31. Lawrence Lockley, *et. al. op. cit.,* p. 111; and *The Annual Report of the Council of Economic Advisors,* p. 239.

32. Lockley, *et. al., op. cit.,* p. 109.

33. *Diagnóstico,* p. 37.

34. U. S. Department of Commerce, OBR 65-46, p. 3.

35. Instituto Nacional de Planificación, *Summary of Franchises and Benefits of the Industrial Promotion Law* (Lima: 1964), Appendix.

36. The material concerning taxation in Peru is taken from Price, Waterhouse, Peat and Company's *Business in Peru* (Lima: 1966).

37. U. S. Department of Commerce, OBR 64-99, *Foreign Trade Regulations of Peru* (September 1964), p. 1.

38. "Texto del Proyecto que el Perú presentó en Panamá sobre integración económica," *El Commercio* (Lima), March 4, 1966.

39. Instituto Nacional de Planificación, *Diagnóstico del sector industrial,* p. 57.

40. The most complete source of information regarding the State's businesses in Peru is *Las empresas estatales en el Perú,* Centro de Documentación Económico-Social eds. (Lima: 1965).

Chapter 3
The Peruvian Market
Environment

1. Joseph A. Tosi, Jr., *Zonas de vida natural en el Perú* (Zona Andina: 1960), p. 261.

2. David A. Robinson, *Peru in Four Dimensions* (Lima: 1964), pp. 170-171.

3. R. J. Owens, *Peru* (London: 1963), p. 3.

4. Robinson, p. 80.

5. Robinson, p. 80.

6. Tosi, p. 261.

7. "What is Happening in Peru, South America?" in *Now,* ed. Richard H. LeTourneau, XX, 3. (March 1966), p. 1.

8. Lockley, *et. al., op. cit.,* p. 3.

9. Vidal, *op. cit.,* p. 10.

10. Cortes, *op. cit.,* p. 35.

11. República Peruana, *Censo nacional de 1940* (Lima: 1941), p. 62.

12. *VI Censo Nacional,* Tomo III, Cuadro 52, p. 48.

13. See, for example, the discussion of these given in Luís E. Válcarcel, "Indian Markets and Fairs in Peru," in Julian H. Steward, ed., *Handbook of South American Indians,* II (Washington, D. C.: 1947), pp. 477-82.

14. Among the more useful studies of these societies are the following: Harry Tschopik, Jr., *Highland Communities of Central Peru* (Washington, D. C.: 1947); Richard N. Adams, *A Community in the Andes* (Seattle: 1959); William W. Stein, *Hualcan: Life in the Highlands of Peru* (Ithaca: 1961); and Henry F. Dobyns, *The Social Matrix of Peruvian Indigenous Communities* (Ithaca: 1964).

15. Oscar Nunez del Prado, "Aspects of Andean Native Life," *Contemporary Cultures and Societies of Latin America,* D. B. Heath and R. N. Adams, eds. (New York: 1965), pp. 106-107.

16. William P. Mangin, "The Role of Regional Associations in the Adaptation of Rural Migrants to Cities in Peru," in *Contemporary Cultures and Societies of Latin America,* D. B. Heath and R. N. Adams, eds., p. 313.

17. *Ibid.*

18. William P. Mangin, "Mental Health and Migration to Cities: A Peruvian Case," in *op. cit.,* p. 549.

19. Whereas *mestizo* refers, strictly speaking, to a mixture of races, the term *criollo* originally meant an American-born person of Spanish ancestry. Today, however, it has come to refer to culture traits which are thought to be distinctively Spanish-American as contrasted with those which are European and those which are Indian. "The Criollo Outlook in the Mestizo Culture of Coastal Peru," in *Contemporary Cultures,* p. 522.

20. Simmons, *op. cit.,* p. 524.

21. *Ibid.,* pp. 518-519. See also Eugene A. Hammel, *Wealth, Authority, and Prestige in the Ica Valley, Peru* (Albuquerque: 1962).

22. Simmons, pp. 525-526.

23. Donald G. Halper, "The Environment for Marketing in Peru," *Journal of Marketing,* XXX, 3 (July 1966), p. 46.

24. Owens, pp. 62-63.

25. *El Comercio* (Lima), March 11, 1963.

26. The workings of this system in the area of labor policy is interestingly analyzed in James L. Payne, *Labor and Politics in Peru* (New Haven: 1965).

Chapter 4
Marketing Infrastructure

1. Lockley, *et al.,* p. 83.

2. *La Prensa* (Lima), May 22, 1966.

3. *Peruvian Times* (Lima), June 11, 1966.

4. República del Peru, Ministerio de Hacienda y Comercio, Dirección Nacional de Estadística y Censos, *Primer censo nacional económico (1963), Directorio de comercio al por mayor* (Lima: 1967), pp. 78, 138.

5. Unpublished student papers, Dr. Konrad Fischer Rossi, Escuela de Administración de Negocios para Graduados, 1966.

6. For a review of the Sears experience in Peru, see William R. Fritsch, *Progress and Profits,* (Washington, D. C.: 1962).

7. *La Prensa* (Lima), April 18, 1966.

8. For a study of the largest of these fairs, that held at Huancayo each Sunday, see the unpublished thesis in economics by Mercedes Vergara Mejía of La Universidad del Centro, Huancayo.

9. Price, Waterhouse, Peat and Company, *Business in Peru* (Lima: 1965), Section 1, Chap. 4, p. 1.

10. The American Institute of Certified Public Accountants, *Professional Accounting in 25 Countries,* 1964, p. 14.

Chapter 5
Research Design
and Sample
Characteristics

1. The sources used to select the sample were *La Fabril* of the Sociedad Nacional de Industrias; *Relacion de Socios 1965* of the Instituto Peruano de Administracion de Empresas; *Padron de Industrias Manufactureras, 1960,* of the Ministerio de Fomento y Obras Publicas; telephone directories; and suggestions from several business contacts.

2. Jon G. Udell, *A Model of Non-Price Competitive Strategy,* Wisconsin Selected Papers, No. 1, Bureau of Business Research and Service, The University of Wisconsin (Madison: July 1963), pp. 4-6.

3. *Industria Manufacturera Peruana* (December, 1965), p. 68.

Chapter 6
Marketing Organizations
in Peru

1. A. A. Sherbini, "Marketing in the Industrialization of Underdeveloped Countries," *Journal of Marketing,* January 1965, p. 29.

2. *Partners in Growth,* Northern Wisconsin Development Center, University Extension, The University of Wisconsin (Wausau: July 1969).

3. Claude McMillan, Jr., *et. al., International Enterprise in a Developing Economy,* Bureau of Business and Economic Research, Graduate School of Business Administration, Michigan State University (1964), pp. 145-146.

4. William J. Stanton, *Fundamentals of Marketing,* (New York: 1967), pp. 12-18.

5. Wayne G. Broehl, Jr., *The International Basic Economy Corporation* (Washington: 1968), passim.

Chapter 7
Marketing Research
in Peruvian
Industry

1. Harper W. Boyd, Jr., et. al., "On The Use of Marketing Research in the Emerging Economies," *Journal of Marketing Research,* November 1964, pp. 20-23.

2. Geoffrey S. Shepherd, "Market News for Farm Products in Peru," mimeographed report, Iowa-Peru Aid Team, March 1967.

Chapter 8
Product and Services
Management
in Peru

1. "Cultivation of [the lower income] market is ordinarily expensive, time-consuming, and highly risky, but the high potential reward for a pioneer is demonstrated by the number of occasions a U. S. brand name has become a generic term for a class of products in a foreign market." John S. Ewing and M. Y. Yoshino, "Some Issues in International Marketing," *Business and Society* (Autumn, 1966), p. 8.

2. *Ibid.* p. 7.

3. Theodore Levitt, "Innovative Imitation," *Harvard Business Review,* Vol. 44, No. 5, (September-October, 1966), p. 65.

Chapter 9
Marketing Communications
in Peru

1. Vincent Norris, "Advertising and Value Added," in Charles H. Sandage and Vernon Fryburger, eds., *The Role of Advertising* (Homewood, Ill.: 1960), p. 151.
2. Alfred H. Saulniers, "Communications and Economic Development: A Descriptive Analysis of Peru," unpublished paper, The University of Wisconsin, May 3, 1968, p. 2.
3. George M. Korb, *Ticaco: An Aymara Indian Community* (Ithaca: 1966), p. 15.
4. J. Reynaldo Roberts, "Comentarias Sobre la Publicidad en el Peru," (Escuela de Administración de Negocios para Graduados (Lima: 1967), pp. 15-21.
5. American Association of Advertising Agencies, *The Advertising Agency Business Around the World: Parts I and II*, (1964), Halper, pp. 43-44.

Chapter 10
Distribution Management
in Peru

1. See, for example, A. Coskun Samli, "Wholesaling in an Economy of Scarcity: Turkey," *Journal of Marketing*, July 1964, pp. 55-58.
2. *Peruvian Times* (Lima), October 15, 1965.
3. David Carson, *International Marketing* (New York: 1967), p. 302.
4. Corporacion de Reconstruccion y Fomento del Cuzco, *Moderno Desarrollo en Un Pais de Antiguas Culturas* (Dortmund, Germany: 1965), p. 9.
5. *Peruvian Times* (Lima), October 15, 1965.
6. *El Comercio* (Lima), March 4, 1966.
7. George Wadinambiaratchi, "Channels of Distribution in Developing Economies," *The Business Quarterly*, Winter 1965, reprinted in John K. Ryans, Jr. and James C. Baker, *World Marketing* (New York: 1967), pp. 263-278.
8. "Good News From the Andes," *Fortune*, August 15, 1969, p. 120.

Chapter 11
Pricing Management

1. A. A. Sherbini, "Marketing in the Industrialization of Underdeveloped Countries," *Journal of Marketing*, XXIX, No. 1, January, 1965, p. 30.
2. Wroe Alderson and Paul Green, *Planning and Problem Solving In Marketing* (Homewood, Illinois: 1964), p. 241.
3. John Kenneth Galbraith and Richard H. Holton, *Marketing Efficiency in Puerto Rico* (Cambridge: 1955), pp. 72-73.
4. Banco Continental, News Letter No. 516, Lima, May 30, 1969.

5. See, for example, David Carson, *International Marketing* (New York: 1967), pp. 446-448.
6. For a good summary of the social legislation in Peru, the reader may wish to consult Lockley, Lockley, and Temple, pp. 97-119.

Chapter 12
Overall Marketing
Strategy

1. Jon G. Udell, "The Perceived Importance of the Elements of Competitive Strategy," *Journal of Marketing*, XXXII, 1 (January 1968).
2. "The 500 Largest U. S. Industrial Corporations," *Fortune*, LXXIV (July 1966), p. 249.

Chapter 13
Synopsis: Marketing Strategies
and Practices in Peru

1. In a study of twenty Wisconsin food and beverage manufacturers that paralleled the *Marketing in Peru* study, small manufacturers were found to be quite unsophisticated in their marketing planning, although they were more aggressive marketers than similar Peruvian firms. J. Estuardo Marrou, *Marketing Strategies and Practices in Small and Medium-Sized Wisconsin Food and Beverage Manufacturers: Comparisons With Similar Manufacturers in a Developing Economy*, Seminar paper in lieu of thesis, University of Wisconsin, January 1968.
2. One such follow-up study which grew out of an earlier version of the present project is Richard H. Wood, "The Agricultural Supply Industries in the Economic Development of the Peruvian Sierras," unpublished doctoral thesis in Economics, The University of Wisconsin, 1969.

Chapter 14
Conclusion: Development
and the Marketing
Concept

1. Walt W. Rostow, "The Concept of a National Market and Its Economic Growth Implications," in Peter D. Bennett, ed., *Proceedings of the American Marketing Association, 1965 Fall Conference*, p. 19.
2. W. Paul Strassmann, Economic Growth and Income Distribution," *Quarterly Journal of Economics*, August 1956, pp.425-440.

3. See A. J. Youngson, *Overhead Capital* (Edinburgh: 1967) for a discussion of these and related situations.

4. The growing connection of the highland economies with the modern coastal economy seems chiefly attributable to the building of railways and, in more recent decades, the spread of highway transport. For an unusually informative report on this process made over 25 years ago, see Harry Toschopik, *Highland Communities of Central Peru, a Regional Survey* (Washington, D. C.: 1947), Smithsonian Institution, Institute of Social Anthropology, Publication No. 5. That small rural communities along the coast have also experienced a growing incorporation into the money economy is illustrated by the case of Moche, wherein traditional handicrafts had largely disappeared by the 1940's. See John Gillin, *Moche, a Peruvian Coastal Community* (Washington, D. C.: 1945), Smithsonian Institution, Institute of Social Anthropology, Publication No. 3.

5. The reference here is to the credit unions developed in the poorer southern parts of Peru. In the central highlands, purchasing power is visibly greater in many communities, a goodly number of which are actively caught up in the process of modernization. For two examples, see Richard N. Adams, *A Community in the Andes* (Seattle: 1959) and Paul L. Doughty, *Huaylas: an Andean District in Search of Progress* (Ithaca, New York: 1968).

6. Stephen Hymer and Stephen Resnick, "A Model of an Agrarian Economy With Nonagricultural Activities," *American Economic Review*, LIX, 4, Part I (September 1969), p. 505.

7. What the agrarian reform program may mean for the Peruvian national market is suggested by the experience in neighboring Bolivia, where an improvised and hastily implemented land reform substantially increased the market participation of the rural populace. See Ronald J. Clark, "Land Reform and Peasant Market Participation on the Northern Highlands of Bolivia," *Land Economics*, XLIV (May 1968), pp. 153-172.

Appendix
Literature on Marketing and Development

1. Richard H. Holton, "Marketing Structure and Economic Development," *Quarterly Journal of Economics*, LXVII, 3 (1953), pp. 344-361.

2. P. T. Bauer and B. S. Yamey, "The Economics of Marketing Reform," *Journal of Political Economy*, LXII, 3 (June 1954), pp. 210-235.

3. Willard F. Mueller, "Some Marketing Structure Considerations in Economic Development," *Journal of Farm Economics*, XLI, 2 (1959), pp. 414-425; George L. Mehren, "Market Organization and Economic Development," *Journal of Farm Economics*, XLI, 5 (1959), pp. 1307-1315.

4. N. R. Collins and R. H. Holton, "Programming Changes in Marketing in Planned Economic Development," *Kyklos*, XVI, Fasc. 1, 1963.

5. A. A. Sherbini, "Marketing in the Industrialization of Underdeveloped Countries," *Journal of Marketing*, XXIX (January, 1965), pp. 28-32.

6. Bennett, ed., *op. cit.*

7. Lawrence Lockley, Noemi Hewes Lockley, Winston Temple S., *A Marketing Guide to Peru*, (Lima: 1965). The study by Frank M. Dunbaugh, *Marketing in Latin America* (New York: 1960), is geographically more comprehensive in scope but also suffers from the deficiency of not explaining precisely how marketing functions within the economic milieu.

8. Philip MacDonald, *Practical Exporting and Importing*, (New York: 1959); and Roland Kramer, *International Marketing* (Cincinnati: 1959).

9. John Fayerweather, *International Marketing* (Englewood Cliffs, N. J.: 1965).

10. David Carson, *International Marketing; A Comparative Systems Approach* (New York: 1967). The approach used, however, is not that of a rigorous systems analysis.

11. Marketing Science Institute, *Marketing Development in the European Economic Community* (New York: 1964).

12. See, for example, Paul Bohannan and George Dalton, eds., *Markets in Africa* (Evanston, Ill.: 1962); Leon V. Hirsch, *Marketing in an Underdeveloped Economy: The North Indian Sugar Industry* (Englewood Cliffs, N. J.: 1961); Alice Dewey, *Peasant Marketing in Java* (New York: 1962).

13. Robert Bartels, *Comparative Marketing: Wholesaling in Fifteen Countries* (Homewood, Ill.: 1963). Unfortunately, not all of the studies included in the volume present comparable data.

14. David Granick, *The European Executive* (Garden City, N. Y.: 1962); and *The Red Executive* (Garden City, N. Y.: 1960).

15. Albert Lauterbach, *Enterprise in Latin America: Business Attitudes in a Developing Economy* (Ithaca, N. Y.: 1966).

16. Personal correspondence with the Marketing Science Institute, October 21, 1965.